010787294

D1356366

THE BRAIN DRAIN

The United Nations Institute for Training and Research was established by the Secretary-General as an autonomous institution within the framework of the United Nations for the purpose of enhancing, by the performance of the functions described hereafter, the effectiveness of the United Nations in achieving the major objectives of the Organizations, in particular the maintenance of peace and security and the promotion of economic and social development.

The two functions of the Institute are training and research.

The Institute provides training at various levels to persons, particularly from developing countries, for assignments with the United Nations or the specialized agencies and for assignments in their national services which are connected with the work of the United Nations, the organizations related to it, or other institutions operating in related fields. These programmes can also include training for staff members of the United Nations and of the specialized agencies as well as training for special United Nations field assignments.

UNITAR's research programme has focused primarily on the structures and procedures of the United Nations which are relevant to the major objectives of the international organization. The Institute's studies and training activities are essentially practical and designed to facilitate action rather than formulate or test theory. Their aim is to facilitate objective appraisal and to clarify alternative modes of action. This by necessity leads to a multidisciplinary approach. Consequently the activities of the Institute are organized mainly in broad problem areas and not on lines of conventional academic disciplines.

THE BRAIN DRAIN: Emigration and Return

Findings of a UNITAR multinational comparative survey of professional personnel of developing countries who study abroad

by
WILLIAM A. GLASER
with the assistance of
G. CHRISTOPHER HABERS

A UNITAR Study
published by

PERGAMON PRESS
OXFORD · NEW YORK · TORONTO · SYDNEY · PARIS · FRANKFURT

U.K.	Pergamon Press Ltd., Headington Hill Hall, Oxford OX3 0BW, England
U.S.A.	Pergamon Press Inc., Maxwell House, Fairview Park, Elmsford, New York 10523, U.S.A.
CANADA	Pergamon of Canada Ltd., 75 The East Mall, Toronto, Ontario, Canada
AUSTRALIA	Pergamon Press (Aust.) Pty. Ltd., 19a Boundary Street, Rushcutters Bay, N.S.W. 2011, Australia
FRANCE	Pergamon Press SARL, 24 rue des Ecoles, 75240 Paris, Cedex 05, France
FEDERAL REPUBLIC OF GERMANY	Pergamon Press GmbH, 6242 Kronberg/Taunus, Pferdstrasse 1, Federal Republic of Germany

First edition 1978

British Library Cataloguing in Publication Data

Glaser, William Arnold
The brain drain. — (United Nations Institute for Training and Research. Research reports; no. 22).
1. Underdeveloped areas — Brain drain
I. Title II. Series
331.127 HD8038.A1 77-30576

ISBN 0-08-022419-9 hardcover
ISBN 0-08-022415-6 flexi

In order to make this volume available as economically and as rapidly as possible the author's typescript has been reproduced in its original form. This method unfortunately has its typographical limitations but it is hoped that they in no way distract the reader.

Printed in Great Britain by William Clowes & Sons Limited London, Beccles and Colchester

The authors dedicate this volume
to their daughters
GILLIAN GLASER and ELISABETH HABERS

CONTENTS

LIST OF TABULATIONS

List of Tabulations

List of Tabulations

FOREWORD

There is much ferment in the United Nations System that has a direct or indirect bearing on the problem of brain drain. The current emphasis within and outside the United Nations System on the necessity of meeting basic human needs and the ongoing dialogue concerning the establishment of a new international economic order will undoubtedly have implications for the brain drain. This is especially true in view of the emphasis placed on the problem by the United Nations General Assembly at its seventh special session.*

The problem has been discussed in the context of the application of science and technology to development, of the promotion of career possibilities and of education and training for development, as well as in terms of the social implications of a new international economic order. It has been suggested that the brain drain should be considered in the elaboration of an international code of conduct for the transfer of technology. It has also been suggested that since the lack of scientific infrastructure in developing countries is one of the underlying causes of brain drain, transnational corporations should, among other things, ameliorate the situation by contributing to the development of the scientific and technological capacity of the host country.

There are variations in the pattern of the international flow of skilled manpower which have been considered. For example, economic conditions in 1974 and 1975 reduced the effective demand in industrial countries for professional personnel. In a report to the Social Commission, the United Nations Secretary-General stated** that while some changes in the level and direction of the outflow are evident, in the medium term its size depends to some extent on the timing and pace of recovery of national and international economies, and

*General Assembly Resolution 3362 (S-VII), section III, paragraph 10.

**E/CN.5/545, para.9.

in the longer term on changes in the international division of labour and industrial activity.

A United Nations Development Programme (UNDP) Working Group on Technical Cooperation Among Developing Countries, outlined the principles and objectives of such cooperation as promoting, among other things, the manner of utilization of the potential human and natural resources. Collective self-reliance through cooperation was seen by the Working Group as relevant to a reduction in the migration of trained personnel in that it could generate a climate of dynamism which would not make emigration so attractive.

Brain drain has been discussed in terms of laissez-faire economics and in terms of disengagement, i.e., "if brain drain is seen as a result of integration into an international market in professional skills then the only way of achieving a substantial impact on the drain (and on the more serious internal distortions that it reflects) is disengagement from that market."* Attention has also been drawn to the fact that while on the one hand brain drain reduces professional manpower in the developing countries it can have the effect of easing population and employment problems in some of those countries and in this respect act as a "safety valve".

* * *

It will be apparent from the foregoing indication of some of the facets of the problem of brain drain that the only way to approach the study of such a vast and complex problem is to study the various aspects of the phenomenon. Such a study would provide information and insights on which policy may be based. This volume reports the findings of a multinational comparative survey carried out under UNITAR auspices. It involves persons from developing countries who study abroad: those who remain abroad either temporarily or permanently after study and finally those who return home. What makes the study unique and of particular relevance to the continuing debate is that the aim of the research has been to discover the motivations and factors that influence the specific choices of these individuals with regard to place of study and subsequent employment. The approach followed in the study adds a new per-

---

*E/CN.5/L.421, par.49.

spective to the debate, which has thus far been mainly economic in content, on the causes of the international flow of professional persons. This volume adds a new dimension to consideration of the problem by taking account of a number of variables such as social origin, class, talent, ability to adjust to social conditions abroad, and income differences between developing and developed countries. Previous studies of the brain drain have, in general, been based on aggregate emigration and immigration statistics; motivations have not usually been investigated, especially on such a wide cross-national basis.

Thirteen surveys that were carried out in eleven countries are reported on. They comprise surveys of students from developing countries who were in Canada, France and the United States; surveys of professionals from developing countries living in France and the United States who received their professional education in a developed country; and surveys in Argentina, Brazil, Colombia, Ghana, Greece, India, the Republic of Korea, and Sri Lanka, of professionals who studied in a developed country and who subsequently, either immediately after study or after a temporary stay abroad, returned to their home country. Surveys are in progress in several other countries and additional surveys may yet be undertaken by research centers elsewhere.

It may be of interest to note that in a report to the Committee on Science and Technology for Development,* the Secretary-General of the United Nations cited twelve developing countries from which brain drain principally occurred and six developed countries that are the principal recipients of the students and professionals from those developing countries. All the surveys reported on in this volume were carried out in countries enumerated in the Secretary-General's report, with the exception of the surveys in Ghana and Greece which were included to give additional perspective.

This study complements but does not duplicate the work done in other parts of the United Nations System. For example, because the World Health Organization is studying the international migration of physicians and nurses, these categories have not been included in the UNITAR surveys. The UNITAR project differs fundamentally from others inasmuch as it involves the range of personal motives, economic incentives and social

*E/C.8/21, para. 16.

influences that govern the decisions of the individual. It will thus be particularly useful as a basis for policy-making and will it is hoped meet an urgent need which has been underlined by the United Nations General Assembly.

The findings of the UNITAR study

In the multinational comparison of the data it has been found that the motives to return home or to remain abroad are diverse. Among other things, it has been ascertained that most students from developing countries plan to return home, that some professionals now working in developed countries plan to return home eventually, and that few of those who return plan subsequently to emigrate. These are important findings but, valid as they are, they should not lead one to lose sight of the fact that in spite of the proportion of actual or potential "returnees", the loss of those who do not return can have unfortunate repercussions for developing countries. While most students may return home, temporary losses can mean a lot to developing countries in urgent need of professional manpower, if counted in accumulated man-years, and a small proportional loss can involve large numbers of people in a country such as, for example, India. Furthermore, the UNITAR data show that the proportion of those who remain abroad varies by country. Some countries lose many persons who obtain their professional education abroad, whilst some lose only a few.

Another consideration that must be kept in mind when reading the findings is the human aspect of what is reported. One of the reasons given for return is discrimination encountered while studying abroad. This can lead to much suffering in human terms. Furthermore, any report on this subject has to be read in the light of the provisions of the Universal Declaration of Human Rights. The needs of developing countries would not be well served if amelioration of the brain drain problem were to depend on arbitrary restrictions which might create new problems for the international community.

Other findings of the UNITAR study are that, among other things:

- many persons from developing countries work temporarily abroad after having completed their education abroad;

- developed countries differ in the extent to which they are hospitable to persons from developing countries and thus in the extent to which they attract immigrants;

- membership in national, religious or racial minority groups is an important reason why some professionals leave developing countries;

- family ties may be an even stronger influence than salary or working conditions upon individuals' decisions to return to the home country or to emigrate. Ties with home are associated with return and the absence of such ties with brain drain;

- professionals will choose to live in the country in which they believe their children will have the best lives and careers;

- perceptions of where income is adequate, where jobs are sufficiently numerous and challenging, and where the individual can make the greatest professional contribution, are important influences on the decision to emigrate or to return to the home country;

- specialists in a few fields may emigrate from developing countries because of lack of equipment, adequate office space, research assistants and contacts with developments in other countries in their profession.

A number of findings are different from currently accepted notions: for example, level of income is not the strongest determinant of a decision to return to the home country or to remain abroad; also a higher level of economic development or rate of growth does not necessarily reduce the brain drain. Paradoxically, it has been found that among developing countries whose nationals go to developed countries for their professional education, it is the nationals of the more prosperous and growing countries that say they plan to remain abroad or who actually emigrate. The factors that account for this are that the less developed countries have a combination of economic and non-economic incentives inducing individuals to return. For example, opportunities are great because professionals are few; in addition the culture and the family structure may make it difficult for the professional to adjust anywhere except in the home country.

It has often been stated that brain drain is a consequence of lack of development. The Committee on Science and Technology for Development has indicated that brain drain is likely to decrease with higher levels of development.* One representative informed this Committee** that as economic conditions in his country improved brain drain ceased to be a problem and in addition skilled personnel from less developed countries were beginning to enter the work force. The oil-exporting developing countries have also found that as their economic situation improves, they, too, have been utilizing skilled personnel from other developing countries. In more general terms, the Director-General of ILO has expressed the view that in the longer term, international manpower movements may diminish because of orderly changes in the international division of labour.*** However, the UNITAR study suggests that in forecasting whether nationals of a particular country might become part of the brain drain a more important factor than the stage of development is the extent to which a country trains an excess of professionals in a particular field. In other words, the brain drain is more likely to be a phenomenon affecting certain economic sectors in a country rather than all economic sectors; a country may have an outflow because of too many persons trained for a certain occupation while at the same time being able to attract persons trained abroad in sectors where there is a scarcity of skilled manpower.

It is not surprising that some of the findings of this study are contrary to conventional wisdom. A United Nations working group on the outflow of trained personnel pointed out that statistics produced from different sources might produce inconsistent results due, for example, to differences in concepts used. As the problem is multidimensional there are many ways of viewing it, each valid in its own context. If a problem is very important it should be looked at from a number of standpoints so that all relevant perspectives may be brought to bear on the consideration of possible solutions.

A careful reading of the volume will reveal findings and their implications that will be of significance for different

---

*Report of the Committee on its Third Session, E/5777, para. 155.

**Summary Record E/C.8/SR.66, para. 35.

***"Employment, Growth and Basic Needs: A One-World Problem" (Geneva: ILO, 1976, page 129).

countries and categories of countries. But some subjects touched upon in the report could not be dealt with comprehensively. For example, no attempt has been made to explain the different effects of the same variables upon men and women. The data indicate that as a general rule women are more likely to contemplate emigration than men and also to possess the motivations that ordinarily lead to emigration. Scholars may wish to avail themselves of the relevant UNITAR data to pursue the question of the different effects of the same variables on men and women as well as other questions with which the report could not deal comprehensively. The author of this volume has subsequently expanded upon some of these findings in a paper entitled "The return of the professional: the value of his education abroad",* addressing himself to such questions as: whether students from developing countries are educated according to the requirements of the developed societies when they study abroad and are thus unfitted for the manpower requirements of their home countries; whether upon return to their home countries they are able to find appropriate jobs; and whether education abroad upsets the balance between manpower supply and demand in the home country.

This volume indicates how the reasons why individuals stay abroad or return vary by country of origin, country of study, and field of specialization. Decisions are determined not only by a combination of reasons and influence at the time of choice but also by earlier reasons and choices as well. The design of the project permitted tracing these kinds of relationships at successive career stages, namely the period in the home country before going abroad for higher education; the period of study abroad; the period of work abroad, if any, whether temporary or indefinite; and the period of work in the home country for those who decide to return home. Furthermore, the project design permitted comparisons of the pressures regarding a particular decision that were exerted in both the home country and the country of study. From this, it has been learned not only what combination of factors is associated with a particular decision, but also what factors were exercising a countervailing influence.

*Paper presented at an International Conference on "Access to Higher Education: Implications for International Manpower Planning", held at the Northeastern University Center for International Higher Education Documentation, published in the Proceedings of the Conference (New York: Institute for International Education, forthcoming).

In a report to the Committee on Science and Technology for Development* the United Nations Secretary-General noted that in spite of the relatively voluminous literature on brain drain, "from an operational standpoint, the problem poses considerable difficulties in that it still lacks an agreed conceptual, factual and statistical basis for action". In clarifying the reasons why professionals of developing countries choose to study abroad and why they take their decisions regarding the locale in which they will pursue their chosen career, this UNITAR study will help to fill some important gaps in the information needed before an agreed basis for action can be achieved. The Secretary-General mentioned, for example, that there is a question as to who should be classified as a "brain drainee".** This volume underlines the complexity of such classification, inasmuch as the data indicate that persons from developing countries who study abroad often remain abroad only temporarily to obtain on-the-job training, to wait until employment that would utilize their skills is available in their home country, and so forth. It is therefore important that, as is the case with this study, there should be a clear and consistent set of definitions as to the persons being considered. One group of persons may be appropriate for the study of certain aspects of the problem and another group for other aspects.

In discussing the UNCTAD Secretariat's report on "The Reverse Transfer of Technology: Its Dimensions, Economic Effects and Policy Implications", one member of the Committee on Transfer of Technology of UNCTAD*** called for practical study of the causes of the brain drain, with suggestions as to how to limit it, while another member**** thought that identifying the causes would be conducive to the formulation of effective international policies that would focus on creating effective host environments in the developing countries for skilled manpower. A member of the Committee on Science and Technology for Development expressed the view***** that although statistics and information on the extent and nature of the brain drain are very valuable, they do not take into account the underlying causes. This volume is designed to meet this need.

---

*E/C.8/21, para.5.

**E/C.8/21, para.13.

***Report of the UNCTAD Committee on Transfer of Technology on its First Session (TD/B/593 - TD/B/C.6/7, para. 70).

****Ibid., para.71.

*****E/C.8/SR.66, para.33.

Among other things, this volume also reports on the actual or prospective earnings in their home countries and abroad of persons from a considerable number of developing countries who studied abroad and either returned home or remained abroad. The data indicate that a number of professionals from developing countries earn a higher real income in their own home country than in a developed country. For future reference, UNITAR has set up the first extensive data file on the effects of differential incomes.

The findings of this study will be of interest to economists, statisticians, policy-makers in scientific and technological fields, and manpower and educational planners and demographers. For example, demographers are now confirming the finding of this study that the magnitude of return migration after a period of work abroad is quite substantial; return migration is much greater for all occupational groups than they had previously estimated. A return migrant often bears a considerable amount of net gain for the home country since much of his education and usually all of his on-the-job training were gained at the expense of the developed country.

It has been said* that the causes of brain drain are closely connected with educational planning and its adjustment to policy objectives in the area of technology. The experience of foreign-educated nationals of developing countries after returning to their home countries is a subject about which very little reliable information has been published, yet it is an important area in relation to educational planning. This volume sheds light on the usefulness of the education acquired abroad which, in turn, is a factor in the consideration of adjusting the educational planning in the home country. In a number of other ways, the report provides facts that may be useful for policy-making not only with regard to the specific problem of brain drain but also with respect to the general question of the further use of human resources for development.

By providing information about motivations this study enables individual developing countries to assess their own circumstances and consider policies that might induce their nationals to study in the home country, or encourage those who might otherwise remain abroad to return.

---

*Report of the Committee on Science and Technology for Development on its Third Session, E/5777, para. 157.

It has been suggested* that thorough consideration should be given to incentives or credit schemes for attracting skilled personnel back to their country of origin. In order to decide how to motivate professionals to return, it is necessary to know what factors in the home country and the country of study influence the "returnees" in different categories. These factors are identified and analyzed in Chapter VII of the study, thus shedding light on the type of incentives that might be effective.

The United Nations Secretary-General has suggested in a report to the Committee on Science and Technology for Development that developing countries might designate a unit with responsibility for a realistic study of the causes of migration.** For any developing countries that have established or plan to establish such a unit in accordance with the Secretary-General's guidelines, this volume will provide relevant data both of a general and a country-specific nature.

The United Nations setting***

Because of the time needed to complete a major multinational survey for this project it may be useful to place the findings in the context of current considerations of the subject at the United Nations. Although the survey was carried out several years ago, its publication is very timely. The United Nations system is in the process of developing a joint approach to the brain drain problem, many aspects of which are being dealt with by a number of its components.

The General Assembly at its Seventh Special Session in September 1975 expressed concern that the outflow of qualified personnel from developing countries is seriously hampering economic advancement of those countries and that there was an urgent need to formulate national and international policies to avoid the brain drain and to obviate its adverse effects.****

---

*Report of the UNCTAD Committee on Transfer of Technology on its First Session (TD/B/593 - TD/B/C.6/17, para. 67).

**E/C.8/21, see para. 78.

***Based on information made available to the Working Party on the Migration of Trained Personnel of the Sub-Committee on Education and Training of the United Nations Administrative Committee on Co-ordination.

****General Assembly Resolution 3362 (S-VII), section III, para. 10.

Members of the United Nations Committee on Science and Technology for Development have requested that the problem be kept on the agenda of future sessions for continuing review. The Committee has already received reports on the subject from the United Nations Secretary-General. The question may be discussed at the forthcoming United Nations Conference on Science and Technology for Development.

The World Health Organization's study of the international migration of physicians and nurses has already been mentioned.

The United Nations Educational, Scientific and Cultural Organization is studying measures with respect to the international exchange of specialists among Member States on a rational basis. Its Secretariat has been requested by the General Conference to assist Member States in defining educational strategies and in developing educational centres, laboratories and research institutions.

The International Labour Organisation's Tripartite World Conference on Employment of June 1975 dealt partly with international migration. The Declaration of Principles and Programme of Action include general objectives of national and international policies, measures to avoid the need to emigrate, measures concerning migrations and equality of treatment, and provisions for insertion in multilateral and bilateral agreements. Research is being carried out in ILO on return migration and alternatives to migration. ILO is also compiling a collection of bilateral and regional agreements having a bearing on those aspects of the migration of trained personnel which are detrimental to the advancement of developing countries.

The Plan of Action adopted by the World Population Conference which took place in Bucharest in 1974 also contained a section on international migration.

The Secretariat of UNCTAD has carried out a study of the economic effects of the outflow of trained personnel from developing to developed countries and also a second more comprehensive study of this phenomenon which it has termed "the reverse transfer of technology". UNCTAD has undertaken additional studies jointly with the United Nations Office for Science and Technology.

The United Nations Economic Commission for Western Asia is undertaking a comprehensive study of the causes, features, consequences and policy implications of the migration of trained personnel within the region as well as to countries outside the region. A recent meeting of an Interagency Working Party on the Migration of Trained Personnel expressed the opinion that Regional Commissions of the United Nations have a critical role to play with regard to the problem.

Two functional commissions of the Economic and Social Council, namely the Statistical Commission which met in New Delhi in November 1976 and the Social Commission which met in Geneva in January 1977 had reports before them on relevant aspects of the outflow of trained personnel from developing to developed countries. The Human Rights Commission has a main concern in the protection and promotion of human rights among migrant workers, including trained personnel. The Commission's Sub-Committee on Prevention of Discrimination and Protection of Minorities has before it a study on "the problem of applicability of existing international provisions for the protection of human rights to individuals who are not citizens of the country in which they live".

The United Nations High Commission for Refugees assists highly trained refugees to find employment in the host country. Both the World Meteorological Organization and the Inter-Governmental Maritime Consultative Organization have taken steps to reduce the possibility that persons trained under their auspices will become part of the brain drain.

UNITAR itself has already published two studies on the question, one entitled "The Emigration of Highly Skilled Manpower from Developing Countries" and the other "The Brain Drain from Five Developing Countries: Cameroon - Colombia - Lebanon - The Philippines - Trinidad and Tobago". UNITAR has also taken active part in discussions of the subject within and outside the United Nations System.

* *
*

A project of the magnitude and scope of the present study could not have been carried out without the help of many institutions and individuals. UNITAR is grateful to all concerned, in particular to those governments, private foundations and research institutes that provided funds; to all the research institutes that participated in the project and contributed the data that made possible the preparation of this study;* and to those experts and scholars throughout the world and especially to those within the United Nations system who have commented on early drafts of the manuscript.

In any cross-national research many tasks have to be carried out. These include selection of topics and guiding ideas as well as countries and participating research centers, developing an organizational structure for the entire collaboration, raising money for field work and for central coordination, designing research methods, gathering, processing and analysing data, writing the results and presenting these to appropriate audiences. It is only recently that surveys of this nature have been initiated and sponsored during the survey phase by international organizations. Research of this type promotes mutual knowledge among social scientists who would otherwise be separated by linguistic, cultural or other divisions, and helps to build a machinery of collaboration as well as produce substantive results. Such research facilitates relations between scholars in developed and developing countries and the exchange of information on techniques of research design and data management and analysis.

This has been a truly international endeavour. The topics and guiding ideas originated in resolutions of United Nations agencies and in proposals of UNITAR staff. It was at UNITAR that the particular approach to this comparative cross-national study was conceived. The motivations and factors governing the decision to study abroad and the decision to remain abroad temporarily or permanently, or to return home, are compared among the nationals of several developing countries in Africa, Asia and Latin America. Similarly, the motivations and factors governing the decisions of those trained in one industrial country are compared with those from the same developing country who study in a different industrial country. The first drafts of all research instruments and sample plans were prepared at UNITAR. However, before the initial surveys were undertaken, interested research centers around the world were consulted and participated in pre-testing and redrafting.

---

*Appendix A contains a list of participating research centers and a description of the design of the research project. Readers are urged to consult Appendix A since an understanding of the character of the data and the limitations of the sample is necessary to an informed reading of the report and will prevent misunderstandings or misinterpretations.

We believe that this has been a most successful example of international and inter-institutional cooperation and that the experience gained in carrying it out will be helpful in the conduct of other similar endeavours. The findings have, we think, demonstrated the value of this type of multinational quantitative sociological research for the study of certain types of problems facing the United Nations.

UNITAR initiated this multinational comparative research project with the encouragement of the United Nations and interested agencies within the United Nations system, in particular UNESCO and ILO. With the help of William A. Glaser, Director of the Program on International and Comparative Research and Senior Research Associate of the Center for the Social Sciences at Columbia University, UNITAR planned and coordinated the cross-national questionnaire survey on which this volume is based. As author of the report, Dr. Glaser has collaborated with UNITAR in organizing the larger volume of data collected for present and future use. Among former UNITAR officials who have been associated with various aspects of the planning and implementation of this project are Gregory Henderson who helped work out the original concept in cooperation with Oscar Schachter and Alexander Szalai. Professor Szalai played a leading role not only in the initiation of the project but also in carrying it out. Annerose Schneider-Hürfeld, Mehri Hekmati (formerly at UNITAR and now at UNFPA), and Margaret Croke have each been associated with the project.

The experience gained by UNITAR in the process of carrying out this project has been discussed in a volume of collected papers on the theory and practice of cross-national comparative survey research.* An article describing the project appeared in "Social Science Information".** The data gathered by UNITAR and the methodology used have already stimulated sociological research in various parts of the world on brain drain. We note with appreciation that several United Nations organizations (particularly the United Nations Office of Science and Technol-

---

*Cross-national Comparative Survey Research: Theory and Practice, Alexander Szalai, et al. (Editors): Oxford, Pergamon Press, 1977.

**"The Brain Drain and UNITAR's Multinational Research Project on the Subject", by Mehri Hekmati and William A. Glaser, in Social Science Information, Vol. 12, No. 2, pages 123-138.

ogy, ILO, UNCTAD, UNESCO, and WHO) now involved in brain drain matters have expressed their acknowledgement of UNITAR's substantial contribution.

It has to be borne in mind that the data in this volume are based on the surveys that have been completed and analyzed. When additional surveys are completed, and if funds are available to analyze and report on these results, it may be that the index values given in this current report will change, perhaps in some cases significantly. Although the great majority of statistics included in the study are based on a fairly large number of observed cases, readers should be reminded that in a few cases a low base was used when the alternative was no information; the findings in these cases should be considered preliminary. The bulk of the relationships reported deal with correlates of migration and they should not vary from time to time. However, the findings should be read in the context of conditions at the time the surveys were conducted, particularly as conditions in the countries that are hosts to students from developing countries, and those in the developing countries themselves, are in constant flux.

UNITAR hopes that the findings of the study and the insights derived from them will be of use to all member states, and to the United Nations System, as well as to scholars, non-governmental organizations and concerned individuals. The findings provide an objective basis for policy decisions. The data on people's motivations and experiences are clear and comprehensive. The information concerning the diversity of factors that influence decisions and the relative strength of these factors, will be of value in the development of policy. Attention is drawn to the implications for policy of certain findings and certain interpretations. The findings and certain interpretations. The effects, side effects, and pitfalls that might result from various measures are discussed. However, no policy recommendations are made. The inferences have been drawn by the author from analysis of the data and in no sense do they constitute formal or official recommendations.

It is impossible to summarize the wealth of data contained in a study of this scope, or to do more than point out the usefulness of certain findings at various levels of planning. This foreword has referred only to some aspects, but the volume itself contains a summary of the findings. However, only a careful reading of the entire volume can do justice to its many useful insights and can suggest ways in which the data could be put to further use for the development of policy.

Drafts of this study were commented upon by all participating research centres some of which are also writing national reports. The interpretation of the data and the opinions expressed are those of the author. It is UNITAR policy to encourage scholarly research without taking an official position on matters studied under its auspices.

UNITAR is indebted to Professor Oscar Schachter of Columbia University who, as Director of Studies of UNITAR, was responsible for institutional supervision when most of the research was done, and to Dr. Robert Jordan, Director of Research, who zealously guided the manuscript during the final stages before publication. Various members of our senior professional staff gave useful advice. The expert contributions of Professor Alexander Szalai, formerly Deputy Director of Studies and now Honorary Special Fellow has already been gratefully acknowledged. We are also indebted to Mr. Gabriel Van Laethem, United Nations Under-Secretary-General in charge of Economic and Social Affairs, and to his colleagues for their interest and advice, especially Mr. Francois Van Hoek, Director, Office of the Under-Secretary-General for Economic and Social Affairs, Mr. Vladimir N. Vasiliev, Deputy Director, Office for Science and Technology, Mr. Theodore S. Zoupanos, Secretary of the Sub-Committee on Education and Training of the Administrative Committee on Co-ordination, and Mr. Bertrand Chatel, Chief of the Technology Applications Section of the Office for Science and Technology.

The depth of scholarship, patience and understanding which Professor Glaser displayed during the number of years spanned by this study was remarkable.

Davidson Nicol
Executive Director

August 1977

SUMMARY OF FINDINGS

The United Nations Institute for Training and Research (UNITAR) has conducted a multi-national comparative study about the migration and return of professionals from developing countries who study in developed countries. This report summarizes the results obtained from analysis of the responses to questionnaires given to: between 500 and 1,600 foreign students in three industrially developed countries; between 100 and 400 foreign professionals who have returned to each of eight developing countries after education in a developed country. Questionnaires were given to the same three groups of individuals in several other countries, as well as to between 50 and 100 employers in several of the developing countries.

The questions are nearly the same in all countries. The research identifies the constellation of economic, social, and other motivations and influences that bear upon decisions to go abroad and to return home. In addition, considerable other information is obtained about the conditions of work and life for such professionals in many countries.

The first results of the survey are based on the answers of the first 6,500 respondents: students in Canada, France, and the United States; stay-ons in France and the United States; returnees in Argentina, Brazil, Colombia, Ghana, Greece, India, the Republic of Korea, and Sri Lanka. Following is a summary of the main findings.

OVERALL PATTERN OF MIGRATION

Commitment to the home country is very strong. Most students from developing countries plan to return home after study abroad. Only small proportions plan to emigrate--but, of course, even small losses can be important to countries with shortages of talent.

Some professional persons from developing countries now working in developed countries plan to return home eventually. For them, work abroad is a form of practical experience after the completion of formal education. Other stay-ons plan to remain abroad.

Having made the decision to go home, few returnees plan to emigrate again. However, some are uncertain about the future.

Attachments to home remain strong even among many who plan to spend most of their careers working abroad. Many plan to return home after they retire. Some hope their children will live and work at home, rather than abroad. On the other hand, some become assimilated into life in developed countries.

The widespread feelings of belonging to one's original home country mean that brain drain need not be irreversible. Many persons work abroad without feeling they have abandoned their home societies completely, and without feeling they have adopted a completely new country. Some persons work abroad only for short periods. Return migration can probably be increased and the time abroad decreased, if the right offers come from home. Working abroad can represent a gain to the home country, rather than a loss, if the professional returns with augmented skills and with savings in hard currencies. Working abroad could become a recognized stage of practical postgraduate training; the type of work and the place (which might be another developing country) could be planned to increase the value of the professional's experience for his home.

VARIATIONS AMONG HOME COUNTRIES

Developing countries differ widely in their permanent losses through brain drain: some attract back nearly all citizens who study abroad, a few lose many persons and their development may suffer. By themselves, higher levels of economic development and higher rates of economic growth do not reduce brain drain. Rather, a crucial criterion is the balance between the education of professional persons and employment opportunities: a country will lose more of its citizens who study abroad if it educates more persons than the economy can absorb, and if the foreign-trained feel their prospects are insecure after return. Improved manpower planning and closer coordination between educational and economic sectors can improve the balance.

Certain other pushes vary among home countries and determine whether brain drain will be high or low. In particular, professionals belonging to minority groups in some societies that have recently adopted policies favoring the majorities in the use of language, employment, education, etc., tend to be apprehensive about their futures and to emigrate.

Certain pulls from the home society vary among countries, and these help determine whether foreign-educated professionals return home and remain there. Particularly important are a sense of confidence in the home country, optimism about future prospects for one's self and for one's children, patriotism, and the strength of family ties. Where these are strongest, students and professionals are most likely to return.

Some developing countries have cultures and institutions that make their citizens less adaptable to life in developed countries, and therefore their students and professionals are more likely to return. Their family ties are strong, they feel lonely and homesick while living abroad, they miss the culture and food from home, the languages of developed countries are unfamiliar, their educational preparation at home is imperfectly adapted to the higher education and jobs in developed countries, or they sense discrimination abroad.

Developing countries differ in whether their returnees have obtained practical experience at work abroad. Students from some developing countries return as soon as formal education ends. Others stay abroad temporarily to work.

VARIATIONS AMONG COUNTRIES OF STUDY

Some developed countries are more open to migrants than others. They issue immigrant visas easily, jobs for foreigners are plentiful, persons of different culture and of different skin color are accepted easily. An example was Canada until recently. Other developed countries are less open to immigration from developing countries.

Students planning to emigrate prefer the developed countries they know best--i.e., the ones where they studied. The United States is the favorite place for emigration, since so many students have been there. However, since persons from particular developing countries gravitate toward particular developed countries for study or work, certain nationalities pick other developed countries for permanent settlement (such as Canada, Great Britain, France, or Australia) in large numbers. Because the flows of students and professionals are most substantial between particular pairs of governments, improvement of educational exchanges and regulation of the brain drain can be conducted through bilateral agreements more efficaciously than through very general policies applying to all countries.

VARIATIONS AMONG SPECIALTIES

Plans to return and remain home are strongest in agriculture, business, and philosophy. Plans to emigrate and remain abroad are strongest in languages, education, architecture, and several of the biological sciences. Persons in the arts and journalism seem to become increasingly discontented after return and contemplate emigrating again.

By itself, specialization in very technical fields does not induce persons to emigrate. Going abroad permanently occurs after study in some highly specialized fields in developed countries, but it occurs among graduates in less technical curricula too. After return, many persons with specialized training customarily work in administration or in more general fields; technical specialization was a phase of their training, not preparation for a career. However, other returnees consciously await the time when the development of their countries creates a demand for their skills. If countries are to take advantage of such resources, these returnees must have chances to refresh their skills periodically and to keep in touch with new developments abroad.

Some stay-ons in very specialized areas work abroad rather than at home because they believe their talents would be wasted at home. But some look forward to the time when their countries will create jobs requiring their skills and when they can return and make their contributions. To take advantage of such potential leadership, developing countries should keep in touch with their nationals working abroad, encourage them to acquire skills useful for the growth of the societies, ask their advice about developing their fields at home, and inform them of new opportunities.

The specialties with the highest rates of emigration (whether highly specialized or less technical) share certain grievances. They feel isolated from the newest events in their field in the world, since their home countries import few journals and provide few opportunities to travel. They say their jobs involve too much burdensome teaching and administration, and not enough research. Poor equipment and facilities motivate emigration among biological scientists and engineers.

MOTIVES TO RETURN HOME OR STAY ABROAD

When foreign students decide to return home permanently or to emigrate permanently, income, the quality of jobs, and the number of jobs seem more attractive abroad. Some believe the greatest contributions to their professions can be made at home, others think they can accomplish more abroad. Developed countries seem far more attractive in their facilities, in the availability of colleagues and of supporting staff, and in proximity to new developments in professional fields.

The most common pulls back home are family, friends, and patriotic feelings. In addition, important pushes by developed countries result from the unfamiliar social settings and from racial and ethnic discrimination.

The foregoing pushes and pulls vary in strength and direction by country of origin, by country of study, and by specialty. After the end of study, as professionals raise families, the interests of the spouse and the children become increasingly important in their decisions to emigrate or return.

The strongest influence upon plans at all stages is the interests of the children--i.e., students and young professionals will return home and stay if they believe the children will be better off there, they will emigrate if they believe the children will have better lives abroad. At several stages of life --such as during study abroad and after return home-- perceptions of where one can contribute most to one's profession, adequacy of income, quality of jobs, and number of jobs are very strong influences upon decisions. The person will remain in or go to the country where he thinks these employment opportunities are best.

The predictive power of many reasons become weaker after return home: commitment to remain for other reasons (such as family attachments) is so strong that, when any reason induces some people to contemplate emigration, often it is over-ridden.

In general, facilities and the quality of professional relationships do not predict migration plans well at any stage: the large majority deem these to be attractions of developed countries, but most return home nevertheless. However, these considerations do influence plans for a few specialties.

It is the person's perception of adequate income and living standards that governs his migration decisions, not the mere income figures alone. Income combines with many other variables in determining migration. The greater the differential in money between home and developed countries, the more likely the professional will emigrate, but the relationship is not as strong as would be predicted from the widespread belief that money dictates brain drain. Many persons return home--for example, to Southern Asia--despite salaries much below the rates in North America, since living standards are adequate at home and since non-monetary reasons push them out of developed countries and pull them back home. Some persons can earn more at home, either because pay for foreigners is low in developed countries (such as France and Great Britain) or because high salaries can be found at home (such as Iran, Brazil, and francophone Africa).

Even though they may not be motivated to leave their home countries and spend their lives abroad, professional persons have complaints about working conditions at home. In some fields (such as the biological sciences) and in some individual cases, however, these grievances may be strong enough to over-ride other ties and induce persons to go abroad again. A common problem is the limited opportunity for research at home, because of heavy teaching loads, limited facilities, and the managerial responsibilities that must be assumed in return for higher salaries. A serious problem in Asian and African countries with non-convertible currencies is loss of contact with international developments. The returnee cannot attend enough international conferences and cannot obtain enough periodicals from abroad. In some countries with rigid hierarchies, seniority systems of promotion, and large numbers of professional persons relative to openings, young returnees complain that they have to wait too many years before they can rise into positions of responsibility, that they must accept subordination to senior people whose knowledge is out of date.

Findings from the part of our survey about motives for brain drain suggest several remedial actions, both to affect flows and to reduce complaints that may not always lead to emigration. Although some increases in pay may be justified in particular countries or in individual situations, many foreign-trained professionals already earn considerable incomes; their serious grievances deal with working conditions rather than pay. Better facilities, more opportunities for research, closer communication with new developments overseas, and more assistants would improve the foreign-trained professional's morale as well as his productivity. The structure of organizations could be altered, so the individual feels he can be promoted or can change his job without risk. At present, too many persons in some developing countries feel trapped in their present jobs. Some remedies for brain drain cost nothing but require national leadership: professionals will stay in countries that have a sense of national purpose, where prospects seem bright for them and for their children, and where they feel wanted.

TIES WITH HOME

Students with scholarships or special grants are more likely to return than those who study abroad privately. The source of the scholarship is crucial: grants from the government or employers in one's home country are associated with return, but grants from the university abroad are associated with emigration.

Bonding may ensure return, but pledges without bonds might be just as effective. It is difficult to attribute higher return to bonds alone, since people who enter such obligations seem to return for many other reasons too. Persons without these financial obligations emigrate much more often. Few persons say they will skip bond; some bonded persons work abroad after return but say they will return eventually.

If a student is on leave from a job, he is much more likely to return home than if he had to quit or was not employed at the time he went abroad.

Contacts while abroad by governments and by private employers concerning employment opportunities are rare. But those who are contacted are more likely to return. Some governments have programs to help overseas students and overseas professionals to find jobs at home, but they do not yet reach many persons abroad.

The closer the ties with home through letters and professional communications, the greater the return.

Persons who keep close ties with compatriots while abroad and who participate in national clubs are most likely to return home after study and work abroad. The greater the association with nationals from the country of study and the lower the association with fellow students from home, the greater the tendency to emigrate. Those who avoid opportunities to associate with fellow nationals are the least likely to return home.

Marriage to foreigners is associated with higher rates of emigration. It is also associated with longer stays abroad before return. In general, foreign spouses much less often than indigenous spouses advise the student and professional to return home. The incidence of intercultural marriage and the effects upon brain drain vary by nationality.

Visits home during study are uncommon. Visits between the end of study and the beginning of work abroad are more frequent for stay-ons. Visits may reinforce rather than alter plans. Visits do not seem to increase the rate of return.

The trend in educational exchanges is to increase the proportions of students who are sponsored by developing countries themselves and who have jobs waiting at home. This will reduce brain drain. Developing countries can further strengthen ties with their students and professionals overseas by helping the work of national clubs abroad, supplying more literature about life and work at home, creating rosters of skilled people who are studying and working abroad, and by informing their citizens overseas about jobs at home. Developed countries can help developing countries create such manpower registries and establish distribution channels among the foreign professionals within the developed countries' borders.

THE DECISION TO STUDY ABROAD

Academic benefits are the most common reason for studying abroad. For many foreign students, the mere prestige of having been abroad is valuable at home. The desire to gain employment experience in developed countries motivates some, but this is not synonymous with emigration. Few students say they studied abroad in order to explore prospects for living there, but this is more common among a few nationalities with higher rates of emigration. Motivations vary by home country and by specialty.

If students go abroad to explore prospects for emigration or to escape personal and political controls, they are more likely to stay abroad permanently. (But even some of these return home.) Going abroad to acquire the prestige of foreign experience is associated with staying abroad temporarily to work, but many plan to return eventually. Academic motivations are associated with permanent return without intervening periods of employment abroad.

The strongest reasons for staying abroad temporarily to work after study are educational, namely, acquiring on-the-job experience. Many hope to benefit by earning higher salaries in harder currencies than they can obtain at home, and then by taking their gains home. Some stay abroad until the job market improves at home or the government changes. Reasons vary by home country and by specialty.

LOSSES AND GAINS

There is no clear-cut tendency for developing countries to regain or lose able persons more than others. But possibly the least able are most likely to return.

A number of highly specialized persons are lost after education abroad, namely, baceriologists, biochemists, engineers in several technical fields, system analysts, chemists and physicists. But there is no clear tendency for developing countries to lose all their narrow specialists and to regain the persons with more general training. Some broader fields produce emigrants too.

Some persons remit money home while working and studying abroad. Most sums are moderate, but a few persons send considerable amounts. Permanent stay-ons send more money home than temporary stay-ons. Although the average person sends home only a limited amount, total remittances from all persons can be a valuable source of hard currency for developing countries.

Chapter I

THE BRAIN DRAIN

The 1950's began amid optimism about the development of Asia, Latin America, and Africa. It was assumed that investment, education, and modern management would be sufficient for their economic growth. The more prosperous countries helped by donating or lending resources, by creating and staffing training centers in those regions, and by welcoming large numbers of foreign students.

By the 1960's, disillusionment spread. The progress of developing countries was uneven, it fell short of aspirations, the developed countries grew faster, and therefore international gaps widened rather than narrowed. The growing output of schools in developing countries was imperfectly related to the job market; consequently many skilled persons found unsatisfactory jobs or no jobs at all. In the developed countries, service industries and complex manufacturing grew at least as fast as the output of their own schools, many attractive jobs were created, migrants were welcomed by employers, and some governments relaxed either the wording or the administration of their immigration laws. Some foreign students stayed on, and policy-makers at home feared a growing trend.

Education abroad for centuries has been widespread in the sciences and professions. Learning from the curricula and faculties of other societies has long been considered an asset for both the individual and his country. Settling abroad has been common. But by the 1960's, complaints about "brain drain" challenged the value of these flows. Writers and officials from developing countries protested that the richer countries were damaging their societies by enticing their professionals. Industrialized countries were said to gain large manpower stocks, representing substantial educational investments by the developing countries; the developed countries' growth was assisted at little cost to themselves, while the developing countries' growth was hampered by losses of their cadres and by waste of their educational investment. Intended as a form of technical assistance, foreign study was said to have become twisted into an instrument for raiding talent.

The "brain drain" issue moved from scholarly analysis and newspaper recriminations onto the floor of the United Nations General Assembly in late 1967. Resolutions introduced by developing countries demanded that richer members--and particularly the United States--change their migration policies, encourage foreign students to learn the skills needed at home, encourage these students to return, and compensate the developing countries for losses. The United Nations community feared that the brain drain was jeopardizing fulfillment of the U.N.'s Second Development Decade. Resolutions were adopted with a view to obtaining reliable facts about the magnitude, causes, and consequences of the brain drain. [See General Assembly Resolutions 2320 (XXII) (1967) and 2417 (XXIII) (1968).] In Resolution 2320 (XXII) the General Assembly requested the Secretary-General

> to assemble and analyse the comments and information that have been received from Governments, specialized agencies, the International Atomic Energy Agency, the Advisory Committee on the Application of Science and Technology to Development and organs in the United Nations system. . . . and when submitting the report, to highlight the advantages and disadvantages accruing to both the developed and the developing countries as a result of the tendency of trained personnel from the latter to remain in the industrialized countries or to leave their country after they have received their training.

Pursuant to this resolution, the Secretary-General submitted to the following session of the General

Assembly a compendium of available facts entitled Outflow of Trained Personnel from Developing Countries (Document A/7294, 5 November 1968). The report was based on a monograph published by the United Nations Institute for Training and Research.[1]

Having considered this report, the General Assembly on 17 December 1968 adopted a resolution entitled "Outflow of Trained Professional and Technical Personnel at All Levels from the Developing to the Developed Countries, Its Causes, Its Consequences and Practical Remedies for the Problems Resulting from It," Resolution 2417 (XXIII), which stated in part:

> The General Assembly . . .
>
> Noting with concern that highly trained personnel from the developing countries continue to emigrate at an increasing rate to certain developed countries, which in some cases may hinder the process of economic and social development in the developing countries,
>
> Considering that among the main causes of the "brain drain" from the developing countries are the technological and economic gaps existing between them and the developed countries and that there is a need to take appropriate interim action at both the national and international levels, until these gaps have been bridged, to tackle the problems resulting from the outflow of trained personnel from the developing countries, . . .
>
> Takes note with interest of the report of the Secretary-General on the outflow of trained personnel from the developing countries and of the important contribution made by the United Nations Institute for Training and Research to the preparation of this study and invites Member States to consider its conclusions and suggestions; . . .

---

[1]Gregory Henderson, Emigration of Highly-Skilled Manpower from the Developing Countries (New York: UNITAR, Research Report No. 3, 1970).

> Requests the Secretary-General to undertake, in consultation with Governments of Member States concerned and taking into account, as appropriate, the work being done by the specialized agencies, the United Nations Institute for Training and Research and other interested organizations and organs of the United Nations system, selective studies of a few developing countries which are seriously concerned with the "brain drain" problem, aimed at clarifying the problem, and in particular to assess its consequences for their economic development and to make appropriate recommendations for practical action at the national and international level in tackling this problem; . . .
>
> Further requests the Secretary-General to draw the attention of the appropriate organizations and programmes within the United Nations system to the need to assist the Governments of the developing countries which are members of the United Nations, at their request, in improving their statistical and research activities aimed at assessing the magnitude and characteristics of the outflow of their trained personnel;
>
> Invites the specialized agencies, the regional economic commissions, the United Nations Institute for Training and Research, the Advisory Committee on the Application of Science and Technology to Development and other interested organs and bodies of the United Nations system to assist the Secretary-General in strengthening coordination of research and operational activities of the United Nations in this field.

In response UNITAR, in cooperation with the United Nations Department of Economic and Social Affairs, arranged for the preparation of five national case studies to clarify the problem, to assess its effects on the development of the countries, and to recommend remedies. National reports were prepared about Cameroon, Colombia, Lebanon, the Philippines, and Trinidad and Tobago. The reports relied on the national statistics about employment, emigration, and return flows that were already available. The

United Nations Social Development Division prepared a general report and a summary of the case studies, and the Secretary-General submitted them to the 49th Session of the Economic and Social Council as documents E/4820 and E/4820 Add. 1.[2]

PREVIOUS RESEARCH

UNITAR's studies were part of a voluminous literature about brain drain[3] and about study abroad[4] that have been inspired recently by the sheer number of educational exchanges and by the controversy over their results. Because of the extent of this material, one would think little remained for new study. However, on close inspection, only a few publications offer firm data and conclusions of wide application. The paucity of theory and of systematic research about persons' decisions characterizes the entire field of migration.[5]

---

[2]Also published as The Brain Drain from Five Developing Countries (New York: UNITAR, Research Report No. 5, 1971).

[3]Stevan Dedijer and L. Svenningson, Brain Drain and Brain Gain: A Bibliography on Migration of Scientists, Engineers, Doctors and Students (Lund: Research Policy Program, University of Lund, 1967); Alice W. Shurcliff, Selected Publications and Research Related to the International Migration of Professional Manpower (Washington: Study Committee on the International Migration of Talent, Education and World Affairs, 1968); and Jarmila Horna, bibliography about the brain drain, International Newsletter on Migration (University of Waterloo, Ontario, Canada), Volume 2, Number 3 (September 1972).

[4]Barbara J. Walton, Foreign Student Exchange in Perspective: Research on Foreign Students in the United States (Washington: Office of External Research, U.S. Department of State, 1967); and Margaret L. Cormack, An Evaluation of Research on Educational Exchange (Washington: Bureau of Educational and Cultural Affairs, U.S. Department of State, 1962).

[5]Critical judgments on the state of the field recur in J. A. Jackson (editor), Migration (Cambridge: The University Press, 1969).

Much of the literature about the migration of professionals consists of essays specifying the nature of the problem, offering hypotheses about the causes and consequences of migration, and citing some national statistics on behalf of an argument.[6] Many studies summarize the statistical magnitude of flows of students and of professionals in particular specialties between pairs of countries. Some estimate the consequences for the losing and gaining countries, by estimating the cost of the professionals' training and the value of their work. Some authors speculate about the weaknesses of countries losing persons and the attractions of other countries gaining them; but the authors can do no more than make wise guesses, since they lack questionnaire responses from the professionals themselves. A few projects create new statistics about aggregate flows from the government records that are not published regularly.[7]

Many surveys of foreign students have been conducted, particularly in the United States. Some have been published; an even larger number are unpublished doctoral projects. Most deal with the problems of adjusting to the host country's schools

---

[6] Some of the best are Walter Adams (editor), The Brain Drain (New York: The Macmillan Company, 1968); Harry C. Johnson, "Some Economic Aspects of Brain Drain," The Pakistan Development Review, Volume VII, Number 3 (August 1967), pp. 379-411; Susumu Watanabe, "The Brain Drain from Developing to Developed Countries," International Labour Review, Volume 99, Number 4 (April 1969), pp. 401-433; Robert G. Myers, "'Brain Drains' and 'Brain Gains'," International Development Review, Volume IX, Number 4 (December 1967), pp. 4-9; and Prakash Awasthi, "Brain Drain from Developing Countries: An Exercise in Problem Formulation," Manpower Journal (New Delhi), Volume II, Number 1 (April-June 1966), pp. 80-98.

[7] Especially The Committee on the International Migration of Talent, The International Migration of High-Level Manpower: Its Impact on the Development Process (New York: Praeger Publishers, 1970); and the secondary analyses of existing sources in Robert G. Myers, Education and Emigration (New York: David McKay Company, 1972).

and society.[8] Some deal with the lasting opinions of the host country that the foreign student is likely to retain after going home and that may influence the home country's foreign policies.[9]

Many surveys of foreign students ostensibly explain the decisions to study abroad, to emigrate permanently, or to return home. On close scrutiny, remarkably few do this by asking thorough questions about what persons plan to do or have already done. Rather, a single question about plans often is correlated with a variety of questions about attitudes toward the home and host countries. Consequently, the data report the correlates of intentions rather than the reasons for these intentions.[10] In a few studies, returnees and nonreturnees are compared by means of the same questionnaire. But since questions deal with attitudes toward the home country and attitudes toward the country of study, again the result is the correlates of emigration and of return rather than explanations of the decision.[11]

---

[8] Many American studies are summarized in Walton, _op. cit._, Ch. V. The principal European surveys are _Colonial Students in Britain_ (London: Political and Economic Planning, 1955); Political and Economic Planning, _New Commonwealth Students in Britain: With Special Reference to Students from East Africa_ (London: George Allen & Unwin, 1965); Jean-Pierre N'Diaye, _Enquête sur les étudiants noirs en France_ (Paris: Editions Réalités Africaines, 1962); and Prodosh Aich, _Farbige unter Weissen_ (Köln: Kiepenheuer & Witsch, Second edition, 1963).

[9] For example, the many unpublished questionnaire surveys of foreign students in the United States, conducted by the United States Information Agency, and now on deposit at the Roper Public Opinion Research Center and in the International Data Library and Reference Service, University of California, Berkeley.

[10] For example, John Alsop Thames, _Korean Students in Southern California: Factors Influencing Their Plans Toward Returning Home_ (Pasadena: dissertations for the Ed.D., School of Education, University of Southern California, 1971).

[11] For example, Josefina R. Cortes, _Factors Associated with the Migration of High-Level Persons from the Philippines_

A few sample surveys have been conducted with questionnaires that ask about migration decisions skillfully, but they are limited in scope. They focus on only one nationality, or they examine several nationalities in only one country of study, usually the United States.[12] Hardly any surveys ask the same questions in the same way, and therefore one cannot generalize reliably across several samples and nationalities. If certain findings seem to recur in several countries, this results from the reader's interpretations rather than from the evidence itself.

UNITAR'S SURVEY OF PROFESSIONALS

When UNITAR planned its program of research about the brain drain, it soon became obvious that the literature contained little reliable information about the reasons why persons studied abroad, why some stayed overseas to work, and why others returned home. And the literature provided almost no trustworthy guidance about whether certain motives, influences, and decisions were universal or whether they varied among nationalities or among sub-groups within the same country. A new survey was not necessary to discover all the possible reasons why anyone might emigrate; the literature contained an exhaustive list of hypotheses. But a survey was needed to discover how students and professionals actually behaved and how their thinking and action

---

to the U.S.A. (Stanford: Stanford International Development Educational Center, Stanford University, 1970).

[12] Paul Ritterband, The Non-Returning Foreign Student: The Israeli Case (New York: Bureau of Applied Social Research, Columbia University, 1968); and John Niland, The Asian Engineering Brain Drain (Lexington: D. C. Heath and Company, 1970). See also Ritterband, "The Determinants of Motives of Israeli Students Studying in the United States," Sociology of Education, Volume 42, Number 4 (Fall 1969), pp. 330-349; and Ritterband, "Law, Policy, and Behavior, Educational Exchange Policy and Student Migration," American Journal of Sociology, Volume 76, Number 1 (July 1970), pp. 71-82.

varied according to circumstances. Governments and the international community could not take policy decisions solely on the basis of the speculations in the literature--despite the tone of finality in many publications--and therefore reliable facts had to be collected.

UNITAR foresaw a project to answer questions such as the following:

Why do persons from developing countries decide to study abroad? How do these reasons vary by country of origin, country of study, and field of specialization?

What are the effects of the different living conditions and different methods of financial support on foreign students' educational experience, orientations, and career plans in developed countries?

What communications do foreign students receive from their home governments and employers? How many are offered or guaranteed jobs at home? What are the effects of these contacts and offers on foreign students' educational experiences, attitudes toward their home countries, and career decisions?

In deciding to emigrate, how many students are influenced by the educational and occupational experiences they encountered abroad, and how many intended to emigrate before leaving home? What were the reasons for such prior decisions to emigrate? How were these prior dispositions weakened or reinforced by study and work abroad?

Are employers in developing countries willing and able to use the skills possessed by returnees? To what extent is the brain drain due to limited opportunities for jobs and promotions in developing countries? How does this lack of fit vary by country of origin, country of study, and field of specialization?

Do returnees return with any attitudes and habits that complicate their adjustments? How do they get along with employers and co-workers? Does their employment create adverse repercussions in the organizations where they work?

What are the personal and occupational experiences of returnees? In what ways were they helped or handicapped by study abroad? Do they think their skills are being used sufficiently and will be used throughout their future careers? How have their experiences after return affected their orientations toward their home countries, their feelings about emigration, and their career plans? What advice are they giving to prospective foreign students and prospective emigrants?

The results of the UNITAR project were expected to bear on such practical issues as the following:

Is the brain drain of those who study abroad large, costly to developing countries, and profitable to developed countries in respect to skills, their use and the motivations behind them? Is foreign study a net gain for the developing countries in that the best students return while the brain drain is concentrated among the less skilled? Is foreign study a net loss for the developing countries in that migration commonly occurs among the most able?

Can any remedies that might be necessary be applied uniformly among all countries or must they be entirely different, depending on country of origin, country of study, and specialty?

Should developing countries improve methods for selecting persons for education abroad? If so, how can one identify potential migrants and potential returnees? Should developing countries try to tailor study abroad more closely to national needs? Should there be more manpower developmental planning and should this be more widely communicated?

Should a closer fit be created between each developing country's occupational structure and the curricula in developed countries? What changes should be made in the economy of the former and the universities of the latter, to ensure that students from developing countries be optimally trained and motivated? Should representatives of the home country play a greater role in the educational and personal experiences of their nationals studying abroad?

Is the brain drain a symptom of a more general lack of fit between a developing country's educational and occupational structure? Should more comprehensive changes be made in both?

Should requirements for exit and entry visas of various types be altered? Should laws on immigration and temporary residence be changed?

Should any machinery be created by governments and employers to communicate with their nationals studying abroad about prospective jobs and life at home?

The design of the research project is described in Appendix A of this volume.

THIS STUDY

The following chapters give an overview of our results. It is based on those data that have been delivered to us by early 1974, viz.: the surveys of students in the United States, Canada, and France; the surveys of professionals from developing countries who have studied abroad and are now working in the United States and France; and the surveys of professionals who have studied in developed countries and have returned to Argentina, Brazil, Colombia, Ghana, Greece, India, the Republic of Korea, and Sri Lanka.

Field work is continuing in several other countries. Therefore, the present manuscript is a progress report. A more complete analysis of all data from the project can be prepared in the future, when all the field work has ended. Future manuscripts can focus on special topics or use more elaborate methods of analysis than we have used here.

The brain drain has many facets, and obviously no single research project can cover them all. Since our task is to explain migration and return between developing and developed countries, we did not survey the large numbers of persons moving from one developed country to another or the flows from one to another developing country. Since we are assessing the effects of education in developed countries, our samples of stay-ons do not include the large numbers of migrants educated entirely in developing countries.

Because the World Health Organization has been planning studies of the brain drain,[13] UNITAR has concentrated on specialties outside of health. Our samples of students omit persons in schools of medicine, nursing, and public health; our samples of professionals omit doctors and nurses. UNITAR and WHO have kept each other informed of their work; the

---

[13] A Multi-National Study of the International Migration of Physicians and Nurses (Geneva: World Health Organisation, HMD/73.5, 1973).

design of the UNITAR project could easily be extended to doctors and nurses without change and with the advantage of full comparability with other professions. However, a few respondents in the UNITAR sample have current or future specialization in health, as our tabulations will show on later pages.

Chapter II

GENERAL PATTERNS

Most students from developing countries plan to return[1]

The widespread and often heated discussion of the brain drain has fostered the impression that it is a common and large problem. Some countries have been singled out as recovering very few of their students who study abroad,[2] and it is easy to assume that many countries suffer from comparable losses.

However, most students from developing countries plan to return home eventually after study abroad. The distribution of all respondents in the surveys of students appears in the first column of Table II-1. Not only do most students expect to return home--75 per cent said they definitely or probably would return--but 51 per cent said their plans were definite.

Of the balance without plans to return to their home countries, not all will be parts of the brain drain. Twelve per cent of the students are undecided about their future plans, and some of these might return home. While 13 per cent plan to emigrate from home permanently, only 4 per cent said their plans were definite.

[1] See Appendix A for "Definition of groups surveyed".

[2] For example, Gregory Henderson, "Foreign Students: Exchange or Immigration?" International Development Review, Volume VI (December 1964) pp. 19-21; and Thomas D. Dublin, "The Migration of Physicians to the United States," The New England Journal of Medicine, Volume 286 (20 April 1972), p. 875.

As Chapter III will report, the proportions planning to return home vary widely among countries.

Is migration too high, or are the proportions tolerable? If several hundred thousand students go abroad, losing even a low proportion may mean losing a substantial number. For countries with unfilled jobs and a scarcity of professional manpower, losing anyone is a sacrifice. Even though few are lost, the damage to the country may be great, if the emigrés are the creative persons. Therefore, Table II-1 is a useful guide to the general order of magnitude of migration and it makes clear that most students return. But the severity of emigration can be judged only by studying the volume, composition, and consequences of flows from each individual country.

Table II-1

Long-Run Plans

Plans	Students	Stay-ons	Returnees
Definitely return home and remain	51%	12%	47%
Probably return home and remain	24	14	33
Uncertain	12	20	16
Probably go abroad and stay	9	29	3
Definitely go abroad and stay	4	25	1
	100%	100%	100%
Total number of respondents who answered the question	(2,924)	(396)	(2,728)

Wording of questions and of response categories varied slightly to fit the situations of students, stay-ons, and returnees. Wording of this question--the most important in the survey--was: "What do you <u>expect</u> to do in the future--i.e., what do you realistically anticipate rather than prefer?" Response categories for students: "I definitely will return to my country of origin," "I probably will return to my country of origin," "I am uncertain whether to return there or to stay abroad," "I probably will remain abroad to live and work permanently," and "I definitely will remain abroad to live and work permanently." This phrasing appeared in the questionnaires for students and stay-ons; slightly different language conveyed the same ideas in the questionnaires for returnees.

The table combines: students in the United States, Canada, and France; stay-ons in the United States and France; and returnees in India, Sri Lanka, Republic of Korea, Greece, Ghana, Brazil, Colombia, and Argentina.

For the method of weighting respondents in the tabulations in Chapter II, see Appendix A, "Statistical Notes and Tabulations", _infra_.

Many stay-ons plan to return[3]

Because so many professionals from developing countries can be found working in developed countries, it is widely assumed that large numbers are leaving home permanently. But these workers have very mixed plans, and some are abroad only temporarily. The distribution of all respondents in the surveys of stay-ons appears in the second column of Table II-1. Twenty-six per cent said they "definitely" or "probably" would return eventually and would remain in their home countries, and 20 per cent were undecided.[4]

Many students from developing countries expect to work abroad temporarily after completing their formal education in developed countries, and they laid such plans even before leaving home. Our questionnaires asked students not only about their long-

---

[3]See Appendix A for "Definition of groups surveyed".

[4]Our statistics about the long-range plans of stay-ons are indicative rather than exact estimates, since we could not take representative national samples. Therefore we cannot be sure what proportion of all stay-ons are definitely committed to remain permanently. However, according to Table II-1, clearly a considerable number of the foreign professional workers expect to return home.

range plans (i.e., the item used in Table II-1) but also about short-range plans immediately after receiving qualifications overseas. The different expected life histories for all students are summarized in Table II-2. The students who expect to stay on temporarily after graduation (25 per cent of all students) outnumber those who expect to become permanent stay-ons (13 per cent of all students).

The average temporary stay-on works abroad only a few years. The observer may think he sees a substantial permanent settlement, but actually the stay-on population has constant turnover. Among the prospective temporary stay-ons in our three student surveys, the median number of years to be spent abroad between the conclusion of education and return home was three. Among the several hundred returnees who had worked abroad, the median number of years between the end of education and return was less than two. (Medians are halfway points in distributions: half the temporary stay-ons were abroad longer and half less.)

As Chapter VIII will report, additional practical experience on the job is the most important reason for staying on temporarily after the end of formal education. Therefore, important policy decisions should be made by governments and employers about how best to organize this form of postgraduate education.

Although many stay-ons say they expect to return, this is not guaranteed. A professional may continue to work abroad until he becomes so assimilated into the culture and economy of the developed country that he postpones return forever. If governments and employers in developing countries wish to recover these temporary stay-ons, they must preserve their ties and their interest in return.

The amount of actual or potential return migration by stay-ons may be surprising, but it has been noticed in several other surveys in recent years. Once it was assumed that every migrant would put down permanent roots. But recent research shows that migrants--ranging from professionals to workers

--are more cosmopolitan and footloose than expected. Much migration has become a form of temporary employment or exploration overseas. More persons return home eventually or can be persuaded to return by attractive conditions.[5]

Table II-2

Expected Life Histories of Students

Plans: Immediately after study	Plans: Permanently	All Students	Type of Person
Stay abroad	(Return home and (stay there	25%	Temporary stay-on
	(Uncertain	10	Uncertain stay-on
	(Stay abroad	13	Permanent non-returnee
Return home	(Leave home and (stay abroad	1	Temporary returnee
	(Uncertain	1	Uncertain returnee
	(Stay home	50	Permanent returnee
		100%	
Total number of students		(2,849)	

The table combines the replies of students in the United States, Canada and France. For the system of weighting the tabulations, see Appendix A, "Statistical Notes and Tabula-

[5]Recent studies on return migration are reviewed in F. Wilder-Okladek, "Research on Return Migration and the Concept of 'Intention of Permanence' in Migration Theory," unpublished paper at the Conference on Policy and Research on Migration, International Sociological Association, Research Committee on Migration, 1973. Among the recent surveys revealing considerable amounts of return migration are Anthony H. Richmond, "Return Migration from Canada to Britain," Population Studies, Volume XXII (July 1968), pp. 263-271; and the Longitudinal Study of the Economic and Social Adaptation of Immigrants, currently conducted by the Department of Manpower and Immigration, Government of Canada.

tions", infra. Table II-2 classifies students by their answers to two questions: long-run plans, previously presented in Table II-1; and plans immediately after the end of study.

Most returnees expect to remain home[6]

Once a professional person has made the crucial decision to return after studying or working abroad, he rarely changes his mind. The distribution of all respondents in the surveys of returnees appears in the third column of Table II-1. Very few expect to emigrate permanently in the future. Four per cent say they "definitely" or "probably" will go abroad and stay. In contrast, 47 per cent will "definitely" remain at home and 33 per cent will "probably" remain.

In our surveys of returnees, a larger group than the prospective emigrants is the 16 per cent who are undecided. Adverse conditions at home might push them abroad. The problem for developing countries is not only to attract persons back but also to alleviate uncertainties about whether they made the right decision.

Many long-term migrants will return home after retirement

The strength of ties with home is demonstrated by lifetime plans. Unless a professional is a religious or political refugee, he may still foresee eventual return, even after a prolonged career abroad. Table II-3 gives the distribution of plans after retirement by students, stay-ons and returnees who expect to work abroad for a substantial time.

---

6 See Appendix A for "Definition of groups surveyed".

Table II-3

Country Where Long-Term Migrant Expects to Settle After Retirement from Work

Country	Students	Stay-ons	Returnees
Home	56%	46%	79%
Abroad	32	36	16
Don't know	14	18	5
	100%	100%	100%
	100%	100	
Number of respondents who answered question	(787)	(284)	(455)

Wording of the question: "If you think you may remain abroad permanently, will you return to your country of origin after retirement from work?" The question was answered by all persons who said they "definitely" and "probably" would go abroad in answer to the item in Table II-1, *supra*, and by many persons who said they were "uncertain." For the samples included in Table II-3 and for the system of weighting the samples when combined, see Appendix A, "Statistical Notes and Tabulations".

Some long-term migrants favor careers at home for their children

Another example of the strength of home ties is the professional's image of where his children would be best off. Those who plan to return home and remain there overwhelmingly favor their home countries as the best places for their children. Most who plan to emigrate also prefer careers abroad for their children. But, nevertheless, substantial minorities believe their children should live and work at home, even though the parents themselves expect to spend most of their lives abroad. According to Table II-4, among persons who expect to emigrate permanently or who are uncertain about their futures, the home countries are recommended for their children by 37 per cent in the surveys of students, 22 per cent in the surveys of stay-ons, and 69 per cent in the survey of returnees.

Table II-4

Preference for Children's Future Country

Respondents' long-run plans for themselves	Percentages of respondents who wish their children to live and work in their home countries		
	Students	Stay-ons	Returnees
	%	%	%
Home and stay	90	79	93
Abroad or uncertain	37	22	69
Total numbers of respondents who answered			
Home and stay	(1,867)	(90)	(2,151)
Abroad or uncertain	(739)	(249)	(491)

Wording of the question about children: "In what countries do you prefer your children to live and work?" The wording of the question about respondent's own career plans appears in Table II-1, supra.

Many tables in the manuscript are constructed like this. First, respondents are classified by their answers to the questions about their own career plans, divided into (1) returning home and (2) staying abroad or uncertain about future plans. The total numbers for these two categories in the student, stay-on and returnee surveys appear in the third and fourth rows in parentheses. The percentages in the first two rows are the members of each category who named their home country as the ideal site for their children, either alone or in conjunction with a foreign country as a second alternative. In the first two rows, the difference between the percentages and 100 per cent consists of the remainder--i.e., proportions of each category who favored only foreign countries for their children.

The table combines: students in the United States, Canada, and France; stay-ons in the United States and France; returnees in India, Sri Lanka, Republic of Korea, Greece,

Ghana, Brazil, Colombia, and Argentina. For the system of weighting the tabulations in the surveys of students, see Appendix A, "Statistical Notes and Tabulations".

Attachments to home and implications for policy

Is the loss from the brain drain irrecoverable? The literature and policy debates about brain drain usually assume that a migrant is gone forever. But our data show that migration and assimilation are variables. Many persons staying abroad expect to return home. Many returnees are uncertain about their futures. Among persons who say they expect to remain abroad "permanently" and "definitely," some retain attachments drawing them home after retirement. Among many students planning to emigrate and among many professionals planning to work abroad for most of their careers, ties of family and cultural affinity remain, and they always feel foreign abroad.[7]

Therefore changing circumstances at home or abroad can cause more changes of plans than is generally assumed. Stronger pulls from home and stronger pushes from developed countries can result in greater return than is generally assumed. Home governments can recover many apparent stay-ons at later

---

[7]One of the most successful expatriates from a developing country happened to fall into our sample and--in response to questions about comparing his home country with the developed country where he worked--he told our interviewers:

> Well, as a social animal here, you can starve to death in this country. There is no social life here. If you love being an individual, this is the best place to be. [My home country] is just the other way around. Nobody really leaves you alone there. Everyone is interested in what you are doing, and sometimes you can feel very smothered by this. I think it depends on the type of person you are. If you are very social or if you are an individualist...
>
> I can say that life in general is extremely comfortable here. But something is missing. I don't know just what.

stages after study, by keeping in touch with them. Later pages of this monograph--and particularly Chapter VII--will mention the principal pulls and pushes that can work to the advantage of the home country.

Staying on temporarily. Many persons working abroad are not permanent migrants. Rather, they are getting practical experience after classroom study, before returning home. This is common in several fields, particularly in architecture, engineering and languages.

Instead of being brain drain, practical experience can be a valuable educational supplement before the professional returns home, and therefore special visas and programs might be developed. Professional schools abroad and subsequent work sites there might be coordinated better than they are now.

At present the favorite place for temporary work experience is the United States. Perhaps societies more nearly resembling developing countries might be better work sites, to facilitate the adaptation of skills learned in North American and European universities. Even if "third country" training does not replace education in developed societies, "third country" postgraduate work experience is more relevant for employment at home than is staying on temporarily in the United States. Enhancing the work of temporary stay-ons requires a more detailed study of employment abroad than has yet been carried out. Research should be conducted about how temporary stay-ons use their work experience abroad after return. (Until now, surveys such as our have asked only about the utilization of foreign formal education after return.) Investigators should examine the feasibility of organized postgraduate work programs in countries constituting good "half-way houses"--i.e., effectively developing societies that combine technology and organization derived from the more developed countries with the problems and resources of developing countries.

Chapter III

VARIATIONS AMONG HOME COUNTRIES

Countries differ widely in their permanent losses

The debate about brain drain is usually conducted in a very general manner, and one might think it besets all developing countries alike. However, some developing countries lose high proportions of their citizens who study and work abroad, while others lose few.[1]

Table III-1 shows the proportions of students in our surveys completed so far, whose long-term plans are to return or to emigrate, and it shows the proportions of those who are uncertain. Some nationalities have large proportions who say they plan to emigrate permanently: at least 30 per cent of the Trinidadians, Haitians, Argentinians, Egyptians, Lebanese, and Indians. Colombians and Koreans are close to this figure. On the other hand, large proportions of Brazilians, Africans, Tunisians, Pakistanis, and students from many small countries report intentions to return.

Students from different countries vary in the certainty of their plans

Besides the direction of future movements, the

---

[1] Such wide variations have been noticed in a few earlier studies, based on comparisons of aggregate national statistics about flows, such as The Committee on the International Migration of Talent, The International Migration of High-Level Manpower (New York: Praeger Publishers, 1970), esp. pp. 475-483.

data show considerable variations in the certainty of plans. In Table III-1, at least 30 per cent of the Venezuelans and Filipinos have indefinite plans. Over 20 per cent of the Turks and Indians are undecided. The fact that direction and certainty of plans can be independent is demonstrated by the Venezuelans and Filipinos: comparatively few definitely plan to emigrate, but many are uncertain and could go either way.

Tabulations not presented here also show variations in certainty of plans among returnees. Over 20 per cent of the foreign-trained professionals in Sri Lanka and Colombia were not sure whether they would stay home or emigrate in the future. The Korean, Greek, and Brazilian returnees were most likely to have made up their minds, and their plans were to remain home.

An index of return. A simple device for comparing groups is a summary statistic that varies between a large positive number if everyone returns, zero if the group is evenly divided or if everyone is undecided and a large negative number if everyone emigrates. The measure should give more weight to the persons with the firmest plans.

From the question quoted in Tables II-1 and III-1, an index number can be calculated with the following scores:

Definitely return	+2
Probably return	+1
Undecided	0
Probably emigrate	-1
Definitely emigrate	-2

Multiply the scores by the numbers of persons giving each response and divide by the total number of all persons. The index number varies between +2.0 and -2.0. Index scores for home countries appear in the last column of Table III-1 and permit clear comparisons of nations with high and low losses.

The nationalities with the strongest intentions

Table III-1

Long-Run Plans of Principal
Groups of Students from developing countries studying abroad

Home country	Definitely return home and remain	Probably return home and remain	Uncertain	Probably go abroad and stay	Definitely go abroad and stay		Total number of students	Index of return
North America	35%	28	14	14	9	100% =	(372)	.66
Trinidad and Tobago	23%	25	19	16	17	100% =	(152)	.21
Jamaica	37%	33	8	20	2	100% =	(67)	.83
Haiti	29%	33	8	13	17	100% =	(63)	.44
Mexico	52%	20	8	12	8	100% =	(25)	.96
South America	42%	21	16	9	12	100% =	(445)	.72
Brazil	69%	13	8	8	2	100% =	(220)	1.39
Colombia	60%	13	1	24	2	100% =	(49)	1.05
Argentina	16%	29	16	37	2	100% =	(30)	.20
Venezuela	63%	5	30	2	0	100% =	(29)	1.29
Greece	33%	31	18	13	5	100% =	(199)	.74
Africa	82%	10	1	4	3	100% =	(280)	1.64
Ghana	89%	9	0	2	0	100% =	(76)	1.85
Senegal	74%	13	3	9	0	100% =	(51)	1.52
Ivory Coast	71%	24	3	0	2	100% =	(48)	1.62
Cameroon	68%	9	3	11	9	100% =	(56)	1.16

[continued]

Table III-1 [continued]

Home country	Definitely return home and remain	Probably return home and remain	Uncertain	Probably go abroad and stay	Definitely go abroad and stay		Total number of students	Index of return
Middle East and North Africa	34%	18	10	13	25	100% =	(664)	.23
Tunisia	61%	21	7	6	5	100% =	(124)	1.27
Egypt	15%	15	9	21	40	100% =	(192)	-.56
Iran	42%	21	18	7	12	100% =	(125)	.74
Lebanon	39%	15	13	15	18	100% =	(135)	.42
Turkey	27%	27	24	0	22	100% =	(35)	.37
Asia	43%	18	18	14	7	100% =	(744)	.76
India	34%	14	22	21	9	100% =	(300)	.43
Pakistan	52%	19	19	8	2	100% =	(116)	1.11
Korea, Republic of	33%	23	17	16	11	100% =	(116)	.51
Philippines	32	11	45	9	3	100% =	(62)	.60
Thailand	84%	9	5	2	0	100% =	(66)	1.75

The table shows all nationalities that had at least 25 respondents in our surveys of students from developing countries in the United States, Canada, and France. The table includes only the surveys of students. The rows for each region--e.g., "North America", "South America", etc.--are not based only on the responses of students from the countries listed within that region (e.g., Brazil, Colombia, Argentina, and Venezuela in South America) but also include the responses of students from other countries of the region that are not listed separately, because less than 25 of their nationals fell into our samples.

to return--i.e., their index numbers come closest to 2.0--are persons from Ghana, the Ivory Coast, Senegal and Brazil. Students from Egypt have negative numbers, indicating predominant intentions to leave home permanently. Several other nationalities include so many potential migrants that their index numbers--while positive--are close to zero, viz., Argentinians, Trinidadians, and Turks.

The index of return will be used to compare different categories throughout this monograph.

Stay-ons from different home countries vary in their plans to remain abroad or to return

Professionals from developing countries working abroad also differ by nationality in their plans to stay permanently or to return home. Following are the scores on the index of return for the largest national groups in our survey of stay-ons in the United States. The groups are ranked by likelihood of returning home; Brazil has the largest number of persons planning to return (their index number is +.05) and the Philippines has the largest proportion planning to emigrate permanently (their index number is -.80).

Stay-ons in United States from:	Index of return
Brazil	+.05
India	-.30
Iran	-.34
Korea, Republic of	-.53
Argentina	-.54
Philippines	-.80

Brazilians were a nationality with very high intentions to return in the survey of the students reported in Table III-1, and they are the group of stay-ons in our data most likely to return. Argentinian students had one of the lower index numbers of return, and so do their stay-ons. There are some deviations in the two rankings; in particular Indian students have one of the lowest rates of return, but their stay-ons rank second highest. Consequently, the correlation between the two lists of countries ordered by rank is positive but not overwhelmingly high.[2]

<u>Levels of economic development of countries have a limited relation to brain drain</u>

The causes and remedies of brain drain usually have been perceived as economic. The central problems always have been thought to be economic growth and employment: countries lose their professionals if they offer too few jobs, and they attract their professionals home through economic growth.

But this explanation is too simple. Table III-2 compares rates of loss by developing countries and their economic strength. The countries are ranked according to the index of return among their students in our surveys in the United States, Canada, and France. The second and third columns give each country's economic wealth and rate of growth. The customary measure of economic wealth is the average value of the national output produced for each member of the society ("GNP per capita"), and it appears in the second column of Table III-2. The average annual increase in a country's economic strength is not synonymous with its wealth but is a measure of its vigor; a comparison of the second and third columns shows that some wealthy countries (i.e., with larger numbers in column 2) have lower rates of growth (i.e., lower numbers in column 3),

---

[2] Spearman's r_S = .54. Spearman's rank coefficient will be used frequently in this chapter. It is a statistical measure showing the amount of agreement between two lists. In this case, a set of countries is ranked in two lists, derived from our surveys of students and stay-ons. +1 means the maximum association, 0 means no association at all, and -1 means lowest on one list is the highest on the other and so on, inversely throughout the list. The method of calculating Spearman's rank correlation coefficient is described in Sidney Siegel, <u>Nonparametric Statistics for the Behavioral Sciences</u> (New York: McGraw-Hill Book Company, 1956), pp. 202-213.

Table III-2

Characteristics of Countries and Return of Students

Country	Index of return, surveys of students	GNP per capita, 1970	Average annual growth, 1960-1970	University students per 1 million inhabitants, 1965	Physicians per 1 million inhabitants, various dates, 1960-1965	Number of scientific journals, 1961	Gini index of inequality, various dates, 1960-1965
Ghana	1.85	310	-0.4	550	75	0	
Thailand	1.75	200	4.9	1,660	132	50	43.0
Ivory Coast	1.62	310	4.5	420	54	0	
Senegal	1.52	230	0.0	790	52	0	
Brazil	1.39	420	2.4	1,890	379	650	36.4
Venezuela	1.29	980	2.3	5,370	767	90	48.7
Tunisia	1.27	250	0.5	1,410	104	15	
Cameroon	1.16	180	3.8	300	38	0	
Pakistan	1.11	100	2.4	2,670	156	90	21.2
Colombia	1.05	340	1.7	2,140	440	75	
Mexico	.96	670	3.7	3,120	553	225	45.7
Jamaica	.83	550	3.0	1,060	490	0	48.7
Iran	.74	380	5.4	1,050	297	10	
Greece	.74	1,090	6.6	6,260	1,408	60	19.5
Philippines	.60	210	2.9	14,410	720	110	37.9
Korea, Republic of	.51	250	6.8	5,000	351	100	17.7

[continued]

Table III-2 [continued]

Country	Index of return, surveys of students	GNP per capita, 1970	Average annual growth, 1960-1970	University students per 1 million inhabitants, 1965	Physicians per 1 million inhabitants, various dates, 1960-1965	Number of scientific journals, 1961	Gini index of inequality, various dates, 1960-1965
Haiti	.44	110	-0.9	370	71	10	
India	.43	110	1.2	2,840	173	670	22.5
Lebanon	.42	580	2.1	8,440	740	20	
Turkey	.37	310	3.9	2,930	316	90	24.7
Trinidad and Tobago	.21	890	3.8	930	419	0	33.1
Argentina	.20	1,160	2.5	10,890	1,466	310	15.7
Egypt	-.56	210	1.7	5,980	419	70	30.9

Sources of data are . . . Index of return, surveys of students in United States, Canada, and France combined: Table III-1, supra. Gross national product (GNP) per capita and average annual growth in per cent: Trends in Developing Countries (Washington: World Bank, 1973), Table 1.4, with missing data supplied from the 1972 edition. University enrollment, physicians, number of journals, and index of inequality: Charles Lewis Taylor and Michael C. Hudson, World Handbook of Political and Social Indicators (New Haven: Yale University Press, Second edition, 1972), pp. 229, 259, 263, and 322.

The list of countries is arranged by descending likelihood of return, according to the index calculated from the survey of students.

Statistics about diverse characteristics of countries are rarely available for the same year. Although the figures come from slightly different dates during the 1960's, the rank order of countries on each variable rarely changes over short periods. Therefore the rank correlations calculated from these data should be no different than if all the data had been gathered during 1970.

while other wealthy countries have higher growth.

If economic strength--whether defined as wealth alone or as rate of increase in wealth--leads to increasing return after study abroad, the numbers would increase from the bottom to the top of columns 2 and 3, just as they increase from the bottom to the top in column 1. But the pattern is irregular: some low figures are at the top and some high numbers are at the bottom. Some poor or stagnating countries have high return; some rich or growing countries have low return. The correlation coefficients between the lists ordered by rank would be large and positive if economic strength determined rate of return. But the coefficients are small and negative; if there is any pattern in the numbers, countries decline in columns 2 and 3 while they get higher numbers in column 1:

Index of return correlated with:	Spearman's r_s
GNP per capita	-0.14
Annual rate of growth	-0.08

In other words, the wealthier the developing country, the greater its loss.[3] More complex measures of development level[4] produce the same results: the higher the rank of the developing country, the lower the return of its students after study abroad. Even expansion does not increase return: the higher the rate of growth, the greater the loss. Other characteristics of countries must be sought to explain differences in their ability to attract back their students and professionals.

---

[3]The unexpected inverse relationship between wealth and return was noticed earlier in Robert G. Myers, Education and Emigration (New York: David McKay Company, 1972), Ch. 4.

[4]For example, Donald V. McGranahan, et al., Contents and Measurements of Socio-Economic Development (Geneva: United Nations Research Institute for Social Development, 1970), Ch. VI; and Theodore Caplow and Kurt Finsterbusch, "Development Rank: A New Method of Rating National Development" (New York: Bureau of Applied Social Research, Columbia University, 1965).

This result is paradoxical only from the perspective of traditional development theories that are now being abandoned. Once it was believed that industrialization, urbanization, and the growth of economic indicators (such as gross national product per capita) would automatically increase employment, general prosperity, social unity, and national stability. But now it is realized that inequality, conflict, and unemployment can spread even when macroeconomic indicators rise. Therefore, the employment, prosperity, and morale of professionals may lag, even when GNP is growing for the economy as a whole.[5] In fact, economic growth and urbanization disrupt the close social relationships that--as we shall see in later pages of this and other chapters--draw persons back to their home countries.

Imbalance and privilege affect brain drain

Structural imbalances in the market for professionals have a stronger relation to brain drain. If a country is producing many educated persons--and, particularly, if it is overproducing them--return by its foreign-trained persons is discouraged. This is one reason why mere level of economic development and rate of growth are negatively related to return: the greatest scarcities of professionals and the greatest certainty of employment occur in the poorest countries, which educate the fewest persons; return is lower to the more prosperous developing countries that educate many professionals.

The relationship can be calculated from Table III-2. The fourth column gives the number of students in institutions of higher learning for every one million inhabitants. The fifth column gives the

---

[5] For a good description of this paradox and a critique of the traditional development policy that assumed automatic benefits from the growth of macrostatistical indicators, see Dudley Seers, "The Meaning of Development" (Brighton: Institute of Development Studies, University of Sussex, 1969). For a case study of a country that raised the statistical indicators but did not expand welfare, see World Bank, Economic Growth of Colombia (Baltimore: The Johns Hopkins Press, 1972).

number of physicians in practice within the country for every one million inhabitants. (No data exist about the total numbers of professionals outside medicine for most countries, but probably the number of doctors correlates highly with the numbers of others.) Although the wealthier countries tend to have more students in universities, these two dimensions are not identical: some less wealthy countries, such as the Philippines, have many students. The rank correlations between return and each of these measures are large and negative:

Index of return correlated with:	Spearman's r_s
Students in higher education per million inhabitants	-0.49
Physicians per million inhabitants	-0.48

In other words, the greater the expansion of university education and professional output in a developing country, the lower the rate of return from abroad.[6]

A country's ability to absorb its educated manpower can be estimated by dividing gross national product (GNP) per capita into the number of university-level students per million inhabitants. The largest figures result for countries with a university system that educates many more people than its economic level can employ; the smallest numbers result from calculations for countries whose university output is modest (thus keeping pace with economic development) or whose economy is very prosperous (permitting it to absorb all its university graduates). The rank-order correlation between the

---

[6]More sophisticated measures of the development of high-level manpower also correlate inversely with return, with nearly identical numbers. For example, the rank order correlation between our index of return and Harbison's composite educational index is -.44. His index is described in Frederick Harbison and Charles Myers, Education, Manpower and Economic Growth (New York: McGraw-Hill Book Company, 1964), pp. 45-48.

index of return and this measure of structural imbalance is -0.42: the greater the oversupply of professionals in a developing country, the lower the rate of return.[7]

This relationship between scarcity and return is strong but not perfect--i.e., -0.42 is closer to zero than to -1.0. Exceptions occur: many persons return to overcrowded countries; some countries lose substantial numbers of professionals abroad, while jobs are unfilled at home.[8] Therefore, even sophisticated economic models of differences in demand and supply of professionals among countries are not good enough by themselves to explain everyone's migration choices. As Chapter VI will show, an individual's decisions are determined by a configuration of professional, monetary, personal, and patriotic motives. How to combine these appeals most persuasively varies among countries.

Another reason why simple measures of demand for professionals are not enough to explain return is that other measures of effective demand may be operating in contradictory ways. For example, essential to the utilization of professionals in a country is the machinery for generating and spreading knowledge and techniques. But it is often weakest when the demand for professionals is strongest. As a result, scarcities in the labor market and traditional social bonds may bring professionals

---

[7]Correlations between brain drain and other measures of overproduction of university graduates have been reported by Michel E.A. Hervé, "International Migration of Physicians and Students" and "Education and Economic Growth" (Washington: Office of Program and Policy Coordination, United States Agency for International Development, 1968 and 1970).

[8]Examples are described in Justus M. Van der Kroef, "The U.S. and the World's Brain Drain," International Journal of Comparative Sociology, Volume XI, Number 3 (September 1970), pp. 227-228; and Jay Ralph Buffenmyer, Emigration of High-Level Manpower and National Development: A Case Study of Jamaica (Pittsburgh: dissertation for the Ph.D. in International Affairs, University of Pittsburgh, 1970).

back, even when the scientific infra-structure seems weak; persons may avoid other countries for social and cultural reasons, even when scientific services are better. One measure of the level of scientific stimulation and demand for scientific output is the number of journals in scientific and technical fields. Column 6 of Table III-2 gives the numbers. The rank-order correlation with the index of return is -0.30: the _fewer_ the journals published in a developing country, the _greater_ the return by those of its students who study abroad.

Professionals may avoid countries whose imbalances are disadvantageous, but they may be satisfied with societies whose imbalances work to their benefit. Column 7 of Table III-2 gives the "Gini index", a measure of the inequality in the distribution of incomes and wealth in a country.[9] The larger the index number, the less equal the distribution of incomes within the population and the greater the monopoly on the society's benefits by elites, including the professional classes. The rank correlation between the index of return and the index of inequality is +0.52: the less equal the distribution of income, the greater the return by those who study abroad.

Citizens of different countries vary in their capacity to adjust to foreign societies

Since countries vary in wealth and in investment policies, they differ in the facilities provided their professionals. Equipment, buildings, and other services are factors influencing a person's decision to return home or emigrate. But, as

---

[9]The Gini index and other measures of inequality are explained in Hayward R. Alker and Bruce M. Russett, "Indices for Comparing Inequality", in Richard L. Merritt and Stein Rokkan (editors), _Comparing Nations_ (New Haven: Yale University Press, 1966), Ch. 16; and Charles Lewis Taylor and Michael C. Hudson, _World Handbook of Political and Social Indicators_ (New Haven: Yale University Press, Second edition, 1972), pp. 211-213.

we shall see throughout this monograph (and particularly in this chapter and in Chapter VI) simple pecuniary and "material" causes are not enough to explain return and emigration: some countries with modest facilities have high return, while other countries with better equipment and services have higher losses.

Several social and cultural factors seem even more important influences upon return and emigration. They will be specified in more detail in Chapter VI. Their strength varies among home countries; students and professionals from some countries more than others feel the pull from home and encounter greater difficulties in adjusting to developed countries.

Our questionnaires contained a list of twenty-six problems of students and professionals, while studying and working abroad. Each respondent checked those that were important difficulties during his study in a developed country.

<u>Ties with home</u>. One cluster of items dealt with feelings of separation from family, friends, and the culture of the home country. Some nationalities, in our surveys of students, missed family, friends, and home far more than others--their average scores on these clusters were 10 per cent or more higher than the averages for all other nationalities. These included several national groups with high rates of return, viz., persons from Senegal, the Ivory Coast, Cameroon and Pakistan. Another group who strongly missed home was the Jamaicans. They have other experiences inducing them to emigrate, but the counter-effects from home ties cause their rate of return to be higher than it would be otherwise.

Another set of items in the battery fell into a distinct cluster measuring loneliness and homesickness while abroad. Again, the nationalities with the strongest complaints had high rates of return, viz., Senegalese, Ivoirians, Cameroonians, Pakistanis, and Thais. The Jamaicans also complained about this problem far more than the average, and this fact seems to have limited their potential rate of emigration.

Educational and language barriers. Incompatibility with the educational system and languages of developed countries inhibit emigration from many developing countries. Several questions asked whether adjusting to an unfamiliar educational system or speaking a new language were troublesome. Among the national groups that experienced such barriers most intensely were three with high rates of return, viz., Brazilians, Thais, and Venezuelans. Two national groups speaking non-western languages also fell among the nationalities with the highest scores on these difficulties (Iranians and Koreans), but they had higher rates of emigration because of countervailing problems in finding jobs at home. For them, the economic push from home contradicted the cultural push from abroad, so that return rates were lower than if no barriers arose from the domestic labor market.

Several nationalities were accustomed to speaking the languages of developed countries at home and in their schools. For citizens of developing countries that were former colonies, their primary and secondary education usually is compatible with the higher education of the former colonial power where they go for foreign study. Therefore, few encounter educational and linguistic barriers when they study abroad. Some have high rates of emigration to those former colonial powers or to developed countries such as Canada, which have many institutions derived from Europe, viz., Trinidadians, Jamaicans, Lebanese, Egyptians, Indians, and Filipinos. Several other nationalities rarely experience such barriers abroad but have high rates of return because of other pushes from abroad and other pulls from home, viz., persons from Ghana, Senegal, the Ivory Coast, and Cameroon.

Discrimination. An important barrier against emigration is skin color or other physical and cultural traits that evoke discrimination by the populations, teachers, and students of developed countries. The nationalities that most often perceived discrimination during study abroad included some with very high rates of return, viz., persons from Ghana, Senegal, the Ivory Coast, Cameroon, Pakistan and Thailand. Discrimination was also commonly reported by several other national groups with lower rates of return, but emigration might have been even greater without such barriers, viz., Trinidadians and Jamaicans.

Many heterogeneous countries have brain drain, since emigration is high among minority groups

Among those from developing countries who study abroad, membership in minority groups is strongly associated with brain drain. Therefore countries with intergroup conflicts (ethnic, religious, racial, etc.) have higher losses.

When developing countries were colonies of European powers or were governed by less nationalistic governments of their own, many attracted considerable migration from other cultural, religious, and racial areas. It was easy for migrants to spread to distant parts of the ruling government's jurisdiction, such as Indians throughout the British Empire and Lebanese throughout the French Empire. In addition, refugees from Turkish, Russian, or German persecution settled in many developing countries. The more Westernized and urbanized minorities strove for more education and property than the indigenous populations, and they became prominent in business and the professions.

Independence and increasing nationalism have unseated the protectors of these groups. The new governments have followed nationalist and homogenizing policies in their hiring policies, in controls over business, and in the curricula and language of instruction in schools. Internal conflict among ethnic, linguistic, racial, and religious groups is common in the world,[10] and the lives of professionals

[10]A subject with such universality and serious consequences has recently generated a vast literature in the social sciences. Two excellent papers about internal conflict in composite societies are Walker Connor, "Nation-Building or Nation-Destroying?", World Politics, Volume 24 (April 1972), pp. 319-355; and Donald L. Horowitz, "Direct, Displaced, and Cumulative Ethnic Aggression," Comparative Politics, Volume 6, Number 1

are affected. Once a substantial amount of migration involved unprivileged and powerless minorities. But uncertainty about the future now results in brain drain by considerable numbers of the newly privileged but still powerless.[11]

Cultural minorities. Many developing countries have substantial minorities who speak languages other than the official or most common tongues. Long before he studies in the country that was formerly the colonial power in his own country, the future professional has lived in its cultural setting at home. But linguistic division during recent decades has replaced religion as the most common basis of conflict between groups, and the professionals are involved: if the members of minority groups return, they may experience intense and unpredictable conflict; many can avoid such conflict and live in a completely congenial setting only by emigration.

According to Part 1 of Table III-3, many members of minority linguistic groups plan to emigrate after

---

(October 1973), pp. 1-16. The increasingly serious linguistic sources of intergroup conflict have been little studied, but notable exceptions are the papers by Herbert Kelman and Johathan Pool in Joshua A. Fishman (editor), Advances in the Sociology of Language, (The Hague: Mouton, 1972), Volume 2, pp. 185-230.

[11] A few earlier questionnaire surveys of foreign students and migrating professionals have noticed that members of minority groups were included in the brain drain. The fact that they are over-represented in these flows has never been examined systematically. For example, Paul Ritterband, The Non-Returning Foreign Student: The Israeli Case (New York: Bureau of Applied Social Research, Columbia University, 1968), pp. 63-66; Robert Myers, Education and Emigration (New York: David McKay Company, 1972), p. 259; and John W. Orton, "An Interview-Based Study of Pakistanis Employed in the Professions in the United States" (New York: Institute for International Education, 1965), pp. 8, 25, 39, and 54.

Table III-3

Long-Term Plans of Minorities

Part 1: Respondents were not asked directly whether they belonged to minority groups. Rather, our questionnaire asked many items about languages spoken and read at different stages of life, including a request to list the "Principal languages used at home, up to ten years of age." We identified the language pattern of each developing country, and the computer compared the respondent and the country, in order to assign him a category. "Western and minority" means that the person spoke one of the European or North American languages in a developing country where it was not widely used; "Western but not minority" means that he spoke such a language, and it was one of the official or most common tongues of the developing country; and "Vernacular" means that the country spoke predominantly one or more non-European languages. A Spanish-speaking Colombian, for example, appears in the "Western but not minority" row; a French-speaking Colombian would be in the "Western and minority" category.

Part 2: Respondents were asked their religions. Published sources helped us identify the religious composition of each developing country, and the computer compared the respondent and the country, to see whether he adhered to one of the principal religions in that country. If he belonged to a less common religion, he was classified a member of a minority.

Parts 3 and 4: Respondents were asked their race. We identified the racial pattern of each developing country, and the computer compared the respondent and the country, in order to assign him to a category. "Minority" means that most citizens were from races other than the respondent's; "majority" means that the respondent belonged to one of the numerically largest races in that country. For example, a "Far Eastern" person is from a "minority" in western Asia, Africa, or Latin America; but he is a member of the "majority" if his home country is Korea.

[continued]

Table III-3 [continued]

The table combines students from the surveys in the United States, Canada, and France; stay-ons in the United States and France; and returnees in India, Sri Lanka, Republic of Korea, Greece, Brazil, Colombia, and Argentina.

	Index of return for			Total number of respondents		
	Students	Stay-ons	Returnees	Students	Stay-ons	Returnees
1. Language spoken during childhood:						
(a) Western and minority	-.30	-.88	1.19	(267)	(20)	(154)
(b) Western but not minority	.68	-.67	1.23	(1,335)	(125)	(1,712)
(c) Vernacular	1.06	-.24	1.25	(1,239)	(244)	(1,049)
2. Religious position in home country:						
(a) Minority	-.09	-.93	.93	(427)	(71)	(231)
(b) Majority	1.03	-.22	1.26	(1,732)	(257)	(2,159)
(c) Atheist, agnostic	.87	-.51	1.17	(296)	(41)	(257)

[continued]

Table III-3 [continued]

	Index of return for			Total number of respondents		
	Students	Stay-ons	Returnees	Students	Stay-ons	Returnees
3. Racial position in home country:						
(a) Minority	.27	----	1.08	(231)	(5)	(43)
(b) Majority	.91	-.44	1.27	(2,410)	(381)	(2,327)
4. Position classified by respondent's race:						
(a) White						
Minority	-.04			(92)		
Majority	.62			(1,659)		
(b) Far Eastern, Oriental						
Minority	.54			(86)		
Majority	1.10			(210)		
(c) Black						
Minority	----			(4)		
Majority	1.42			(470)		

foreign study.[12] For them, study abroad is the first step in a move with deep roots. The division is most obvious in the surveys of foreign students: if they grew up in families speaking a language not generally used in their home country, half plan to emigrate; if they spoke European languages that were among the official languages of the country (for example, French in francophone Africa, English in Commonwealth countries, Spanish in Latin America), smaller but substantial proportions expect to leave; if their families used the non-European vernaculars, they were likely to return. The index numbers of return involving language show one of the strongest relationships in our data: in the surveys of students, the minority group members have an index of -.30, showing a substantial tendency to emigrate; the speakers of vernaculars have an index of 1.06, showing a strong intention to return; and the users of Western languages widely spoken at home fall between (.68). The tendency for minority groups to emigrate far more than speakers of vernaculars is apparent among stay-ons as well.

Because of these differences, returnees include comparatively few members of linguistic minorities; the ones who returned despite their minority status

---

[12] Our methods of classification tend to underestimate the amount of brain drain associated with minority status. The questionnaire asked respondents for languages spoken during childhood, for their religion, and for their race. We classified countries by their linguistic, religious, and racial composition. The computer assigned the individual to a "minority" status if he did not share the common characteristics of the country. If a society was mixed in language, religion, and race, it was so identified, and anyone possessing any common trait was classified as part of the "majority." For example, most Indians were treated as members of the "majority" at home. But a more thorough study of each individual's life might show that many persons in mixed societies really experience minority status. If so, the correlation between minority position and brain drain should increase, since emigration from such countries is higher than average, and since our present classification methods increase the count for emigration by members of "majorities."

have had strong attachments and seem determined to stay. The returnee samples contain many persons who grew up speaking European languages that were also used by the governments, by the elites, or (less often) by entire populations.

Additional tabulations not presented in this manuscript show particular groups that are most likely to emigrate. The brain drain consists partly of French-speaking minorities moving out of Africa, the Middle East, and Asia toward North America. In addition it includes members of Greek, Italian, Eastern European, and German families from Latin America; Greeks and Armenians from the Middle East; and Western minorities from Asia.

Religious minorities. Part of the brain drain consists of religious minorities, according to Part 2 of Table III-3. In the surveys of students, nearly half the members of religious minorities planned to emigrate, while the majority groups planned to return. (In Table III-3, the index numbers of return among students are -.09 for members of minorities and 1.03 for members of majorities.)

In the stay-on sample as well, minority groups are much less likely to return than majority groups. (Judging from our small sample, many nonreturnees in France are Jewish refugees from francophone Muslim countries.)

Members of religious minorities in the returnee samples had strong enough ties to return home. But their commitment to remain is weaker--i.e., their index of return is .93 while the index for the followers of numerically larger religions is 1.26. Over one-quarter of the members of religious minorities in the returnee surveys were uncertain about their futures.

Among the religious groups included in our surveys, the most likely to emigrate from developing countries are Jews from the Middle East and Iran, Eastern Orthodox from any country, Muslims from any non-Islamic country, Protestants from the Catholic countries of Latin America, Christians from Egypt and India, and Catholics from the English-speaking West Indies.

Race is one of the most important influences upon migration: in general, membership in a racial minority results in emigration, according to Part 3 of Table III-3. But race operates in diverse ways.

Emigration by minority races is most true of whites in darker-skinned societies, according to Part 4 of Table III-3. Black minorities in white societies rarely obtain the opportunity for foreign study, so we do not know whether they would use it as a channel of emigration. Probably they would not be as likely to emigrate to developed countries, since they would still be members of minorities in Europe or North America. Much as they might dislike conditions at home, blacks are not easily accepted by the white populations of the developed countries, according to our tabulations concerning adjustment problems during study. Members of Far Eastern races are also more likely to emigrate if they belong to minorities than if the rest of the population is Far Eastern as well. In short, emigration after study abroad is greatest among the lighter-skinned minorities in darker-skinned societies.

More detailed tabulations suggest that the minorities most likely to emigrate are: white persons from Trinidad and Tobago, and Africa; Orientals from the West Indies, the Philippines, and Indonesia; and a sprinkling of other persons.[13]

---

[13] The simple conception of race breaks down when applied to many populations in South Central Asia. Although darker than Europeans, they are usually classified as "Caucasians." Table III-3 includes them in the "Caucasian majority" in their home countries. We reran Table III-3 without citizens of India and of other Southern Asian countries, and the statistical conclusions were the same.

Other motives for emigration and return vary by home country

Economic level, balance between the number and demand for professionals, family ties, the strength of cultural attachments, and intergroup relations are only some of the characteristics of countries that affect brain drain. Crucial causes are a sense of confidence in the home country, a feeling that one's efforts will be appreciated, patriotism, and optimism about the future of the country for oneself and for one's children. As Chapter VI will show, these attitudes are associated with migration and return: if they are weak, persons are more likely to leave home; if they are strong, persons are more likely to return. And, as Chapter VI will report, these attitudes vary among developing countries: those with higher rates of return in Table III-1 more often have the leadership, sense of national purpose, or organizational growth that generate high morale among professionals.

Working abroad temporarily varies by home country

So far, this chapter has described differences among developing countries in permanent emigration. Table II-2 and the accompanying text showed that many professionals work abroad temporarily after the end of foreign study. This sequence too varies widely by country. The proportions of our samples of returnees who worked abroad before return are:

India	36 per cent
Ghana	25 per cent
Korea, Republic of	23 per cent
Greece	20 per cent
Sri Lanka	17 per cent
Argentina	16 per cent
Colombia	5 per cent
Brazil	5 per cent

In other words, over one-third of the Indians have had practical experience abroad, but nearly every Colombian and Brazilian returnee goes straight home after getting his foreign degree.

These differences are confirmed in our surveys of students. Half the Indian students in our survey in the United States say they plan to work abroad after study and then return to India. Only one-quarter of the Indian students in the United States plan to return home at once after obtaining degrees, and only 11 per cent plan to emigrate permanently after study.[14] Thirty-two per cent of the Korean students in the United States plan to work abroad for a while and return rather than emigrate permanently.

The surveys of students suggest several additional nationalities (for which we do not yet have surveys of returnees) that often stay abroad to work temporarily before return. They do not undertake temporary work as often as the Indians and Koreans, but at least one-fourth of their foreign students contemplate it. They are students from Trinidad and Tobago, Jamaica, and Tunisia.

Many students go abroad for study, intending from the start to stay on temporarily before return. On-the-job experience is part of their educational plans. The questionnaire presented a long battery of reasons why students went abroad for study. (A complete analysis will appear in Chapter VIII.) One item was:

> Practical experience of working abroad in my specialty is important, and the only way I could get it was by a visa as a student there.

---

[14] An earlier survey also found that many Indians seek jobs in the United States but say they plan to return home. The authors suspected that the proportions who actually remain permanently in the United States exceed the proportions originally intending to stay. Temporary work can be prolonged, as the individual becomes integrated into the occupational system and social structure of the United States, while his contacts with the job market in India remain weak. Marjorie H. Klein _et al_., "The Foreign Student Adaptation Program: Social Experiences of Asian Students in the U.S.", _International Educational and Cultural Exchange_, Volume VI, Number 3 (Winter 1971), pp. 87-88.

The proportions of respondents who checked this reason as "very important" or "important" in their original decision to study abroad are:

Surveys of students in:

France	30 per cent
United States	27 per cent
Canada	22 per cent

Surveys of stay-ons in:

France	42 per cent
United States	26 per cent

Surveys of returnees in:

Argentina	46 per cent
Sri Lanka	35 per cent
India	33 per cent
Ghana	31 per cent
Greece	25 per cent
Colombia	20 per cent
Brazil	17 per cent
Korea, Republic of	14 per cent

Constant turnover occurs among foreigners working abroad temporarily before return. The years worked abroad are few. Following is the median number of years between the end of study and return in our surveys of returnees. Persons who never worked abroad were excluded from the calculations.

India	2 years
Korea, Republic of	2 years
Ghana	2 years
Sri Lanka	1 year
Greece	1 year
Colombia	1 year
Brazil	Less than 1 year
Argentina	Less than 1 year

The characteristics of developing countries and their implications for policy

Developing countries differ widely in their losses of professionals and in their ability to attract back students after completion of study abroad. Therefore brain drain is not a universal problem requiring universal policies applying to all developing countries. Rather, the situation must be examined in each country, and remedial actions must be attuned to each.

Certain characteristics of the social structure, economy, government, and culture determine whether a developing country loses many or few of its professionals educated abroad. This book will describe the general principles. The particular configuration of strengths and weaknesses varies among countries, accounting for high or low retention of their foreign-trained professionals. Policy-makers for a particular country need to assess both the strengths and weaknesses of that society.

Simple assumptions about reasons for brain drain should be revised. Wealth, level of development, and rate of growth do not automatically govern brain drain. Merely increasing wealth is no panacea. Rather, it is the structure of the economy and the structure of the society which govern the motives of professionals. For example, imbalances between the educational system and the economy, so that the number of professionals outstrips opportunities, will result in many departures.

Another feature of the country which policy-makers must note, is the position of professionals in the group structure of society and how the structure is affected by government policies. If professionals are heavily recruited from linguistic, cultural, religious, or racial minorities, brain drain will result from policies that make the majority's languages and customs the official standards or that reserve higher ranks in organizations to members of the majority. In such societies, greater toleration of minorities will reduce the brain drain.

Developing countries differ widely in whether their students trained abroad stay on temporarily for practical experience at work. This is so common for some countries that their manpower and educational planners should consider how such overseas experience can best fit their countries' domestic needs.

Chapter IV

VARIATIONS AMONG COUNTRIES OF STUDY

Developed countries vary in receptivity to immigrants from developing countries

Developed countries are not equally open.[1] Some are closed societies; in their immigration procedures and culture, they accept few foreigners as citizens or permanent residents. They have many foreign students from Africa and Asia, but--unless they can appeal as stateless refugees--such persons usually can settle only temporarily as outsiders to solve shortages in jobs that citizens avoid.

Some developed countries are hospitable only to foreigners of similar culture, language, and color. Asians and Africans are not easily accepted. Considerable numbers of foreign professionals work, including many from Africa and Asia. They alleviate labor shortages in particular sectors. But most live in their own segregated groups, believe the indigenous population is inhospitable, and worry about restrictive government policies.

---

[1] Variations in law are described in Richard Plender, International Migration Law (Leiden: A. W. Sijthoff, 1972). Some comparisons of practices appear in Freda Hawkins, "Canadian Immigration Policy and Management" and W. R. Böhning, "Immigration policies of Western European Countries," International Migration Review, Volume VIII, Number 2 (Summer 1974), pp. 141-164.

A few developed countries are open to immigration by professionals from developing countries. Immigrants even from non-white societies can move around the country, find many jobs, and encounter many enclaves speaking their own or other languages. Immigrant visas and citizenship are obtained easily. Such a comparatively open environment is unusual; it results from a particular combination of economic expansion, geographical space, underpopulation, dependency on external infusions to produce indigenous culture, and the absence of jingo nationalism. But no society is completely open; mass entry (or rumors of future mass entry) by foreigners of quite different cultures and colors will generate resistance and occasional tightening of immigration and visas.

The United States illustrates the fact that no country is ever completely open, enabling foreign professionals to work on an equal basis as its own citizens, and that periods of apparent hospitality do not last forever. Good jobs have been available for immigrants only in certain fields during periods when the economy expanded faster than domestic university output, but native-born citizens received the more permanent, prestigious, and rewarding posts. High immigration of professionals was not a deliberate and open policy but was arranged circumspectly through little publicized amendments creating loopholes in the visa laws, through relaxed administration of the regulations, and through special bills for individuals. Some foreign professionals entered in sufficient numbers to create communities enabling newcomers to adjust, but they could never forget they were different from the rest of the society, and many remained nostalgic for home. Economic recessions and the overproduction of doctorates held by native-born persons eventually, during the 1970's, led to rumors that jobs would become more scarce. This set of market conditions, government policies, and cultural conditions bred considerable insecurity. Most foreign students from developing countries retain ties with home and plan to return, despite their appreciation of the advantages of work in the United States.

Variations in receptivity to persons from developing countries appear in our survey data. As we said in the last chapter, our questionnaires included a battery of twenty-six items about problems of adjustment, while students and professionals were studying abroad. The list fell into a few clusters, representing types of adjustment problems. The respondent was given a score of "high" if he fell into the upper half of the distribution of answers to all items in that cluster. A "high" score resulted if most of his answers to the items belonging to that cluster rated them as "very important", "important", or "of slight importance." His score was "low" if he said the items were "unimportant" or "did not apply to him.[2]

Table IV-1 shows the proportions in each survey of students who scored "high" on those clusters reflecting the hospitality of developed countries to persons from developing societies. As a general rule, Canada is perceived by the students as most open, France is most closed, and the United States is intermediate. I.e., for each set of problems, the proportions with high scores are lowest in Canada and highest in France.

Two deviations exist from these general patterns. France offers fewer barriers than the United States with respect to educational and linguistic difficulties. Most foreign students come to France from countries that use the French language and have school systems heavily influenced by France. Many foreign students come to the United States from Asian and Latin American countries whose school systems are European or indigenous in conception and where English is not common. Therefore, educational and linguistic problems for students are greater in the United States than in France.

---

[2]"High" really means that the item had some effect on the respondent, while "low" means it had no effect. If the responses are divided into only two approximately equal groups by the usual methods of scale construction--as we try here--the answer "of slight importance" falls into the same group as "very important" and "important". The other group consists of persons who were not affected at all by the variable.

Another exception to the general pattern involves discrimination. Canada and the United States are perceived as having comparable and lower levels of discrimination (23% and 22%), while students in France report more (31%).

Table IV-1

Adjustment Problems of Students by Country of Study

Problems of adjustment	Proportions with high scores on each cluster from surveys of students in		
	Canada	United States	France
	%	%	%
Educational and linguistic difficulties	20	30	22
Loneliness	30	37	45
Separation from home	36	48	51
Discrimination	23	22	31
Total number of students	(922)	(1,566)	(491)

Potential migrants gravitate toward certain countries for study

Because of its more open immigration policies, Canada slightly more than other developed countries attracts persons who use study abroad as an opportunity to explore the prospects for emigration. As the last chapter mentioned and as Chapter VIII will report in full detail, questionnaires for all students and professionals presented a battery of items eliciting reasons for going to a particular developed country for study. In the surveys of students, the respondent was asked his reasons for going to the country where he was currently enrolled. Three possible answers were:

> I was seriously considering emigrating and I thought it best to try it out first as a student.
>
> I wanted to establish rights of citizenship or of permanent residence abroad.
>
> I needed the qualifications to have a good career abroad in case I stayed there.

Comparatively small proportions checked the boxes that indicated the serious migration plans (i.e., the first two items) were "very important" or "important" in the decision to study abroad rather than at home. The more tentative exploration (i.e., the third item) was mentioned by larger numbers. For all three motives, slightly more students in Canada said the reasons were "very important" or "important":

	Explore migration	Acquire rights	Qualifications for career abroad
	%	%	%
Canada	12	14	37
United States	8	8	33
France	8	1	15

According to Table III-3 and the accompanying text, an important reason for emigration is membership in a minority group. Because of Canada's reputation as a tolerant multi-ethnic society and because it has both French-speaking and English-speaking universities, Canada attracts far more foreign students from minority groups than other developed countries do. The proportions of the samples of students belonging to minority groups are:

	Canada %	United States %	France %
Ethnic minority, reflected by language during childhood	11	5	5
Religious	24	12	13
Racial	16	7	3
Any type of minority group, including the above	46	24	21

The goals of these minority groups are jobs in the United States and Canada. Many find Canada an ideal combination of European culture and the more open American economy. French-speaking minorities might prefer France, but it is difficult to settle there and obtain good jobs. Economic and housing opportunities are more favorable in Canada, part of the country is French-speaking, and English-speaking Canada contains many unassimilated European enclaves where an immigrant can feel at home.

Immigration doors are more open in some countries than in others

Type of visa is often thought closely associated with permanent migration of students. Therefore, it is said, brain drain can be reduced by limiting the number of entry visas that enable persons to settle in developed countries.[3]

Type of visa is associated with migration plans in our data. A much higher proportion of foreign students in Canada than in other developed countries

---

[3]For example, International Migration of Talent and Skills (Washington: Hearings before the Subcommittee on Immigration and Naturalization of the Committee on the Judiciary, United States Senate, 90th Congress, First Session, 1967), esp. pp. 113-132 and 161-174.

plan to emigrate, because it is much easier to enter Canada with immigrant papers. In our survey, one-third of the students in Canada arrived on immigrant visas; by the time of the survey, an additional one-sixth had acquired them. Less than one-twelfth of the students in our survey in the United States had applied for American citizenship when they arrived, and the number increased to only one-eighth at the time of the survey. A stay-on sample, of course, includes many applicants for citizenship.

Table IV-2 classifies respondents in the student and stay-on surveys by the visa held upon arrival in the developed countries where they studied and by the type held at the time of the survey. The table gives the index of return for each category. The immigrant visas and other "welcoming" or "loose" arrangements are associated with much higher immigration--i.e., their index numbers of return are close to zero or are negative.

Table IV-2 shows another pattern described in Chapter II. Many students and professionals move back and forth among countries; even permanent residence rights or citizenship abroad are not automatically followed by life-long stays in Europe or North America. The index numbers of return for holders of these papers are not -2.0 but are closer to zero; for certain groups, they are even positive. Many persons acquire permanent resident visas or immigrant visas not in order to migrate permanently but in order to work, either to supplement their stipends during study or to gain practical experience after the end of formal instruction. Acquiring permanent rights in a developed country permits wider options.[4]

---

[4]A recent survey of stay-ons in the United States also found that obtaining foreign citizenship is often a method of ensuring wider opportunities, rather than a guarantee of permanent emigration. Several persons obtaining American citizenship planned to return home nevertheless. <u>Immigrant Scientists and Engineers in the United States: A Study of Characteristics and Attitudes</u> (Washington: National Science Foundation, 1973), p. 20.

A policy problem is whether some persons harbor plans to enter a developed country, obtain a student visa while concealing their intentions, and then change the visa after arrival. The "exchange" or Section J visa of the United States is supposed to prevent this. It is designed for participants in organized educational programs and is not to be changed to any other visa until the person has been out of the United States for at least two years. The "student" or Section F visa can be changed without the two-year departure requirement, but it shares with the J visa the requirement that it be given only to "an alien having residence in a foreign country which he has no intention of abandoning."[5] In our data, the J visa seems to accomplish what was intended, but largely because their holders are committed to their home countries regardless of the regulations: high proportions of the holders of J's expect to return, and few change their statuses after arrival in the United States. Of course, some losses occur: thirty-nine of the applicants for American citizenship in the stay-on survey had first entered on J visas, seventeen planned to remain abroad,

---

[5] In practice, the rules are ambiguous in their texts and uneven in their administration. The applicant merely seeks to enter the United States and has no control over the type of visa issued to him. Some American consulates issue J visas where others might give F's, and vice versa. As we can see from our data, some persons obtain visas while planning to emigrate, but this is more common among the F's than among the J's. After arrival in the United States some holders of J visas change them to F or H without leaving, by persuading the Immigration and Naturalization Service that they or their dependents will suffer "hardships" or that their employment will contribute to the "public interest" of the United States. On the history of visa law in the United States since World War II and on the steady widening of loopholes, see Rosemary Stevens and Joan Vermeulen, Foreign Trained Physicians and American Medicine (Washington: Bureau of Health Manpower Education, National Institutes of Health, 1972), Ch. 3.

Table IV-2

Visa and Future Plans*

	Type of visa held at start of education abroad				Type of visa held at time of survey			
	Index of return in surveys of		Total number of respondents		Index of return in surveys of		Total number of respondents	
	Students	Stay-ons	Students	Stay-ons	Students	Stay-ons	Students	Stay-ons
United States:								
Student (F)	1.14	-.25	(979)	(200)	1.21	.71	(947)	(6)
Exchange (J)	1.58	-.26	(241)	(56)	1.61	.85	(248)	(11)
Tourist (B)	.90	-.59	(144)	(8)	1.05	----	(9)	0
Residence (H)	.69	-.71	(27)	(13)	.82	.36	(49)	(25)
Immigrant, awaiting citizenship	-.03	-.56	(97)	(46)	.07	-.21	(194)	(228)
Family of diplomat (A or G)	1.45	----	(41)	0	1.43		(45)	0
Spouse of student (F2 or J2)	.91	----	(7)	0	----	----	(5)	0
United States citizen	.92	----	(6)	0	.30	-1.20	(10)	(54)

*Some foreign students arrive with full citizenship rights in the country of study. Usually one parent was born there, and therefore the student has dual citizenship. If any category has fewer than six respondents, the index of return has not been calculated. As in all our data, statistics based on very few cases should be interpreted cautiously. We have included small categories from the stay-on survey, since the alternative is no information at all.

[continued]

Table IV-2 [continued]

	Type of visa held at start of education abroad				Type of visa held at time of survey			
	Index of return in surveys of		Total number of respondents		Index of return in surveys of		Total number of respondents	
	Students	Stay-ons	Students	Stay-ons	Students	Stay-ons	Students	Stay-ons
Canada:								
Student	1.08		(521)		1.26		(385)	
Tourist	.30		(49)		----		(2)	
Immigrant	-.54		(307)		-.28		(446)	
Canadian citizen					.08		(15)	
France:								
Touriste	.71	-1.52	(127)	(12)	----	----	(3)	0
Visa of long duration (*Visa longue durée*)	1.51	-1.27	(178)	(9)	1.32	----	(155)	0
Residence permit (*Carte de séjour*)	1.39	-1.04	(106)	(30)	1.22	----	(214)	(2)
Work permit (*Carte de travail*)	1.35	----	(6)	0	.44	-.54	(9)	(6)
Residence and work permit (*Carte de séjour and carte de travail*)	----	-1.10	(3)	(8)	1.44	-1.14	(8)	(47)
None	1.76	----	(28)	(3)	1.39	----	(23)	(1)
French citizen	----	----	(2)	0	----	----	(2)	(5)

eleven were uncertain, and eleven planned to return.[6]

The discussion of visa regulations and brain drain usually concentrates on the various permits officially intended for education. But Table IV-2 shows that considerable numbers of foreign students arrive with tourist visas. They have weaker intentions to return than the holders of educational visas. As in the case of many less skilled migrant workers, the tourist visa often becomes the first step in prolonged stays.

Persons without obligations or guarantees gravitate toward certain countries for study

Some persons go abroad for foreign study under pledges to return home: they have signed bonds, so that their families forfeit money if they emigrate without repaying the cost of their education; others have received scholarships and have promised to return. The host country most open to immigrants--Canada--attracts fewer of these persons. The United States and France educate more students from developing countries under some form of obligation to return:

	Canada	United States	France
	%	%	%
Bonded	9	10	5
Pledged to return, but not bonded	10	21	25

[6]The correlation between certain types of American visa and migration plans appears in previous surveys, reported in Robert G. Myers, Education and Emigration (New York: David McKay Company, 1972), pp. 120-122 and 254; in Josefina Bulatao Jayme, Demographic and Socio-Psychological Determinants of the Migration of Highly Trained Filipinos to the United States (Pittsburgh: dissertation for the Ph.D in Psychology, Carnegie-Mellon University, 1971), pp. 30, 32, and 44; and in Paul Ritterband, "Law, Policy, and Behavior: Educational Exchange Policy and Student Migration," American Journal of Sociology, Volume 76, Number 1 (July 1970), pp. 71-82. Our data cover other visas as well. Ritterband describes the legal theory and the actual practice in changes of status.

Compared to those studying in the United States and France, fewer foreign students in Canada have scholarships and fellowships under an organized program. More go abroad under their family's money, and therefore they are not obligated to governments or employers about their futures. The proportions of each sample who ever held any scholarships or fellowships from any source are:

Canada	42 per cent
United States	50 per cent
France	55 per cent

During study abroad, fewer foreign students in Canada had jobs waiting for them at home. The proportions of each sample with such employment guarantees are:

Canada	20 per cent
United States	28 per cent
France	22 per cent

<u>Proportions of students planning to migrate vary widely among countries of study</u>

Because of these differences in willingness to accept persons from developing countries and because of differences in the composition of student bodies, brain drain varies among host countries. In Table IV-3, Canada contrasts with other developed countries. Apparently Canada's policy of more liberal immigration attracts many persons who intend to stay abroad: 13 per cent of the foreign students in Canada said they "definitely" would stay abroad, 13 per cent said they "probably" would stay abroad, and 15 per cent were undecided.

Since so much has been written about the size and value of the brain drain into the United States, the low proportions in our survey may be surprising. Twelve per cent in the American student survey say they will stay abroad and 12 per cent are undecided. But an important distinction exists between proportion and volume: because so many persons study in the United States, the low rate results in a large volume. Of all professionals from developing countries who have ever studied in the United States, the migrants are a small proportion.

Rates of migration by students from developing countries are higher in Canada than in the United States but--since Canada has fewer students--the total number is lower. Canada provides an attractive combination of American economic institutions, personal freedom, and Old World cultural enclaves. The number of immigrants to Canada will grow along with the numbers of foreign students in the future, if the motives of the students persist and if Canada's normally hospitable immigration laws are not tightened.

The exact percentage of all foreign students in the United States intending to settle outside their home countries varies widely in previous questionnaire surveys about brain drain to that country: most report proportions about equal to or lower than ours; a few discovered higher frequencies.[7] We attempted to record the "true" migration plans by asking long-range intentions; similar questions in other surveys have elicited comparable proportions. Higher rates of emigration in some earlier American studies often resulted from different ways of asking questions or of drawing samples: some projects defined as brain drain, any change of visa or any stay for work after study, two acts that are more common than true permanent migration; surveys with higher rates often included the Europeans, who migrate to North America more often than do students from developing countries.[8]

[7]A list of the proportions of non-return in many surveys appears in Luiz Rocha Neto, "Some Remarks on the Methodological Aspects of Research on the International Migration of Scientists," unpublished paper prepared for the Collaborative Research Training Project on "Migration and Return of Students and Professionals in Latin America," sponsored by the Foreign Area Fellowship Program, Rio de Janeiro, 1973, pp. 30-33.

[8]The difference between rates of return to Europe and to developing countries are reported in Myers, Education and Emigration (op. cit., fn. 6), pp. 129-138; and in Steven E. Deutsch, International Education and Exchange (Cleveland: The Press of Case Western Reserve University, 1970), p. 86.

The proportion of potential migrants in the survey of students in France in Table IV-3 slightly exceeds the frequency in the one earlier study of the subject in that country.[9] The lower figure is probably a better estimate than ours: our sample in France concentrated on fourteen principal nationalities, thereby slightly oversampling the Lebanese, whose emigration rates are higher than others'.

Table IV-3

Long-Run Plans by Country of Study

Plans	Surveys of students in Canada	United States	France
Definitely return home and remain	41%	49%	63%
Probably return home and remain	18	26	16
Uncertain	15	12	8
Probably go abroad and stay	13	8	8
Definitely go abroad and stay	13	4	5
	100%	100%	100%
Total number of students	(889)	(1,561)	(474)
Index of return	.61	1.04	1.24

Variations by sex. As a general rule, women are more likely to contemplate emigration than men and to possess the motivations that ordinarily lead to emigration.[10] An important difference between

[9]Unpublished data supplied to us by Professor Otto Klineberg from Klineberg and Jeanne Ben Brika, Etudiants du tiers-monde en Europe (The Hague: Mouton, 1972).

[10]Comparisons between men and women in our data are reported in G. Christopher Habers, The Universal Minority: A Study of the Female Brain Drain of Students from Developing Countries in Three Developed Countries (New York: Essay for the Master of Arts in Sociology, Columbia University, 1972).

Canada and the other countries of study is that Canada attracts many women who are thinking of emigrating. The indexes of return of men and women in the three surveys of students are:

	Men	Women
Canada	.67	.24
United States	1.12	.99
France	1.23	1.28

Women either emigrate permanently or return home immediately after study. More men remain overseas temporarily for work.

Persons contemplating emigration prefer the country where they studied

The literature on the brain drain usually pictures the world's professionals hungering to enter the United States. While it is true that many students look forward to staying in or returning to the United States--as Table IV-4 confirms--this is not universal. Potential emigrants prefer the country where they studied. Many professionals pick the United States because so many throughout the world have been educated there. Persons educated in other developed countries usually prefer them over other foreign destinations,[11] but the United States often is the second choice.

Among persons planning to emigrate, Canada ranks very high. Canada is not merely a "parking lot" for persons awaiting a move to the United States; many persons prefer it, including nearly

---

[11]Among respondents educated primarily in the United States and contemplating emigration, 89 per cent picked the U.S.A. first. Canada was the first choice of 91 per cent of the Canadian-trained potential migrants, while France was the first preference of 76 per cent of the potential migrants who had been educated there. In our surveys of returnees completed so far, a substantial number of the British-educated prefer the United States over the United Kingdom.

everyone who has received most of his education there. Although many foreign students in Canada plan to emigrate, few (8 per cent) say they selected it as the country of study with an eye toward going later to some other developed country. (The proportions giving such an answer were slightly higher in the United States and slightly lower in France.)

The United States attracts temporary stay-ons

Different developed countries have different immigration patterns. Many stay-ons in the United States retain close ties with their home countries. Over half the prospective stay-ons in the sample of students in the United States are temporary. They plan to gain post-graduate practical experience at work and then return home.

The weaker ties with home produce a different migration pattern in Canada. Its prospective stay-ons are more permanent than the stay-ons in the United States: in the data summarized in Table IV-5, 348 of the 688 prospective stay-ons in the United States "definitely" or "probably" expected to return, but 292 of the future 576 stay-ons in Canada expected to remain there permanently.

Surveys of professionals working abroad. Since we were unable to take representative national samples of foreign professionals in each country, and since we have conducted only two small stay-on surveys so far, generalizing about the permanence of settlements must be cautious. But, clearly among the stay-ons who were willing to fill out our questionnaires in the United States and France, those in America include more temporary persons. The long-term plans of the two samples are in Table IV-6. The indexes of return are -.27 for those in the United States and -1.34 for those in France.

Migration for life. Developed countries differ in the commitment of their permanent migrants. Just as the United States is the country for temporary stays abroad, so it is the country of eventual return even among immigrants of longer time. The migrants into Canada and France more often expect to

Table IV-4

Where Emigrants Intend to Go Permanently*

Prospective country of stay	Students from developing countries in			Professionals from developing countries in		Foreign-trained returnees in							
	United States	Canada	France	United States	France	India	Sri Lanka	Republic of Korea	Greece	Ghana	Brazil	Colombia	Argentina
United States	285	208	18	230	19	145	41	28	17	19	54	59	46
Canada	90	408	8	41	6	91	40	15	8	11	11	22	8
United Kingdom	51	19	5	15	2	48	35	2	11	10	21	11	11
France	26	16	66	2	49	6	1	1	3	2	12	12	10
Federal Republic of Germany	23	5	8	10	1	26	3	2	28	3	9	9	10
Australia	15	13	1	2	--	35	20	1	3	1	--	5	2
Other European countries	42	19	7	23	2	18	3	3	24	8	21	26	19

*Respondents who intended to emigrate or were uncertain were asked to list the countries where they planned to go. Most listed one, some two or three countries as alternatives. The table lists the second and third choices as well as the first. Entries are numbers of choices and not percentages.

[continued]

Table IV-4 [continued]

Prospective country of stay	Students from developing countries in			Professionals from developing countries in		Foreign-trained returnees in								
	United States	Canada	France	United States	France	India	Sri Lanka	Republic of Korea	Greece	Ghana	Brazil	Colombia	Argentina
Other developed countries	5	4	1	2	--	6	3	3	1	--	2	--	--
Other developing countries in:													
North America and Caribbean	8	4	1	3	--	1	--	1	--	--	3	6	--
South America	10	8	--	5	1	4	2	1	1	--	11	18	28
Africa	11	2	3	--	--	13	2	--	3	5	--	--	--
Middle East and North Africa	5	8	4	41	11	4	--	--	--	--	2	1	1
Asia and Pacific	6	4	2	--	--	7	6	2	2	1	--	--	--
Total number of respondents listing countries	(305)	(417)	(77)	(231)	(50)	(182)	(64)	(31)	(52)	(26)	(73)	(77)	(71)

remain abroad permanently. The proportions of long-term stay-ons in each country planning to return home after retirement are:

Surveys of students in:	%
United States	62
Canada	36
France	34
Surveys of stay-ons in:	
United States	49
France	17

Table IV-5

Expected Life Histories of Students by Country of Study

Migration Plans: Immediately after study	Migration Plans: Permanently	Surveys of students in: United States	Canada	France	Type of Person
Stay abroad	Return home and stay there	28%	18%	10%	Temporary stay-on
	Uncertain	11	13	5	Uncertain stay-on
	Stay abroad	12	27	12	Permanent non-returnee
Return home	Leave home and stay abroad	0+	0+	1	Temporary returnee
	Uncertain	1	1	1	Uncertain returnee
	Stay home	48	41	71	Permanent returnee
		100%	100%	100%	
Total numbers of students		(1,551)	(840)	(458)	

Table IV-6

Long-Run Plans of Stay-ons

Plans	Surveys of Stay-ons in United States	France
Definitely return home and remain	13%	7%
Probably return home and remain	15	10
Uncertain	23	4
Probably go abroad and stay	30	23
Definitely go abroad and stay	19	56
	100%	100%
Total number of respondents	(334)	(62)

Characteristics of developed countries and implications for policy

Developed countries differ widely in acceptance of migrants from developing countries and in their attractiveness to persons from developing countries. Just as developing countries vary in their losses, developed countries vary in their gains. The flows of students and--even more clearly--the flows of migrants are from particular developing countries to particular developed countries. Where the situation requires planning and amelioration, universal policies applying to all developed countries are not as efficacious as policies applying to the particular situation in each one. Bilateral agreements about educational exchanges and migration will be more attuned to each situation than universal policies are.

Whether immigration of professionals into a developed country is high or low depends on many characteristics of its social structure, employment market, and government regulations. This book will describe their effects. Characteristics of some developed countries make them attractive for study but not for immigration; characteristics of some countries result in considerable immigration; for other reasons, certain developed countries attract persons interested in practical work experience between the end of foreign study and return home. Any policy decisions about educational exchange and immigration must be made in the light of how all the pertinent characteristics of that particular developed country attract or deter persons from developing countries.

Regulation of educational exchange attracts persons who intend to return home and discourages changes of plans. Some developed countries have stricter systems of sponsorship and of visas than others, and more of their foreign students return home. In practice, some developed countries' visas are administered permissively, and foreign students can arrange changes that allow temporary work or permanent immigration. The system of entry visas in developed countries at present is designed for tourists, students, or permanent immigrants. If practical experience at work after the conclusion of formal study is to become part of educational exchange, a new category of visas should be devised.

Chapter V

VARIATIONS BY SPECIALTY

A serious question for developing countries is whether the brain drain is concentrated in essential occupations. Wide variations occur among specialties. Slight differences appear according to career stage--i.e., the association between speciality and migration varies among the student, stay-on, and returnee surveys.

Plans of students

The first column of Table V-1 gives the plans of all students by specialty. Plans to return are strongest in agriculture, philosophy, and business--i.e., they have the highest indexes of return. Plans to emigrate are highest in languages, education, and architecture--i.e., they have low indexes of return. Uncertainty about future plans is most common in home management, mathematics and law--i.e., these three categories have the highest percentages of persons checking the "undecided" box.

In the last chapter, we noted that women are more likely to emigrate than men. This intention was more evident among the students. Women are found in large numbers in the specialties with low indexes of return, particularly languages, education, and home management.

Plans of stay-ons

The second column of Table V-1 shows the future plans of foreign professionals working in the United States and France. Most persons expect to stay abroad permanently, and therefore their indexes of re-

Table V-1

Long-Run Plans by Career Specialty

Specialty	Index of return			Total number of respondents		
	Students	Stay-ons	Returnees	Students	Stay-ons	Returnees
Agriculture	1.46	----	1.35	(72)	(5)	(142)
Architecture	.33	----	1.21	(59)	(4)	(109)
Art, music, drama	.95	----	1.00	(37)	(2)	(33)
Biology	.52	-.60	1.03	(119)	(26)	(194)
Business	1.05	-.23	1.14	(386)	(52)	(277)
Education (primary and secondary)	.32	-.38	1.36	(185)	(18)	(153)
Engineering	.72	-.39	1.29	(671)	(82)	(758)
Health	.42	----	1.27	(82)	(2)	(124)
Home management, child development, foods	.23	----	1.30	(20)	(1)	(23)
Journalism, mass media, publishing	.82	----	1.04	(34)	(1)	(26)
Languages, literature	.18	-1.54	1.13	(140)	(8)	(138)
Law	.93	-.59	1.42	(75)	(7)	(91)
Mathematics	.90	-.37	1.17	(154)	(41)	(84)
Philosophy, religion	1.13	----	1.30	(45)	(4)	(56)
Physical sciences	.85	-.41	1.28	(253)	(63)	(253)
Social sciences, public administration	.87	-.25	1.15	(394)	(49)	(373)

The question asked the respondents' "anticipated career field." The answers were very specific, as later pages of this chapter will show. They are grouped into broader categories in this table.

The table combines: students in the United States, Canada, and France; stay-ons in the United States and France; and returnees in India, Sri Lanka, Republic of Korea, Greece, Ghana, Brazil, Colombia, and Argentina. The index of return was not calculated for specialties of stay-ons with too few persons.

In one or two instances a low base was used when the alternative was no information. Those entries should be read with caution.

turn are negative. However, variations exist among specialties.

The persons most likely to return--i.e., those with index numbers closest to zero or above--are the stay-ons in business and the social sciences. Those most likely to emigrate permanently--i.e., those with index numbers closest to -2.0--work in languages, biology, and law.

Plans of returnees

The long-range expectations of returnees appear in the third column of Table V-1. Most members of each profession plan to remain at home, and the tendency is most pronounced for lawyers, persons in education, and agriculturists; their index numbers of return are highest. The artists, biologists, and journalists have the highest rates of prospective migration and uncertainty--i.e., their index numbers for return are lowest.[1] As we shall see later in this monograph, these groups experience frustrations after return, in the form of inadequate facilities (which bother the biologists) and social and political dissatisfactions (which affect many artists and journalists).

Despite variations in plans at the student, stay-on, and returnee stages, a few consistant patterns appear. Persons in agriculture, business, and philosophy are committed to return and stay at all stages. (As the next section will show, however, one sub-group within agriculture weakens in its commitment to remain after it has returned.) On the other hand, biologists have lower intentions to return and remain home at all stages.

Persons in a few specialties seem to adjust to whatever situation they experience during study and work. During the student and stay-on stages, specialists in education and law are among the groups

[1] As in all our data about returnees, "low" is comparative. Most returnees expect to remain home. For them, "low" indexes of return are closer to +1.0 than to +2.0.

more likely to consider emigration. After return, they are most likely to remain.

Extreme specialization does not automatically produce high emigration

A fear among many policy-makers is that highly specialized training abroad causes brain drain, because students are educated beyond the needs of their home countries or because they require facilities available only in developed countries. Table V-2 gives the indexes of return of persons who expect to work throughout their careers in the particular fields in the list. (Table V-1 groups together in general categories,(e.g., engineering) the individual fields,(e.g., metallurgical engineering and mechanical engineering) given by respondents, such as are listed separately in Table V-2.)

Part 1 of Table V-2 shows the ten fields with the lowest indexes of return (i.e., the greatest propensities to emigrate) in the surveys of students. These are the groups whose numbers are negative or close to zero. Part 2 of the table shows the ten fields with the lowest indexes of return in the surveys of returnees. All figures are positive, since most persons expect to remain home, but these are the specialties with the highest degree of uncertainty or largest numbers of potential migrants.[2]

According to Table V-2 some very specialized and technically advanced fields have lower rates of return, but specialization in complex areas is not convincingly related to emigration. Less specialized fields have even lower rates of return--i.e., in both halves of the table, the less specialized fields constitute majorities of the ten areas with

[2]Besides asking long-term career field, our questionnaires also asked the exact specialties of all degrees earned at home and abroad. Nearly every person's expected career field is the same as his highest degree. Therefore, classifying respondents by the highest degree they have earned abroad so far--another way of learning extent of possible "over-specialization" during foreign training--produces results nearly the same as Table V-2.

Table V-2

Specialization and Long-run Plans

	Index of return	Total number of respondents
Part 1. Surveys of students:		
(a) More specialized fields:		
Metallurgical engineering	-.18	(16)
Education of the handicapped	-.18	(8)
Bacteriology	.04	(21)
Aeronautical engineering	.07	(24)
(b) Less specialized fields:		
Teaching French in secondary school	-.51	(10)
Teaching English in university	-.31	(22)
Secondary or primary education in general	-.23	(24)
Teaching English in secondary school	.04	(12)
Teaching French in university	.20	(20)
Mechanical engineering	.21	(110)
Part 2. Surveys of returnees:		
(a) More specialized fields:		
City planning	.84	(26)
Bacteriology	.96	(25)
Biochemistry	1.03	(33)
(b) Less specialized fields:		
Journalism in general	.64	(11)
Botany	.75	(12)
Industrial engineering	.90	(31)
Linguistics	.90	(29)
Physiology	.91	(12)
Agriculture in general	1.00	(11)
Zoology in general	1.00	(12)

The table combines: students in the United States, Canada and France; and returnees in India, Sri Lanka, Republic of Korea, Greece, Ghana, Brazil, Colombia, and Argentina.

In one or two instances a low base was used when the alternative was no information. Those entries should be read with caution.

the lowest return; and the lowest index numbers are among the less specialized groups. Most very specialized and technically advanced fields have higher rates than the groups in the table.[3]

Therefore, mere specialization by itself does not lead to substantial migration. Many other non-occupational variables are at least as important in determining where individuals live and work. Many persons with very specialized training and career plans return to countries currently lacking all the appropriate facilities, because they expect their skills will eventually become useful.

The specialties with the lowest indexes of return among students (in Part 1) are not identical with the specialties with the lowest index numbers among returnees (in Part 2). Differences between the answers of students and returnees are common throughout this manuscript, even when home countries are matched. The two populations are not the same: the returnees do not include the types of person who are still part of student samples but who emigrate. Even when they are comparable on many traits, age and experience at home cause returnees to answer many items differently from students.

The problems of particular specialties in developing countries

What adverse conditions in home countries discourage return by persons with foreign training? What are the particular barriers encountered by specialties with the lowest indexes of return? Chapter VI will present a complete discussion of the attitudes, influences, and experiences that induce certain persons to emigrate and others to return home and stay. The principal battery of questions about reasons appears in Table VI-1 and in the text accompanying it. This section will present a brief

[3]The very specialized agriculturists have high indexes of return at all stages, including after return. So the broad category of "agriculture" has a high index number in Table V-1. The small group of generalists in agriculture had one of the lower index numbers in Part 2 of Table V-2, but they are outnumbered by the more specialized persons in that area.

overview of the strongest reasons for avoiding home countries by the specialists who (in Table V-2) had the lowest index numbers of return.

Table V-3 is based on the proportions of persons who gave each reason as a motive for going abroad rather than returning home. Large numbers of respondents tended to select certain factors as inducements to emigrate; examples are income and library facilities, which are generally perceived as far better in developed countries. The entries in the table show whether that specialty mentioned that reason for emigration far more often than the combined total of all other specialties that had higher indexes of return. Some categories have small numbers of respondents, since Table V-3 focuses on the specific fields with the lowest rates of return, and therefore the findings should be interpreted cautiously.

In each half of Table V-3, the symbol "+" means that the specialists in that field gave the reason from 10 to 19 per cent more often than all other respondents (outside the fields listed in the table) as reasons for going abroad. The symbol "++" shows a very widespread complaint in that specialty: the persons in the field give the reason at least 20 per cent more often than others as a reason for emigrating. Since this is a table of deviations from the average, the first step is looking at the two rows that show the proportions saying that the reason on balance made them consider work abroad. Row 1 (a) lists the proportions of all other students giving each reason for emigration; row 2 (a) consists of the proportions of all other returnees citing each reason. One can conclude that a reason is very powerful for a specialty only if the average percentage is high and the symbols + or ++ appear for that specialty. Otherwise, + and ++ merely show that the reason affects that specialty more than it motivates emigration in other fields; but that specialty might be motivated primarily by other reasons with much higher proportions.

Reading across each line in Table V-3 reveals the principal problems of that specialty in develop-

Table V-3
The Above-Average Reasons for Emigration by the Specialties with Lowest Return*

Specialties	Number of jobs	Quality of jobs	Income	Potential contribution to one's profession	Laboratory or office space	Equipment	Library facilities	Research workers for discussion of common problems	Skilled assistants	Contact with developments in the profession throughout world	Sufficient time for one's professional development	Status of professionals in pay and prestige	Total number of respondents
1. Survey of students:													
(a) Proportion of all other specialties giving this as a reason for staying abroad	39	48	55	35	28	48	55	43	49	56	36	25	(2,274)

*The symbol "+" means that the persons in that field gave the reason from 10 to 19% more often than all other respondents (outside the fields listed in the table) as reasons for going abroad. The symbol "++" means that the person in that field gave the reason at least 20% more often than all other respondents (outside the fields listed in the table) as reasons for going abroad. If a cell is empty, persons in that field gave the reason about as often as the average respondent in the survey. For example, in our data, 39 per cent of students in specialties other than those in rows 1(b) through 1(h) said that "number of jobs"

[continued]

Table V-3 [continued]

Specialties	Number of jobs	Quality of jobs	Income	Potential contribution to one's profession	Laboratory or office space	Equipment	Library facilities	Research workers for discussion of common problems	Skilled assistants	Contact with developments in the profession throughout world	Sufficient time for one's professional development	Status of professionals in pay and prestige	Total number of respondents
(b) Bacteriology		+	+		+	++		++		++		+	(21)
(c) Accounting	+	+	+									++	(59)
(d) Primary or secondary education:													
(1) English										++		+	(10)
(2) French	++	++	++	++	+	+	++		+		+	++	(8)
(3) History, social studies			+	+		++	++			+			(10)
(4) General	+		++	++									(20)

was a reason for emigrating abroad; 47 per cent of the bacteriologists said this (and therefore their cells are empty); 55 per cent of the accountants said this (and their cell contains a "+"); and 90 per cent of the teachers of French said this (a weighted percentage meriting the symbol "++"). The specialties in this table are those with the lowest rates of return in Table V-2. The footnote to Table V-2 lists the surveys included in the calculations.

[continued]

Table V-3 [continued]

Specialties	Number of jobs	Quality of jobs	Income	Potential contribution to one's profession	Laboratory or office space	Equipment	Library facilities	Research workers for discussion of common problems	Skilled assistants	Contact with developments in the profession throughout world	Sufficient time for one's professional development	Status of professionals in pay and prestige	Total number of respondents
(e) Education of handicapped	++	++	++	++	++	++	++	++	++	++	++	++	(8)
(f) Engineering													
(1) Aeronautical	+		+	+		+		++		+			(24)
(2) Mechanical					+	++	+	++		+	+		(109)
(3) Metallurgical		+		+		+		+					(16)
(g) University teaching:													
(1) English							+			++			(21)
(2) French	+		+	++		+					++		(18)
(h) Librarianship												+	(15)
2. Surveys of returnees:													
(a) Proportion of all other specialties giving this as a reason for going abroad	27	41	47	33	31	45	49	48	41	56	42	34	(2,503)
(b) Agriculture, general	+	+					+	++					(11)

[continued]

Table V-3 [continued]

Specialties	(c) Biology: (1) Bacteriology	(2) Biochemistry	(3) Botany	(4) Physiology	(5) Zoology	(d) City planning	(e) Industrial engineering	(f) Journalism in general	(g) Linguistics	(h) Music	(i) Political science
Total number of respondents	(24)	(31)	(9)	(12)	(11)	(26)	(30)	(10)	(28)	(12)	(16)
Status of professionals in pay and prestige	+	+	+	++				++	+	++	+
Sufficient time for one's professional development	+	+	++	++				++	+	++	
Contact with developments in the profession throughout world	++	+	+	++		+			+	++	+
Skilled assistants	++		+	++					+		
Research workers for discussion of common problems	++	+	++	++	++					+	
Library facilities	++		++	++	+			+	+		
Equipment	++	+	++	++	+						
Laboratory or office space	++		+	++	+						
Potential contribution to one's profession	+		++	++	+			+			
Income	+			++				++	+		
Quality of jobs	+			+	+	+		+		+	
Number of jobs	+	+		++	++		+	++			

ing countries. Reading down each column shows the professional problems that recur in developing countries.

Table V-3 lists only the items in the battery pertaining to conditions of professional work. The respondents checked other non-occupational reasons for preferring home or foreign countries, and these results will be analyzed in full in Chapter VI.

Specialties among students. Several groups have numerous complaints about conditions at home and large proportions believe the situation far superior abroad: bacteriologists, teachers of French in schools and universities, educators of the handicapped, and aeronautical engineers. A few groups have a limited number of grievances, but these may be intense: for example, teachers of English in schools and universities are particularly bothered by isolation from developments in their field abroad. Librarians have only one unusual occupational complaint; the persons who become librarians are probably influenced to emigrate in large numbers by non-professional reasons.

Specialties among returnees. Part 2 of Table V-3 summarizes the answers of persons who have already experienced work at home, after their training abroad. The specialties with lower indexes of return differ from those in the student samples, because some members of fields with high rates of emigration (such as aeronautical engineers and teachers of French and English) never went home. Certain fields, such as the biological sciences, experienced problems at home that may have exceeded their expectations.

The one specialty with a low index of return in both surveys--bacteriology--has the same complaints after return. New grievances have been added.

The specialists with the greatest numbers of frustrations beyond the average are bacteriologists, botanists, physiologists, zoologists, and journalists.

<u>The most common reasons for emigration among different specialties, and their implications for policy</u>.

It is no surprise that improving the number and quality of jobs is urgent to induce greater return. These reasons are strongly associated with migration and return in general (according to Table VI-3 in the next chapter) and they are mentioned particularly often by the specialties with high rates of loss (in Table V-3).

Certain reasons not so powerfully associated with migration and return for professionals in general (in Table VI-3) seem particularly important for the specialties with high losses (in Table V-3). One is maintaining contact with news in the profession. Remaining <u>au courant</u> is particularly difficult in many developing countries. Scarcities of hard currency limit subscriptions to foreign journals, prevent attendance at distant conferences and prevent study tours. The isolation is particularly troublesome to biological scientists, persons in languages, and musicians; but it handicaps others as well. If only limited numbers of books and periodicals can be bought from Europe and North America, a need is better dissemination within the developing country. Feelings of isolation can be reduced by sponsoring more exchanges of information and conferences among the developing countries themselves.

Better communication with stimulating colleagues is a stronger reason for emigration among the specialties with high losses (in Table V-3) than among all professionals (in Table VI-3), even though it is a complaint common to all. In Table V-3, scarcities of colleagues particularly bother the biological scientists and engineers. One remedy is better machinery for discussion and exchanges of scientific papers within organizations that employ these specialties and within entire countries. Another remedy is more time for intellectual exchanges, a need expressed by many persons in our survey. The burdens of teaching and administration are so heavy in developing countries that opportunities for research and shoptalk are reduced under present conditions. The specialists in Table V-3 adopt the solution of emigrating to countries where conditions are better.

Physical facilities--such as equipment and libraries--are almost unanimously considered better in developed countries but are only weak predictors of emigration for most (in Table VI-3). Most persons return home for other reasons, and therefore facilities are an object of complaint for them rather than a controlling reason for emigration. However, facilities seem important reasons for the losses of biological scientists and engineers in Table V-3.

Some reasons for emigration become less salient after return home while others increase in effects, due to practical experience on the job. The shifts can be noticed by comparing Parts 1 and 2 of Table V-3. Income expectations are an influential reason for emigration while a student, but are cited as a problem less often after return. One reason may be the satisfaction with other rewards after return; another, as the next chapter, will show, may be the professionals' discovery that real incomes at home often are not as far below the pay in developed countries as they previously believed. A new complaint becomes common and is an important determinant of emigration after return: burdensome routines reduce the time available to develop one's professional interests.

This chapter points up the grievances and high migration rate of an area usually neglected in the discussions about brain drain, viz., the biological sciences. Compared to others, biologists feel more neglected in opportunities, facilities, and recognition. Clearly they require attention by policymakers in science and education.

Other groups that feel deprived on many counts --and react not merely by complaining but by leaving--are teachers of languages and of handicapped persons.[4] Because of the rapid recent improvement in medical and social services in developing countries, many citizens now survive but with some handicaps from prior accidents and diseases. According to Table V-3, the teachers necessary for their rehabilitation are being lost for many reasons.

---

[4]The small numbers of teachers of the handicapped in our survey yield conclusions that are suggestive but not yet definite. Their consistent pattern for emigration merits more extensive examination with larger numbers in future research. They constitute one of the specialties that developing countries need.

Chapter VI

THE INDIVIDUAL'S MOTIVES AND EXPERIENCES

As in all important decisions, the professional is affected by a great number and range of influences and inducements, when deciding whether to return home or to remain abroad. Some pull him one way, some point him in another direction, others have mixed results. Stimuli that affect one person are ignored by another; individuals differ widely in the motives and experiences affecting their migration plans.

To measure the direction of the varied influences and orientations, we wrote a list of twenty-nine items under the following categories:

1. Economic and professional:
   - (a) Suitable job
   - (b) Income and living standard
   - (c) Working conditions: facilities, autonomy, career prospects, relations with superiors and with co-workers

2. Personal influences:
   - (a) Spouse
   - (b) Feelings and interests of the children
   - (c) Family
   - (d) Friends
   - (e) Colleagues at work

3. Living conditions in society:
   - (a) Where life is more interesting and more pleasant
   - (b) Discrimination by the public

4. Political situation:
   (a) Government controls
   (b) Nationalist feelings of respondent

Each factor may operate as a push or pull from the home country; and at the same time, it may exercise a push or pull from another country. The full battery was used to describe the choice of countries at three different times: as foreign study was concluding; as a period of foreign work (if any) was ending; and the returnee's current choice of countries. The response categories for each item were the following. (The present tense was used when a current decision was involved, the past tense for an earlier decision.)

Influences me to return to (stay in) my country of origin.
Influences me to stay for a substantial time in a foreign country. Each time you give this response, please enter the name of the country where you consider staying.
This factor leaves me undecided, since it influences me both on behalf of my country of origin and on behalf of a foreign country.
No influence on me.
This factor does not apply to me at this time. [Category not provided for some items.]

This battery was mentioned in the last chapter, in the explanation of high emigration by certain specialties. The following pages are a more extended analysis. Like many other parts of our survey, an even more thorough examination of certain special problems is possible.

Reasons for return home or for prolonged stay abroad just after conclusion of study

Since every respondent was asked how the list of twenty-nine items affected him during study abroad, that battery gives the largest number of responses showing the effect of various reasons on migration. For all respondents together and in the separate samples, the answers fell into nine main clusters.

Each cluster combined items that affected respondents similarly.[1]

1. Working conditions
2. Professional needs
3. Colleagues
4. Societal setting
5. Alienation and discrimination
6. Politics
7. Citizenship rights
8. Influence of others
9. Interests of children

Table VI-1 gives the proportions who said that each factor influenced them in the direction of home (the percentage in the column headed "home") and the proportions who said that each factor influenced them to emigrate (the percentage in the column headed "abroad"). The difference between each pair of numbers and 100 per cent consists of persons for whom the factor left them undecided, had no influence, and did not apply. The surveys of students, stay-ons, and returnees are presented separately; each group is describing its state of mind at the time of study abroad. The questions were not answered in the order they appear in the table but are rearranged by cluster.

The numbers in Table VI-1 report only how each factor pointed in one or the other direction. Not until we reach Table VI-3 can we conclude how each factor actually predicts migration.

---

[1]The division of the battery into clusters and the assignment of each question to a cluster was performed according to the method described in Louis L. McQuitty, "Elementary Linkage Analysis for Isolating Orthogonal and Oblique Types and Typal Relevancies," Educational and Psychological Measurement, Volume XVII, Number 2 (Summer 1957), pp. 207-229; and McQuitty, "Capability and Improvements of Linkage Analysis as a Clustering Method," ibid., Volume XXIV, Number 3 (Fall 1964), pp. 441-456. More complex non-hierarchical clustering techniques produce essentially the same results, as we have established in test runs.

The most common reasons for return or migration

Reading down each pair of columns in Table VI-1 identifies the attitudes and influences most salient in forming judgments about countries: these are the items with the largest totals when "home" and "abroad" are added. If "home" is much larger than "abroad," the factor is a big reason for preferring developing countries. If "abroad" is much larger than "home," the factor operates strongly on behalf of North America or Europe.

As we shall note in the next section of this chapter, students, stay-ons, and returnees are somewhat different types of people. They perceive the advantages and disadvantages of home and of developed countries differently in several respects, and, therefore, they differ in recollections of how they compared countries at the time they were finishing their education abroad. In the next section, we will compare these differences among students, stay-ons, and returnees. The next paragraphs will list those reasons in the battery that most persons interpret alike.

Working conditions. Several items in the first cluster in Table VI-1 make developed countries more attractive. For students, stay-ons, and returnees, these are income, the quality of jobs and the number of jobs (items 1b, 1c, and 1d).

Professional needs. Among the greatest attractions of developed countries are the material facilities for work, viz., libraries, equipment, laboratory space, and office space. (For items 2c, 2d, and 2e in Table VI-1, the "abroad" per cent is much higher than the "home" per cent.)

Developed countries seem better than home because of closer involvement in world-wide professional events. At home, the professional has less chance to attend international meetings and sees fewer journals. (Throughout Table VI-1, the "abroad" per cent is much higher than the "home" per cent for item 2a.)

Table VI-1

Reasons for Choosing Destinations Just After Study Abroad

Reasons	Surveys of Students		Surveys of stay-ons		Surveys of returnees	
	Home	Abroad	Home	Abroad	Home	Abroad
	%	%	%	%	%	%
1. Working conditions:						
a) "Potential contributions to my profession"	35	35	7	64	39	29
b) "Potential income and living standards"	13	56	3	71	10	40
c) "Quality of jobs available"	19	48	4	74	14	34
d) "Number of jobs available"	19	40	4	59	15	23
e) "Satisfactory housing at a reasonable price"	35	11	10	15	16	11

The list of reasons gives the exact wording of the items in the questionnaires. Next to each item are two percentages. As the text explained, "Home" is the proportion who checked that the item "Influenced me to return to my country of origin." "Abroad" is the proportion who checked that the item "Influenced me to stay for a substantial time in a foreign country." The difference between these two figures and 100 per cent are those who said the factor had conflicting influences, no influence, or did not apply

All respondents are combined from the surveys of students in the United States, Canada, and France; from the surveys of stay-ons in the United States and France; and from the surveys of returnees in India, Sri Lanka, Republic of Korea, Ghana, Greece, Brazil, Colombia and Argentina. Students answered about how each factor influenced them "now"; stay-ons and returnees told how each factor influenced them at the end of foreign study.

[continued]

Table VI-1 [continued]

Reasons	Surveys of students		Surveys of stay-ons		Surveys of returnees	
	Home	Abroad	Home	Abroad	Home	Abroad
	%	%	%	%	%	%
2. Professional needs:						
a) "Contact with developments in the profession through travel, access to current publications, etc."	8	56	1	73	4	51
b) "Sufficient time for professional development, free of routine work"	20	36	4	58	9	42
c) "Library facilities"	3	54	1	61	3	47
d) "Equipment"	3	49	1	53	3	41
e) "Laboratory or office space"	8	28	2	33	5	28
f) "Status or professionals in pay and prestige in comparison with other occupations"	26	26	8	39	14	31
3. Colleagues:						
a) "Research workers with whom I can discuss common problems"	9	43	2	57	6	46
b) "Skilled assistants in my specialty"	5	47	2	43	4	38
4. Societal setting:						
a) "Cultural level of some countries"	22	22	10	22	11	27
b) "Challenge of life in some countries"	20	20	7	28	18	9

[continued]

Table VI-1[continued]

Reasons	Surveys of students		Surveys of stay-ons		Surveys of returnees	
	Home	Abroad	Home	Abroad	Home	Abroad
	%	%	%	%	%	%
5. Alienation and discrimination:						
a) "Feelings of strangeness in some countries"	36	2	10	3	29	1
b) "Discrimination against people like me"	36	4	12	6	13	1
6. Politics:						
a) "Political conditions"	12	24	3	22	5	8
b) "The government's language policies"	7	7	0+	10	3	3
7. Citizenship:						
a) "Maintain my existing citizenship rights or my existing rights of permanent residence"	20	8	5	9	15	1
b) Acquire new citizenship status or acquire new rights of permanent residence"	5	13	2	19	5	3
8. Influence of others:						
a) "Patriotism"	56	1	29	2	54	1
b) "Obligations to my family"	39	7	29	9	43	1
c) "Influence of members of my family"	34	6	26	8	36	1
d) "Influence of my friends"	22	3	13	6	13	2

[continued]

Table VI-1 [continued]

Reasons	Surveys of students		Surveys of stay-ons		Surveys of returnees	
	Home	Abroad	Home	Abroad	Home	Abroad
	%	%	%	%	%	%
9. Interests of spouse and children:						
a) "My spouse's or fiancée's (fiancé's) feelings"	16	8	8	19	19	5
b) "Education of my children"	10	13	4	17	15	4
c) "Careers of my children"	10	9	3	17	9	3
d) "Matrimonial prospects of my children"	10	2	5	4	6	1
Total number of respondents	(2,787)		(386)		(2,853)	

A common belief is that professionals in developing countries are burdened by too much administration and other distractions. This is confirmed in our data. Most respondents say that work in developed countries is more attractive in that it has fewer nonprofessional chores. (For items 2b, the "abroad" per cent exceeds the "home" per cent.)

Colleagues. The quality of associates makes developed countries more attractive. Compared to conditions at home, Europe and North America can supply more persons to talk to and have better assistants. (The "abroad" per cent is much larger than the "home" per cent for both items 3a and 3b.)

Alienation and discrimination. Motivation to return in large part is determined by pushes from developed countries. Over one-third of students from developing countries feel out of place abroad. Fewer are pushed in like manner from their home countries (item 5a). Racial, religious and ethnic discrimination by the populations of developed countries is reported by many foreign students. (I.e., for item 5b, the percentage on behalf of "home" exceeds the percentage on behalf of "abroad".)

Politics. An important reason for emigration is the push from a distasteful government at home. But politics is not a push for everyone: small numbers feel their duty is to return and work for improvement; others have been active in politics at home and wish to resume. (I.e., while the "abroad" percentage exceeds the "home" percentage for item 6a, some respondents pick "home".)

Influence of others. The most powerful attractions of the home country are nonprofessional personal relations. (In Cluster 8, the "home" per cent consistently exceeds the "abroad" per cent.) Patriotism induces many to return (item 8a). Many respond to the persuasion of family and friends at home (items 8b, 8c, 8d).

Comparisons of students, stay-ons, and returnees

Comparisons of students and stay-ons. The first four columns of Table VI-1 permit comparisons of the pattern of motivations between students and stay-ons. Table VI-1 summarizes the states of mind during study in all our student surveys and the thinking at the end of study of all stay-ons and returnees, and one might hypothesize that each factor should influence all persons in the same way at different times. If so, the percentages in the two sets of columns would be identical; the variables inducing temporary or permanent emigration would control stay-ons' behavior, while the variables influencing return would exert predominant effects on the many students planning to go home.

But actually the percentages in the first four columns of Table VI-1 differ in the ratios between "home" and "abroad": for nearly every reason, the "home" percentage is lower for stay-ons and the "abroad" percentage is higher. In other words, the effect of each factor on return is weaker for stay-ons, and the influence on emigration is stronger. Compared to students, stay-ons seem to "interpret" each reason more strongly in favor of emigration and less strongly in favor of home.

Comparisons of students and returnees. Columns 1, 2, 5 and 6 of Table VI-1 permit comparisons of the motivational profiles of students and returnees. Because so many students plan to return, they resemble the returnees more closely than they resemble the stay-ons. The percentages in the "abroad" column are usually substantially lower for the returnees than for the students--i.e., fewer returnees interpreted these factors as reasons for avoiding their home countries or preferring foreign countries.

Shifts in reasons during work abroad by stay-ons

A comparison of columns 3 and 4 with columns 1 and 2 in Table VI-1 is not a true test of how work abroad affects the orientations of persons toward their home and foreign countries. Most persons in columns 1 and 2 have not been and will not be exposed to work in developed countries.

The ideal test is a panel (or "longitudinal") study: the stay-ons who answered the battery about reasons for emigration and return should have filled out the students' questionnaire at the time they received their foreign degrees. Since our project could not conduct follow-ups, we had to ask for earlier states of mind retrospectively: the stay-ons answered how the items in the barriers affected their preferences at the time of the survey and, in an earlier question in the same survey, how each item governed their choice of countries when completing their studies abroad. Since both batteries were answered in the same questionnaire, present states of mind probably biased answers about past decisions somewhat, even though we urged the respondents to answer the questions independently. That many tried conscientiously is demonstrated by substantial turnover in responses. Even if many answers are the same, this is not entirely an error: even if the questions had been asked at different times, the answers should show some correlation, since an individual's thinking persists. (To conserve space and to simplify this manuscript, the complete tabulations are not printed here.)

The structure of motives. The following paragraphs summarize persistence and change in the outlooks of the _same_ stay-ons between the end of study and the time of the survey, when they had experienced employment abroad. Certain viewpoints have not changed since their student days. Working conditions and professional assets (the items in Clusters 1, 2 and 3 of the table) seem more attractive in developed countries--i.e., the "abroad" per cent exceeds the "home" per cent. The influence of family and friends is a pull homewards--in Cluster 8, the "home" per cent exceeds the "abroad" per cent. Unfamiliarity of life and discrimination in developed countries are pushes against staying--in Cluster 5, the "home" per cent is larger than the "abroad" per cent. Unstable or dictatorial governments are strong obstacles to return--for item a in Cluster 6, the "abroad" per cent is larger than the "home" per cent.

Certain reasons form new patterns at the stay-on stage. Compared to the student stage, more of the stay-ons have acquired or are seeking citizenship or residency rights abroad; therefore maintaining and seeking these rights are more common reasons for emigration. (In Cluster 7, the "abroad" per cent has increased.) Having acquired families they might not have had before and having given them the experience of life abroad, the stay-ons report that family considerations influence emigration more than respondents at the student stage did. Percentages increase in favor of both "home" and "abroad," particularly in favor of emigration to developed countries.

A general shift in motives. For many reasons in the list, stay-ons are less favorable toward developed countries between the time they finished study and the time of the survey. I.e., the proportion in favor of home for each reason has increased, while the proportion in favor of developed countries has decreased. But the stay-ons started with a strong bias in favor of developed countries, and this persists for most reasons in the battery.

Shifts in reasons after return

The returnees answered the battery of reasons not only about their states of mind at the end of study (presented in columns 5 and 6 of Table VI-1) but also in a later part of the questionnaire concerning their attitudes at the time of the survey. (The complete tabulations are not presented here.)

The structure of motives. As in the case of the stay-ons, the family becomes a greater influence on decisions whether to remain at home or to go abroad again. Because more returnees are married and have children since they finished study, the total proportions influenced by them in any direction are greater. Compared to the period of study, the effects of spouse and children are substantially in the direction of staying in the home country.

Changes in other motives. Shifts between time of study and the time of the survey after return are small. Often the proportions increase slightly in favor of both home and abroad, reflecting greater awareness of the determining factors as professionals become more experienced. But influence on behalf of home for some persons often is matched by influence on behalf of emigration for others. Therefore, no trend either more favorable or less favorable toward home occurs among all the surveys of returnees.

Shifts of returnees who worked abroad. The returnees who were employed in developed countries after study filled out the battery of reasons three times in the questionnaire, to describe their states of mind after study, after the completion of work, and at the time of the survey after return. Compared to the stay-on samples, they were more favorable toward home in the battery at the time of completing work and less favorable toward developed countries. I.e., for each reason, their proportions at that time were higher in the "home" column and lower in the "abroad" column.

Like the stay-ons, these returnees had become more favorable toward home and less favorable toward developed countries during the period of work abroad. But they began with the strong dispositions on behalf of home in columns 5 and 6 of Table VI-1, and their additional shifts were small.

Reasons for migration and return vary widely among home countries

Considerable differences occur among neighboring countries, and therefore simple generalizations cannot be made about different regions of the world. Presenting the statistics of Table VI-1 for each home country would result in a very long and cumbersome document. The following paragraphs will summarize how reasons vary in strength among countries.

Acceptance ratio. To simplify the discussion, the numbers in Table VI-1 should be combined. A simple measure of the net effect of each factor is the "acceptance ratio," calculated in our data by the formula (Home - Abroad) divided by (Home + Abroad). This statistic gives the relative difference between two responses, when there remains a third (or more) response conveying mixed feelings or uncertainty. In our data, an acceptance ratio for a motive or influence is a positive number when more persons are influenced by that factor toward home and a negative number when more are influenced by it to emigrate. It can vary between +1.00, if the effect of the reason upon choice of country is in favor of home for everyone, and -1.00, if the only persons affected by the reason are persuaded on behalf of foreign countries. The ratio is 0.00, if choices of home equal the choices of foreign countries.[2] The first column of Table VI-2 gives the acceptance ratio for all respondents, based on the numbers in Table VI-1.

Comparisons among countries. The following paragraphs summarize how reasons vary in strength among countries, based on complete tabulations not presented in this manuscript. Table VI-2 supplements this exposition by giving the extreme cases, viz., national groups with very positive or very weak (or even negative) reactions to that basis for prefer-

---

[2]The acceptance ratio should not be confused with the index of return, introduced in Chapter III. Both involve choices between countries: a positive number of both indicates preference for the home country; a negative number indicates preference for foreign countries; and zero reflects mixed feelings or indifference. But the index of return is based on the question about plans to return or to emigrate, while the acceptance ratio measures whether a motivation or influence persuades people to prefer the home country or foreign countries. The index of return is based on five possible responses and therefore varies between + 2 and - 2; the acceptance ratio is calculated from three possible answers and therefore varies between + 1 and - 1. Since most persons say they will return home, most groups have positive index numbers of return; since many persons are critical of home countries, the acceptance ratios associated with many reasons are negative. The acceptance ratio is the most common statistic to report the results of another cross-national survey with many national samples and with questions involving three possible responses: Johan Galtung, "The Future: A Forgotten Dimension," in Images of the World in the Year 2000 (The Hague: Mouton, 1974).

ring home. The following text, therefore, includes some patterns that do not appear in Table VI-2.

By reading down each column in Table VI-2, one can quickly see the reasons that affect persons from that national group to an exceptional degree. By reading across each row, one notices the countries that are affected in unusual ways by that reason for returning or migrating.

Working conditions. Most reasons are perceived by students and professionals as pointing clearly either toward return or emigration--i.e., the acceptance ratios are substantially above or below zero. But this is not true of judgment about where the professional can make the greatest contribution (item a in Cluster 1). This provides one of the principal contrasts among countries in our data. Many developing countries are perceived as better places for professional contributions than developed societies; others are rated worse; and the variations average out for everyone to a total acceptance ratio of zero.

The nationalities believing they can make greater professional contributions at home than abroad are the Jamaicans, Mexicans, Brazilians, Argentines, Colombians, Venezuelans, the large majority of Africans, South Koreans and Thais.[3] (I.e., for them, the "home" per cent exceeds "abroad" for item 1a.) Those who believe they could accomplish more abroad are the Haitians, Egyptians, Lebanese, Turks, Iranians, Indians, Ceylonese, Pakistanis, and Filipinos. (For them, the "abroad" per cent exceeds "home".) The extreme above-average and below-average groups appear on the first row of Table VI-2; the Venezuelans, Ghanaians, and Thais are most convinced they can contribute to their professional fields at home; the Indians and particularly the Egyptians are the nationalities most pessimistic about making such contributions in their home countries.

---

[3] As in the case of all nationalities mentioned in this manuscript, our findings are based on the responses of those sampled at the time of our surveys.

The division of countries on item 1a demonstrates the difficulty of finding any simple explanation of difference between countries in the orientations and behavior of their professionals. Each group--i.e., those preferring their home countries and those preferring developed countries--is mixed. Each category contains more or less industrialized economies, saturated and uncrowded labor markets, democracies and dictatorships.

Nearly all nationalities report that income and living standards are more attractive in developed countries (item 1b). The principal exceptions are Venezuelans, who prefer pay at home. Only small pluralities of the Ivoirians and Thais think they would do better financially overseas.

The quality and number of jobs are different dimensions: in the first column of Table VI-2, more persons rate the quality rather than the number as a reason for emigration; in many home countries, it seems easy to get a job, but the good ones are said to be overseas. A few nationalities (such as Jamaicans, Brazilians, and Turks) thought they could get jobs of some sort more easily at home than abroad, but the better jobs were said to be overseas.

Persons from Venezuela, Senegal, the Ivory Coast, Cameroon, Tunisia and Thailand are exceptions to the general belief that the quality of jobs is better abroad (item 1c). Some nationalities--particularly the Egyptians, but to a lesser extent the Trinidadians, Indians, Ceylonese, and Filipinos--say that foreign working conditions are far superior.

Professional needs. Contact with world-wide developments, libraries, equipment, and space are almost universally deemed far superior in developed countries and therefore are very strong arguments to work abroad. (I.e., the acceptance ratios are large negative numbers for items 2a through 2e.) A few nationalities seem less persuaded to contemplate emigration by these considerations. For example, Thais, Ghanaians, Cameroonians, and (particularly) Venezuelans rate a few of these factors less attractive abroad than do other nationalities; for some of

Table VI-2

Reasons for Choosing Destinations Just After Study Abroad
--Home Countries with Wide Divergencies from Average *

*All respondents were combined from the surveys of students, stay-ons, and returnees. The battery gave the reasons for return or emigration at the time of study abroad. Each reason can operate in any of four ways: for the home country; for developed countries; against the home country; against developed countries. The wording of each item appears in Table VI-1, <u>supra</u>. The first column of Table VI-2 shows the acceptance ratio for each item for all respondents, calculated by the method described in the text. The table shows only those national groups with at least 29 respondents and with acceptance ratios much higher or lower than the average: If a cell is empty, that national group had an acceptance ratio that was within .50 above or below the number in the first column. The other symbols show the groups that exceeded this deviation from the average:

++ = +.70 higher than the average,
in the direction of return

+ = +.50 higher than the average,
in the direction of return

- = -.50 lower than the average,
in the direction of emigration

-- = -.70 lower than the average,
in the direction of emigration

If an average acceptance ratio in column 1 is very large--i.e., over +.50 or under -.50--and some national groups have ratios of +1.0 or -1.0, the table carries the entry of + or -, even though the difference between them and the average is less than .50. The footnote to Table V-3 explains how to read tables like this.

Because the table only shows the extreme values, the text describes several patterns that do not appear in the table.

Table VI-2 [continued]

Reasons	Average acceptance ratio	Caribbean and Central America				South America				Africa				Middle East and North Africa					Asia						Greece
		Trinidad and Tobago	Jamaica	Haiti	Mexico	Brazil	Argentina	Colombia	Venezuela	Ghana	Senegal	Ivory Coast	Cameroon	Tunisia	Egypt	Lebanon	Turkey	Iran	India	Sri Lanka	Pakistan	Korea, Republic of	Philippines	Thailand	
1. Work conditions:																									
a) Contribution to profession	.00								+	+					--				-					+	
b) Income and living standards	-.55								++																
c) Quality of jobs	-.39								+		+	++	++	+	-									++	
d) Number of jobs	-.23					+			++	+	+	++			-				-				-	++	
e) Housing	+.42						-				+	+							-						
2. Professional needs:																									
a) Contacts	-.82																							++	
b) Sufficient time	-.45				+			+	+		+	++	++	+			+							++	
c) Libraries	-.90				-								-				-						-		
d) Equipment	-.87				-							-	-				-						-		
e) Space	-.63				-				++																
f) Status of professionals	-.14								++				-		-		++	+						+	

[continued]

Table VI-2 [continued]

Reasons	Average acceptance ratio	Caribbean and Central America				South America				Africa				Middle East and North Africa					Asia						
		Trinidad and Tobago	Jamaica	Haiti	Mexico	Brazil	Argentina	Colombia	Venezuela	Ghana	Senegal	Ivory Coast	Cameroon	Tunisia	Egypt	Lebanon	Turkey	Iran	India	Sri Lanka	Pakistan	Korea, Republic of	Philippines	Thailand	Greece
3. Colleagues:																									
a) Fellow workers for discussion	-.69										++	++	++											+	
b) Assistants	-.80							+																+	
4. Societal setting:																									
a) Cultural level	-.23				+			--		+		--	+						++		++		+	++	
b) Challenge of life	+.15						+						+		--								--		
5. Alienation and discrimination:																									
a) Feel strange	+.90		+		+								+				+								
b) Discrimination	+.79				+						+	+	+		-										

[continued]

Table VI-2 [continued]

Reasons	Average acceptance ratio	Caribbean and Central America				South America				Africa				Middle East and North Africa					Asia						Greece
		Trinidad and Tobago	Jamaica	Haiti	Mexico	Brazil	Argentina	Colombia	Venezuela	Ghana	Senegal	Ivory Coast	Cameroon	Tunisia	Egypt	Lebanon	Turkey	Iran	India	Sri Lanka	Pakistan	Korea, Republic of	Philippines	Thailand	
6. Politics:																									
a) Political conditions	-.27		+	–	++					+	++	+					+							+	
b) Language policies	-.06		++			+		+		+									–	–		+		+	
7. Citizenship:																									
a) Maintain existing rights	+.62		–								+	+	+		––		+					––	––		
b) Acquire new rights	-.29		–	–		++								–	–	–							–		
8. Influence of others:																									
a) Patriotism	+.97																								
b) Obligations to family	+.85			––							+	+	+		––								–	+	
c) Influence of family	+.86			––	+						+	+	+		–								–	+	
d) Influence of friends	+.76				+				+		+	+	+		–		+						–	+	

[continued]

Table VI-2 [continued]

Region	Country	9. Interests of spouse and children: a) Spouse feelings	b) Education of children	c) Careers of children	d) Marriage of children	(Total number of respondents)
	Greece					(661)
Asia	Thailand					(68)
	Philippines	--	--	-	--	(83)
	Korea, Republic of					(402)
	Pakistan			+		(111)
	Sri Lanka					(194)
	India					(1,076)
Middle East and North Africa	Iran		--	--	--	(148)
	Turkey					(39)
	Lebanon	-	--	-		(142)
	Egypt	--	--	--	--	(170)
	Tunisia					(126)
Africa	Cameroon			++	+	(45)
	Ivory Coast			++	+	(41)
	Senegal	++	++	++	+	(34)
	Ghana		++	+		(218)
South America	Venezuela	++			+	(31)
	Colombia			-		(323)
	Argentina		+	+		(509)
	Brazil					(864)
Caribbean and Central America	Mexico	-		-		(29)
	Haiti			--	+	(67)
	Jamaica					(76)
	Trinidad and Tobago			-		(163)
Average acceptance ratio		+.37	+.32	+.16	+.70	(6,031)

the factors, these groups think the situation at home is good enough. (I.e., for them, the "abroad" per cent is not so high.)

Some nationalities believe that routine work, such as burdensome administration, is greater at home, and therefore the need for time for professional development makes overseas jobs more attractive. (I.e., for item 2b, their acceptance ratios are large and negative.) The contrast between developed countries and home seems greatest to Indians, Ceylonese, and Egyptians. (I.e., the "abroad" per cent is higher than the "home" per cent for item 2b.) But others believe that it is the North American and European jobs that are most demanding and that they would have more flexible and more rewarding experiences at home. These groups include most Africans, Thais, Turks, Mexicans, Colombians, and Venezuelans. (I.e., the "home" per cent is much higher for them than for the other respondents, and their acceptance ratios are closer to zero.)

Nationalities differ over where professionals enjoy better income and more respect (item 2f). Because of these divisions, the average acceptance ratio for everyone is only slightly below zero (-.14). Indians, Ceylonese, Filipinos, Egyptians, Cameroonians, and several others deem the status of professionals superior abroad. Venezuelans, Ghanaians, Iranians, Turks, Thais, and some others believe that pay and prestige are sufficiently better at home to make this an important reason for return.

Colleagues. Most nationalities think that work abroad is far more attractive in the intellectual companionship from colleagues and in the quality of assistants (Cluster 3). Pakistanis, Indians, Ceylonese, Haitians, Jamaicans, and several others consider the difference between domestic and foreign working conditions particularly wide. Thais and Ghanaians also find that overseas conditions are more attractive, but the contrast is not so one-sided. (I.e., for both items 3a and 3b, the "aboard" per cent is lower than for other national groups, and their acceptance ratios are closer to zero.)

<u>Societal setting</u>. If the professional comes from a developing country with long traditions and much current output in the arts and letters, he often prefers it to the developed countries on grounds of higher culture and better quality of life. Examples are Mexico, India, Pakistan, and Thailand. (For them on item 4a, the "home" per cent exceeds the "abroad" per cent.) But in the eyes of some others, particular developed countries are more attractive than home: for example, Latin Americans are drawn to the United States, while many francophone Africans believe France is culturally superior to their homelands. (I.e., "abroad" per cent exceeds "home" per cent, and respondents mention the United States and France in answer to the supplementary question soliciting further details.)

Nationalities vary in perception of where life is more challenging, where more can be accomplished. On balance, more students and professionals prefer their home countries, and therefore this is one of the few reasons pertaining to work that has a positive acceptance ratio in Table VI-2. The homeland often is picked if it is rapidly developing (e.g., Brazil, Iran, and Turkey) or if its development is still at such an early stage that much can be created (e.g., Senegal and Cameroon). (I.e., for them, the "home" per cent exceeds the "abroad" per cent on item 4b.)

In contrast are some countries where many of our respondents believe that red tape, uncertain internal conditions, and favoritism prevent things from getting done. In such cases, our respondents believed that work abroad was more attractive. (I.e., in these cases, the "abroad" per cent exceeds the "home" per cent.)

<u>Alienation and discrimination</u>. These pushes from the developed country vary by nationality: they are very strong for most Africans but are hardly noticed by the Venezuelans. The darker one's skin, the greater the push of racial discrimination from North America and Europe, and therefore the greater the preference for the home

country (Cluster 5).[4]

Discrimination is usually a push by a developed country inducing return home. But in one case in our data (Egypt), so many foreign students are drawn from minority groups that their perception of discrimination at home becomes an important reason for emigration.

Political conditions. In those cases where the political situation anywhere affects the individual's migration decisions, most nationalities on balance say that these conditions induce them to emigrate. Therefore, in the first column of Table VI-2, line 6a has the entry -.27, reflecting a substantial pressure to emigrate. For several nationalities, the inducement was even stronger than this average, although only one group has a minus score on line 6a, reflecting such an exceptionally strong response. (Table VI-2 is designed to show the cases that differ very widely from the average.)

The political situation--presumably the need to maintain contacts and to play a role in future developments--is a strong reason Senegalese give for returning. The Senegalese are the unusual case with a positive acceptance ratio for item 6a. Otherwise, the nationalities with + or ++ entries in Table VI-2 for Cluster 6 find governmental actions irrelevant to their migration decisions rather than a reason for return--i.e., the + and ++ entries result from low response to political motives, in contrast to the responses in favor of emigration by other groups.

---

[4]The countries with predominantly black populations have the highest acceptance ratios--i.e., the strongest statements that discrimination is a reason for returning home. But the same association between race and perceptions of discrimination can be calculated when individual respondents are classified by their own race. The acceptance ratios for the item about discrimination are:

Race of respondent	Ratio
Black	.94
Far Eastern, oriental	.74
White	.73

Several governments recently have spread vernacular languages throughout the schools and official business. It is widely believed a chief reason for brain drain, but the assumption is not supported by our data. In a few countries where this is taking place--such as India and Ceylon--our respondents cite government language policies as a reason for leaving, but the proportions are not as high as might have been expected (item 6b).

Citizenship. Egyptians, Filipinos, and South Koreans seem particularly interested in obtaining second citizenship or second residency rights abroad (Cluster 7). The same motive appears among Jamaicans, Haitians, Tunisians, and Lebanese, but not as strongly.

Influence of others. Family relations and the influence of friends are among the most powerful reasons for return. In Table VI-2, the average acceptance ratios are very high and positive for items b through d in Cluster 8. Only the Haitians give family and friends as influences for emigration.

For some nationalities with strong family systems, such as Pakistanis, the pull homeward for these reasons is very one-sided. The pull is less powerful for certain other groups with higher emigration rates, such as Trinidadians, Egyptians, and Filipinos.

In our cluster analysis of the battery of reasons, feelings of patriotism were part of the set of items measuring attachments to family (item 8a). It is always one-sided on behalf of return: hardly anyone says he considers emigrating for patriotic reasons. The difference is between those who are drawn home by patriotism and those who are not affected by it, a distinction not measured by the acceptance ratio. Those who cite patriotism most frequently are persons from Ghana, Senegal, the Ivory Coast, Cameroon, Pakistan, Greece, Jamaica and Haiti. The national groups who mention it least often are the Mexicans, Argentines, Egyptians, Lebanese, and Filipinos.

Interests of spouse and children. Most students and professionals believe that the interests of their spouses and children are best served at home (Cluster 9). This is particularly true for Venezuelans, Ghanaians, and Senegalese. The force of this set of reasons is demonstrated by groups under cross-pressures, such as the Argentines: on many reasons they prefer foreign countries; for other reasons they prefer home; but for their children's futures, they are strongly committed to return and stay in Argentina.

Professionals from some countries seem so pessimistic about their own future prospects at home that they consider emigrating in order to facilitate the careers of their children as well as of themselves. They include Haitians, Trinidadians, Egyptians, Iranians, Filipinos, and several others. (For them, the percentage favoring "abroad" exceeds the percentage favoring "home" on items 9b and 9c, and therefore their acceptance ratios are negative.)

Reasons and actual plans to return home or stay abroad

The list of reasons in the questionnaire obtained each person's criteria for preferring his home country or a foreign country. The decision to migrate or return is the net result of all these motivations and personal influences, some pulling him one way and others pulling him in an opposite direction. Tables VI-1 and VI-2 showed whether each reason operated on behalf of return or emigration, and whether each reason was common or rare in frequency. Even more important is to estimate each reason's strength, i.e., its effect upon return or emigration. In order to predict a student's or a professional's future movements, the reasons having the strongest association with plans for return or emigration should be identified.

The association between these attitudes and plans is complicated, because we have data about persons' attitudes and plans at three different stages, viz., during study abroad, during work abroad after the end of study, and after return to the home countries. A few relationships are consistent, but many vary. The following pages summarize the general patterns. The complete results, including all the variations at different stages, appear in Appendix B. The numbers measuring the association between all reasons and persons' plans are in Table B-1 in the appendix. Table VI-3 in the text gives the highlights of Table B-1, i.e., it shows the reasons that are most strongly associated with plans at each stage.

Consistent patterns. A few reasons seem to control the decision to return home or to remain abroad at every stage, particularly the perception of the country that is best for the education and careers of one's children. If the respondent believes the home country is best for the children, he returns; if he thinks a foreign country is best, he emigrates. These reasons appear in all three groups of strong motives in Table VI-3.

Certain reasons have weak effects on plans throughout, particularly preferences between countries because of their equipment, office space, libraries, and other facilities. Most persons say these properties are superior in developed countries and, by themselves, would persuade them to emigrate. But these persons return home for other reasons.

Differences in strength of reasons. Several reasons are strongly associated with plans to return or to stay abroad at certain stages, but seem weaker than other motives at other stages. For example, the cluster of reasons concerning working conditions--i.e., income, quality of jobs, number of jobs, and opportunity to contribute to one's profession--are among the strongest influences upon return or emigration at the end of study and after actual return home. But our respondents during work abroad --while affected by these motives--seemed even more influenced by the political situation at home and abroad, by a desire to maintain citizenship and residency rights, and by a desire to avoid discrimination.

[Text continues on page 116]

Table VI-3

The Strongest Reasons for Returning Home or for Staying Abroad

1. During or at the end of study abroad:

Acquire new rights
Careers of children
Education of children
Patriotism
Maintain existing rights
Quality of jobs
Number of jobs
Income

2. During or at the end of work abroad:

Careers of children
Education of children
Acquire new rights
Language policies
Feel strange (alienation)
Patriotism
Political conditions
Maintain existing rights

3. After return to home country:

Income
Quality of jobs
Number of jobs
Contribution to profession
Careers of children
Spouse feelings
Education of children
Language policies

Complete wording of the items is in Table VI-1. Appendix B describes how the association was measured between each item and plans to return home or to emigrate. The three parts of Table VI-3 list the reasons most strongly associated with plans in the first three columns of Table B-1 in the appendix. For example, the first column of Table B-1 gives the measures of association between plans and the reasons for return or emigration in the battery asking about attitudes during or at the end of study abroad. Part 1 of Table VI-3 lists the eight reasons with the largest numbers, ranked in descending order.

In general, comparative judgments about countries seem to weaken as influences upon plans after return--i.e., in Table B-1, the numbers show weaker statistical associations in the third column (the stage after return home) than in the first two columns (the stages of study and work abroad). After he has returned home, the professional develops many ties and obligations, going abroad for a career is too risky, and inertia takes effect. Therefore, increasing numbers of persons expect to stay at home regardless of any perceptions that things might be better elsewhere.

Comparison with previous research. Many essays suggest reasons why some persons return and others emigrate.[5] But the authors do not specify the comparative strength of the motivations and influences; nor do they suggest what reasons are particularly important for what types of persons.

Since earlier studies have been simple, our results confirm them. But such confirmation is limited to the modest finding that a particular motive or influence is related to the decision to migrate or return. For example, previous research has found that a student is more likely to return if he believes his income will be adequate, if economic prospects at home are favorable, and if he will obtain a good job.[6] And our data--reported in Tables

[5] Cited in Chapter I, footnote 6, supra.

[6] For example, John Niland, The Asian Engineering Brain Drain (Lexington: Heath Lexington Books, 1970), pp. 59-89 passim; Man Singh Das, "The 'Brain Drain' Controversy in a Comparative Perspective," International Review of Sociology, Volume 1, Number 1 (March 1971), p. 3; Paul Ritterband, The Non-Returning Foreign Student: The Israeli Case (New York: Bureau of Applied Social Research, 1968), p. 89; Tai Keun Oh, The Role of International Education in the Asian Brain Drain (Madison: dissertation for the Ph.D. in Industrial Relations, University of Wisconsin, 1970), pp. 123-131, 138-147, and 273-274; Josefina Cortes, Factors Associated with the Migration of High-Level Persons from the Philippines to the U.S.A. (Stanford: Stanford International Development Research Center, Stanford University, 1970), pp. 50-57 and 83-85; Josefina

VI-3 and B-1--confirm the association of these reasons with return. Our confirmation varies: for example, some previous samples did not seem to rate income as one of the stronger predictors of migration, while others did.[7]

In the last chapter and in this one, we reported the very common complaints by returnees about the lack of facilities, staff, and time to conduct research. One of the few surveys done of stay-ons discovered that the opportunity to do research was one of the principal motives for migration, particularly among Indians.[8]

Earlier studies found that family ties at home are important forces bringing the person back. If he has few family members in the country of origin, his chances of return are smaller.[9] Some popula-

---

Bulatao Jayme, Demographic and Socio-Psychological Determinants of the Migration of Highly Trained Filipinos to the United States (Pittsburgh: dissertation for the Ph.D. in Psychology, Carnegie-Mellon University, 1971), pp. 39 and 41; Iraj Valipour, A Comparison of Returning and Non-Returning Iranian Students in the United States (New York: thesis for the Ed.D., Teachers College, Columbia University, 1962), pp. 80-87; and Keshav Dev Sharma, "Indian Students in the United States," International Educational and Cultural Exchange, Volume IV, Number 4 (Spring 1969), p. 52.

[7] Surveys in which income and living standards were strong motives are Immigrant Scientists and Engineers in the United States: a Study of Characteristics and Attitudes (Washington: National Science Foundation, 1973), pp. vi and 1; Niland, The Asian Engineering Brain Drain (op. cit., fn. 6), pp. 60-65; Ritterband, The Non-Returning Foreign Student: The Israeli Case (op. cit., fn. 6), pp. 89-90; and Valipour, A Comparison of Returning and Non-Returning Iranian Students in the United States (op. cit., fn. 6), pp. 86-87.

[8] Immigrant Scientists and Engineers in the United States (op. cit., fn. 7), pp. vi, 1, and 18.

[9] Cortes, Factors Associated with the Migration of High-Level Persons from the Philippines to the U.S.A. (op. cit., fn. 6), p. 78; Mehri Hekmati, "Non-Returning Foreign Students: Why Do They Not Return Home?" Die Dritte Welt, Volume 2, Number 1 (1973), pp. 32-40 passim; Oh, The Role of International Educa-

tions, such as Koreans, place strict obligations to help parents upon older sons, and these ensure return.[10] One study found that the interests of children can be a principal reason for emigration, if the professional believes the home country offers them a poor future.[11] No studies yet identify which reasons are sufficiently powerful to over-rule others pointing in the opposite direction, but we suspect that family ties is one.

Previous studies have identified qualities that foreign students find overwhelmingly superior in developed countries. The authors' implications usually are that these reasons lead to emigration.[12] Examples are libraries, laboratories, office space and staff. But actually these are complaints rather than reasons for migration, except possibly for those specialties described in Chapter V. As motives they are weak for most persons and in most cases are over-ridden by strong home ties of other kinds. At best, these complaints predict only whether the average professionals will work abroad a short time after completing study.[13]

A set of complaints about conditions at home that may have somewhat greater predictive power are the seniority system, the conflict of generations, and scarcity of jobs at the top, which afflict some

---

tion in the Asian Brain Drain (op. cit., fn. 6), pp. 207-218; and Valipour, A Comparison of Returning and Non-Returning Iranian Students in the United States (op. cit., fn. 6), pp. 36 and 93-94.

[10]John Alsop Thames, Korean Students in Southern California: Factors Influencing Their Plans Toward Returning Home (Pasadena: dissertation for the Doctor of Education, University of Southern California, 1971), pp. 64 and 114.

[11]Immigrant Scientists and Engineers in the United States (op. cit., fn. 7), pp. vi, 1, and 18-19.

[12]For example, Niland, The Asian Engineering Brain Drain Drain (op. cit., fn. 6), pp. 59-89 passim.

[13]Noticed also by Oh, The Role of International Education in the Asian Brain Drain (op. cit., fn. 6), pp. 153-158.

countries, such as India. These barriers were criticized both in previous surveys[14] and in the interviews that supplemented our questionnaires.

Feelings of discrimination have been found associated with decisions to return, while distaste for political conditions at home have been reported to foster emigration, but neither has seemed as strong as other influences.[15]

Need for more complex analysis. Appendix B is the first step in developing better prediction of migration. It shows that some reasons are strong predictors of migration, but none by themselves are complete. Better predictive power might be achieved by combining the stronger items from these batteries into multiple regression equations.[16] Other causes mentioned in other chapters should also be included in such explanations. Particularly important is whether an individual belongs to a minority group.

Besides the complications from the need for many causes in explaining migration, reasons apparently depend on location and stage of life. Contrary to our expectations when we began, the same explanations cannot hold true for students, stay-ons, and returnees. If they did, the columns in Table B-1 would show the same numbers. But the numbers differ: some reasons have the same importance for all groups, others fluctuate. Therefore, different prediction equations--possibly even with different variables--will be necessary for students, stay-ons, and returnees.

---

[14] Oh, The Role of International Education in the Asian Brain Drain (op. cit., fn. 6), pp. 165-172.

[15] Oh, The Role of International Education in the Asian Brain Drain (op. cit., fn. 6), pp. 184-185, 188-190, 198-199, and 204-205.

[16] Our staff has begun to apply the methods of multivariate path analysis to our data. See Orlando Rodriguez, Social Determinants of Non-Return: A Study of Foreign Students from Developing Countries in the United States (New York: dissertation for the Ph.D. in Sociology, Columbia University, 1974).

Income difference among countries do not determine brain drain as strongly as is generally believed

A common belief is that[17]

> the decision to emigrate may obviously result from a number of motives, which may differ in each individual case. But generally speaking, among these motives an economic consideration, the desire to become better off, has been predominant. The liberal theory of the economic effects of migration is...based on this assumption, on the abstraction of the "economic man" who always wants to act in accordance with his best economic interests and also knows how to do so. This simplification may be regarded as a fairly realistic first approach to the problems of migration.

The brain drain is usually discussed in the context of manpower economics, and it is frequently attributed to the higher salaries available in developed countries. Elegant mathematical models have been published, predicting how increases in migration are functions of increased differentials between countries in income expectations.[18]

---

[17] Julius Isaac, Economics of Migration (London: Kegan Paul, Trench, Trubner & Company, 1947), p. 23.

[18] For example, Gopalakrishanan Dorai, Economics of the International Flow of Students: A Cost-Benefit Analysis (Detroit: dissertation for the Ph.D. in economics, Wayne State University, 1968); and Herbert G. Grubel and Anthony D. Scott, "Determinants of Migration: The Highly Skilled," International Migration, Volume V, Number 2 (1967), pp. 127-139. For a very able summary of the literature of economists about brain drain, see Anthony Scott, "The Brain Drain--Is a Human-Capital Approach Justified?", in Education, Income, and Human Capital (New York: National Bureau of Economic Research and Columbia University Press, 1970), pp. 241-284.

But this favorite explanation of brain drain founders on the facts. "Everyone knows" income differences to be the most important determinant except the persons involved in the flows themselves. On the rare occasions when they are asked, the professionals usually pick income gains less frequently than many other considerations in controlling their choice of country.[19] When respondents have been classified according to possible income gains from migration, the differences have little or no statistical association with plans.[20]

Our data about the effects of perceptions. In Table B-1 in the appendix, professed interest in money was one of the strong predictors of migration. Item 1b--"potential income and living standards"--had measures of association with migration plans between .35 and .54. In other words, respondents generally planned to go to (or stay in) the countries with the income prospects they deemed most attractive. The measures fall short of 1.0, of course, because some persons incline toward countries with less advantageous money and living standards, as the result of other and stronger pulls and pushes.

But these questions elicited respondents' perceptions of where income was better. Are any precise income differentials or ratios identified with high emigration?

---

[19] Niland, The Asian Engineering Brain Drain (op. cit., fn. 6), pp. 60-65; Robert G. Myers, Education and Emigration (New York: David McKay Company, 1972), p. 280 (our recalculation of Table 45); John W. Orton, "An Interview-Based Study of Pakistanis Employed in the Professions in the United States" (New York: Institute for International Education, 1965) p. 8; and Oladejo O. Okediji, "Nigeria 'Brain Drain' to the United States of America: A Sociological Perspective," Journal of Eastern African Research and Development, Volume 2, Number 2 (1972), pp. 150-151.

[20] Ritterband, The Non-Returning Foreign Student: The Israeli Case (op. cit., fn. 6), p. 90.

Comparisons of expected income. Our questionnaires asked about the monthly salaries respondents might expect if they worked at home or abroad. We converted all answers into standard currency units to correct for differences in exchange rates and in living costs. Then we examined the differentials between the home country and the developed country where the respondent studied or worked. The questions and our manipulations of the answers are summarized in Appendix C of this monograph.

Table C-1 in the Appendix shows the monthly incomes expected at home and abroad, expressed in our standard currency units that correct for variations in living costs. Most respondents expect to earn more abroad than at home, but this is not true of everyone; the Greek, Brazilian, and Colombian returnees expect to earn more at home. Among students and stay-ons, even after correcting for the higher prices in the United States, pay rates in employment abroad are highest in the United States and lowest in France. Among the returnees, domestic pay rates are highest in Greece and South America and lowest in Asia and Ghana.

Proportional gains. Table C-2 in the Appendix shows the gains expected from work abroad. Wide variations occur by country of study and by country of origin. Respondents expect larger gains from work in the United States and Canada than in France or the United Kingdom.[21] Several nationalities expect larger gains in Canada than in the United States because they come to Canada with lower expectations of what they can earn at home. (One reason is that

[21]The literature on brain drain assumes that migrating professionals can earn very high salaries in all developed countries. But this is possible only for a few specialties in a few developed countries, such as the United States. Even there, rent, taxes, and other high costs reduce the real value of these salaries. In most developed countries, professionals from developing countries earn low salaries, particularly at first. See, for example, Geoffry Oldham and Oscar Gish, "Survey of Immigrant Professionals in the Fields of Science and Technology" (Brighton: Science Policy Research Unit, University of Sussex, 1970), pp. 6-7.

Canada attracts undergraduates with lower immediate expectations than the graduate students from those same countries, who usually go to the United States.)

Several of the Asian nationalities--such as Indians, Pakistanis, Ceylonese, and Koreans--expect low incomes at home and might earn three or even four times as much in the United States or Canada. They expect less in France or the United Kingdom. Most nationalities expect smaller gains from foreign studies. Many persons from home countries with better pay--such as Iran, Brazil, and Colombia--expect to earn more at home.

Effects of income differentials on migration plans. Increased salaries abroad are associated with a greater intention to emigrate, but the relationship is very limited, and clearly other influences operate as well. Among no group of persons--whether students, stay-ons, or returnees from any country--is there a strong tendency for larger income prospects abroad to produce increasing increments in plans to emigrate. Many persons are committed to return and remain in developing countries despite the belief they could earn two or three times as much overseas. Small variations in income expectations do not produce shifts between the strength of intentions to return--i.e., between the categories "definitely" and "probably" return. Table C-3 in the Appendix presents the figures describing how increased gains relate to plans for migrating or returning.

As a result of the positive but weak relation between higher income prospects and migration plans, migrants think they can earn more abroad than non-migrants. But the gains are small and are absent from some samples. The data are in Table C-4.

Our calculations use units of currency that correct for higher prices in some countries. If all respondents' income estimates are converted into one country's money at official exchange rates, the numerical differences between salaries expected abroad and at home are larger, and only one-sixth of all persons expect to earn more money at home. But the statistical conclusions are the same: increases in the absolute gain or relative gain through foreign employment are associated with greater plans to take those jobs, but the tendency is weak.

The meaning of money. At first sight, the findings about income are paradoxical. Foreign students' and professionals' perceptions of where incomes are better predict where they go more strongly than most other motives and influences, according to Table B-1. But the actual measurements of differences in income in Appendix C seem to affect movements only slightly.

It has long been fashionable to say that persons' patriotic attachments, their family loyalties, their perceptions of where society provides better opportunities, and such attitudes and personal ties are "subjective" while market conditions and their resulting income offers are "objective." Economic explanations of the brain drain dismiss the "subjective" causes as unmeasurable and less important, while the differentials in income are the truly fundamental and sufficient explanations. But when professionals make decisions about migration and return, money is no more objective and no less subjective than anything else. They seek a satisfactory life in all aspects. Little money may seem satisfactory under some conditions; much money may seem unsatisfactory under other circumstances.

Everyone probably would be pleased to accept more money, and therefore receiving little is a favorite subject of complaint. But a person can become reconciled to a living standard that appears normal to his peers. Even though incomes in a developing country appear low by world-wide standards, the professionals are still well paid in comparison to the rest of the populations and are on a par with the small élites. Even if living standards are stringent, the frustrations are shared by the rest of the élites. So, even the professionals who could earn relatively much more abroad might not let income by itself affect their migration decisions and might think that salaries at home are adequate enough to justify staying.

Implications for policy: making appeals that attract students and professionals home

Some factors affecting individuals' migration plans require expensive investments that developing countries can make only with difficulty. Others require not a reallocation of scarce resources but a better sense of national purpose.

Salaries. The most common belief about brain drain is that raising income will bring more persons back. Our respondents agree, but apparently they mean to work in those countries where incomes are satisfactory, rather than automatically move to societies where real income is highest.

Since developing countries with attractive salaries have higher rates of return, governments and employers often try to give especially favorable rates and fringe benefits to foreign-trained professionals. But problems often arise. Many developing countries lack the means to pay wages even in nonconvertible currency that can compete with rates in North America. If the professionals are guaranteed the right to buy consumer durables that must be imported, scarce hard currency is lost. High pay for new returnees may be resented by other employees with more seniority. High pay for the foreign-trained professionals will accentuate the class differences in income that are already too wide in developing countries and that may produce much class conflict in the future.[22]

---

[22] Discussion of the very high salaries, the hard-currency imports, and the severe budgetary problems that result from matching incomes the professionals can earn abroad, can be found in an unpublished report by Paul B. Sack, L'émigration du personnel qualifié camerounais: un cas africain d'exode des cerveaux, pp. 35-40 and 55-56; and in Richard Jolly and Dudley Seers, "The Brain Drain and the Development Process," in Gustav Ranis (editor), The Gap Between Rich and Poor Countries (London: The Macmillan Company, 1972), p. 374.

If pecuniary differentials alone controlled migration, developing countries would have insoluble problems: they could keep their best professionals only by matching the pay offers from overseas, and their economies would become increasingly unbalanced by heavy cash flows into the salaries of the élite.[23] However it appears as if adequate salaries rather than very high figures would be attractive enough to keep most persons at home, provided they are accompanied by a variety of non-monetary incentives. The investment of money in both salaries and the complete setting of the job is essential. In several countries with low salaries, professionals complain at least as much about jobs that are stifling in their routines and primitive in their facilities.[24]

Reforms in payment should include revision of the rank structure as well as increases in salary. At present in many countries, the hierarchy of rank confers higher pay only upon managers. Talented stay-ons and students often get high pay offers at present, but at the price of a heavy schedule of administration. Often this leaves little time for the expert and innovative professional work that was the purpose of their foreign study and is their unique contribution after return. Complaints about too much teaching and administration and few opportunities for research were common in the interviews given by the returnees after they filled out our questionnaires.

Increasing employment. Another determinant of flow also requires heavy investment by the developing country, viz., the number of jobs. Respondents say they will go to those countries with the more

---

[23] Dudley Seers, "The Brain Drain from Poor Countries" (Brighton: Institute of Development Studies, University of Sussex, 1969), pp. 4-5.

[24] A combination of problems noticed also by Justus van der Kroef, "The U.S. and the World's Brain Drain," *International Journal of Comparative Sociology*, Volume XI, Number 3 (September 1970), pp. 232-233.

attractive employment market. This confirms the familiar recommendation that developing countries must improve their economic growth to absorb professional manpower.[25]

But, as Chapter III showed, merely increasing statistical indicators at a fast rate is not enough. Even if overall growth occurs, certain fields may lag. For these specialties and even for the entire economy, the number of professionals may outstrip the number of jobs. Therefore many observers have recommended better planning of domestic university enrollments and of support for foreign study, so that the numbers in particular fields correspond more closely to the country's current absorptive capacities and future needs.[26] This would frustrate persons not admitted to particular curricula at home and abroad, but at present they are frustrated by uncertain job prospects after long and expensive education.

---

[25] Committee on the International Migration of Talent, The International Migration of High-Level Manpower (New York: Praeger Publishers, 1970), pp. 678-682 and 700-706; Walter Adams (editor), The Brain Drain (New York: The Macmillan Company, 1968), pp. 251-254 and 261-263; and many other sources. On the need to expand private as well as public employment, see Alberto Sánchez Crespo, "La emigración de profesionales universitarios desde America Latina" (Washington: Organization of American States, 1969), pp. 31-32.

[26] UNESCO, "The Problem of Emigration of Scientists and Technologists ('Brain Drain' or 'Exode des Compétences'): General Appraisal of the Phenomenon" (Paris: United Nations Educational, Scientific and Cultural Organization, Science Policy Division, SC/WS/57, 29 February 1968), p. 32; Susumu Watanabe, "The Brain Drain from Developing to Developed Countries," International Labour Review, Volume 99, Number 4 (April 1969), pp. 428-430; Committee on the International Migration of Talent, The International Migration of High-Level Manpower (op. cit., fn. 25), pp. 268 and 703-704; and Adams (editor), The Brain Drain (op. cit., fn. 25), pp. 254-256.

Because some countries have shortages of jobs and many students overseas, one may think that attracting back more persons will increase the problem.[27] Despite rhetoric about combatting all forms of emigration, most governments seem to take practical action only concerning fields with unfilled jobs. For their part, the overseas students and nonreturnees worry about the risks of going back. Even under these conditions, bringing the ablest persons back might still be worthwhile. Instead of taking jobs away from others, they might generate new jobs for the unemployed. Some of these people might be exceptionally able managers and mobilizers of resources; others might be innovators in science and applied research.

The growth of science and applied research in developing countries would alleviate the brain drain not only by creating new employment both in the fields of application and in the research centers themselves, but it would reduce the common complaints by returnees about too much routine teaching and administrative work without opportunities for scientific creativity.[28]

Strengthening national purposes. Some effective motivations are cheaper in national resources but depend on leadership and national morale that might be equally hard to generate. The foreign-trained professional tends to go where he thinks jobs are more interesting, where he can make the greatest contributions to his profession, where life generally seems more challenging, and where he thinks he is wanted.[29] Some developing countries arouse in their

[27] Research on the phenomenon of unemployment among the educated is now appearing. For example, Mark Blaug, The Causes of Graduate Unemployment in India (London: Allen Lane, 1969).

[28] On the importance of science policy as a remedy for brain drain, see Migration of Health Personnel, Scientists, and Engineers from Latin America (Washington: Pan American Health Organization, 1966), pp. 47-48; and Allan McKnight, Scientists Abroad: A Study of the International Movement of Persons in Science and Technology (Paris: UNESCO, 1971), Ch. 11.

[29] On the importance of feeling wanted, see McKnight, Scientists Abroad (op. cit., fn. 28), pp. 115-119.

citizens images that the societies are superior to North America and Europe in these respects, and they enjoy higher rates of return. In addition, the stronger the nationalistic and patriotic feelings that a country can evoke among its overseas students, the higher their return.

Generating these pulls from home requires leadership not only from governments but from the leaders of the professions themselves. Ultimately, only they can give full meaning to employment in their fields; only they can be effective role models for their younger colleagues considering return from abroad. Professional associations can safely be organized in a decentralized and *laissez faire* manner in developed countries, but a more dynamic sense of purpose must be fostered by professional leaders in developing countries. At present, some leaders of professions serve on governmental planning commissions and address the public about policy questions, but this should become more common. In some developing countries, leaders of professions are ignored by governments and the mass media, and low morale and high emigration cannot fail to result.

Appealing to the family. As strong a determinant as professional considerations is the person's family, and particularly judgments about the long-term best interests of children. While longer stays may never lead to the full assimilation of the adult into foreign societies and may correlate with migration plans only within limits, the children can become Westernized. Therefore, governments trying to attract valued professionals back should woo their wives and children as well with programs of education and recreation. Returnees need to be satisfied with the schooling and future prospects for their children.

Since marrying a foreigner is such a strong correlate of emigration--as the next chapter will show--governments and employers must succeed in interesting the spouse in the country and in making stays pleasant. Ease in conferring work permits and citizenship will help convince the foreign spouse that the professional's home country is also his or hers. Work permits and citizenship may reduce the "brain drain" of women and result in "brain gain", by attracting foreign husbands; at present in mixed marriages, husbands rarely go to the wife's country, and therefore the foreign spouse in a developing country is usually the wife.

Improving working conditions. Several working conditions are sources of mass complaint rather than of mass emigration. Nearly all professionals consider them superior in developed countries but return anyway for other reasons, viz., opportunities to keep in touch with professional developments abroad, libraries, equipment, office space, the quality of professional relationships, and the quality of assistants. After several years of experience at home, the returnees are more affected by these considerations: to a greater degree than earlier, the returnees plan to go to countries where these facilities seem best. Some developing countries with high rates of growth, enough hard currency, and new construction create facilities attractive enough to supplement the other pulls homeward, but usually these are pulls from developed countries that must be over-ridden by the other attractions at home. A very common grievance of professions is isolation, because of inability to travel and the scarcity of foreign journals; governments can remedy this only by using the hard currency in demand for many other purposes.[30] As in the case of income and numbers of good jobs, developing countries cannot compete with developed societies in all these areas without purposeful and balanced growth.

---

[30] A beneficial trend to reduce isolation is the growing number of regional professional associations and regional professional conferences. Professionals in neighboring countries can learn from each other and might collaborate on projects. With proper financial management, the drain on hard currency can be minimized. The next steps are communication among the regional professional groups in different parts of the world, and creation of more regional professional journals that are sufficiently respected to attract enough subscribers.

If improvements are too expensive to be made in all fields, they should start in those specialties with the highest losses due to these reasons. According to Chapter V, these fields are the biological sciences, the teaching of languages, and certain areas in engineering. Making similar improvements in other fields with higher return rates may pay off there in higher morale and higher productivity.

The uneven character of educational systems is reflected in the common complaint about the number and quality of assistants. Developing countries produce too few technicians and technically proficient college graduates, at the same time that many are overproducing mandarins. Economic growth depends as much on repair men as on doctors of engineering; the latter cannot function without the former. Sound educational planning may require fewer domestic and foreign university students in some fields and more primary and secondary school students from the working classes in technical curricula. This requires concerted leadership by government and by other opinion leaders to induce populations to respect the technicians as much as the mandarins and literati.

Sharing lessons among developing countries. Developing countries can learn more from each other's examples than from the written reports of committees and experts. An important contribution of multinational surveys like ours is to identify the countries that might become models. With respect to brain drain, some countries motivate higher return than others; certain reasons induce their nationals to return, while the same factors cause persons from other countries to prefer North America or Europe.

Chapter VII

TIES WITH HOME

If a student or professional working abroad is obligated to return or frequently communicates with persons at home, he is much more likely to go back. But if these pulls are weak or if he develops new connections with foreign countries, his chances of emigrating increase. The association between pulls from home and intention to return and stay is strong, but of course the causal influences may work in both directions: ties with home may increase and reinforce intentions to return, while intentions induce the person to increase his ties and to notice the appeals from home. Our survey contains some evidence that adding extra pulls from home increases the certainty and speed of return, and therefore extra efforts by organizations at home will pay off.

Sponsored students are more likely to return, particularly if the money comes from home

A world-wide trend is increased control over foreign study, largely out of fear of the brain drain. If a foreign student stays abroad, he takes not only the original domestic educational investment in building up his talents but also the foreign exchange that paid for his ticket and education abroad. So, many countries now discourage private foreign study through exchange controls and exit visas, include their students in official programs of educational exchange, and require some form of pledge to return.

Scholarships and other grants. In our data, academic scholarships or grants from employers were held by 52 per cent of the foreign students in the United States, 56 per cent of those in France, and 40 per cent of those in Canada. Most likely to be sponsored are Mexicans, Africans, Tunisians, Turks, Indians, and Koreans. Least likely are West Indians, Lebanese, Egyptians, Filipinos, and Thais. The specialties with the highest proportions of sponsorship are agriculture, biology, mathematics, physical science, and social science. The specialties where private payment is most common are architecture and business management.

Students on scholarships--whether from their own or from the host country--are more likely to return than the privately supported, according to Table VII-1. The difference appears in each of our surveys of students and confirms earlier research on brain drain.[1] Emigration is greater in our Canadian sample in large part because fewer students there are sponsored--i.e., three-fifths of the Canadian students are personally funded, compared with less than half in the United States and France.

Source of support. Merely having a fellowship or grant does not guarantee return: a crucial question is the source of the money. According to Table VII-2, support from one's home country is most strongly associated with return. Scholarships or grants from the country of study are associated with

---

[1] Robert G. Myers, *Education and Emigration* (New York: David McKay Company, 1972), pp. 113-116 and 253; Josefina Cortes, *Factors Associated with the Migration of High-Level Persons from the Philippines to the U.S.A.* (Stanford: School of Education, Stanford International Development Education Center, Stanford University, 1970), p. 58; Josefina Bulatao Jayme, *Demographic and Socio-Psychological Determinants of the Migration of Highly Trained Filipinos to the United States* (Pittsburgh: dissertation for the Ph.D. in Psychology, Carnegie-Mellon University, 1971), pp. 32, 35-38, and 44; and John Alsop Thames, *Korean Students in Southern California* (Pasadena: dissertation for the Doctor of Education, University of Southern California, 1971), pp. 84-85.

Table VII-1

Holding a Scholarship or Grant and Long-Run Plans of Students

Sponsorship	Index of return of students in			Total number of respondents		
	United States	Canada	France	United States	Canada	France
Sponsored	1.16	.84	1.47	(842)	(373)	(260)
Personally funded	1.02	.43	1.02	(716)	(508)	(206)

lower rates of return, particularly if they come from the university attended by the respondent. During their study, the large majority of the stay-ons in the United States had such emigration-associated fellowships from their host universities.

Previous surveys also have found that getting money from the university in the country of study is associated with higher emigration than is support from official sources in the governments of the home country or of the country of study.[2] Tabulations presented later in this chapter will show that some faculty members in developed countries advise students to stay abroad rather than return. Therefore, instead of reinforcing students' intentions to serve their home societies, foreign universities sometimes attract students into careers abroad.

[2]Tai Keun Oh, The Role of International Education in the Asian Brain Drain (Madison: dissertation for the Ph.D. in Industrial Relations, University of Wisconsin, 1970), pp. 72-75; Cortes, Factors Associated with the Migration of High-Level Persons from the Philippines to the U.S.A. (op. cit., fn. 1), p. 58; and Godwin C. Chu, "Student Expatriation: A Function of Relative Social Support," Sociology and Social Research, Volume 52, Number 2 (January 1968), p. 178. A recent survey of permanent stay-ons in the United States found that half had received full or partial support from American universities: Immigrant Scientists and Engineers in the United States: A Study of Characteristics and Attitudes (Washington: National Science Foundation, 1973), p. 8.

A few exchange programs rely on loans rather than grants. Since education abroad is often thought to increase the person's life-time earnings at home, it is assumed that he is able to repay; requiring the élite to pay for their own benefits is considered more just than placing the burden on the mass of poor taxpayers. However, this method may boomerang by weakening commitment to the home country and by producting an incentive to seek better pay abroad.[3] In our survey, persons with problems of debt repayment after return had higher rates of emigration. One reason for the greater emigration and uncertainty by Colombians in our data might be the greater reliance on loans in their educational exchanges. Compared to all other nationalities, Colombians most often reported that debts would be a problem after return.

Bonds are associated with return, but any pledge may be equally effective

Sponsorship without strings may not inspire strong convictions about returning, particularly if the money comes from the universities or cultural programs in the host country. Substantial numbers of persons expecting to stay abroad permanently report having received scholarships and fellowships during overseas study, according to Table VII-2. Therefore, some developing countries try to impose pledges, as a condition for receiving scholarships, foreign exchange, and exit visas. Some governments have considered adopting bonding systems for the first time, as a remedy for brain drain.

Bonds--i.e., forfeits of money by the family if the student does not return--are less common than

[3]Nevertheless, the country is guaranteed compensation for its educational investment. If loans can be paid off by several years of service at home--a method resembling bonds--then the country is compensated by return. Some economists favor this combination of freedom in the employment market and protection of the country's educational investment. For example, Harry G. Johnson, "An 'Internationalist' Model," in Walter Adams (editor), The Brain Drain (New York: The Macmillan Company, 1968), p. 87.

Table VII-2

Types of Scholarship or Grant and Plans to Return Home or Stay Abroad

	Index of return among				Total number of respondents			
	Students in		Stay-ons in		Students in		Stay-ons in	
	United States	France	United States	France	United States	France	United States	France
A. Sources of support at start of foreign study:								
1. International and regional organizations	1.31	1.40	-.37	-	(48)	(15)	(7)	(3)
2. Home country								
a) Government	1.85	1.37	-.54	-	(75)	(121)	(13)	(6)
b) Private, including universities	1.36	1.32	-.65	-	(51)	(20)	(8)	(1)

Persons supported only by their families or by personal funds are omitted. Each source is related to its beneficiary's plans to return home or stay abroad. Some respondents are counted more than once if they had two or more fellowships from different sources. The question about source of support was omitted from the survey of students in Canada and from all surveys of returnees. As usual in our tables, we do not include statistics in the first four columns if base numbers are too small for accuracy. We have included some statistics based on few cases, when the alternative was a complete loss of information, but these figures should be interpreted cautiously. Columns five through eight give the total numbers of persons on which the indexes are based--i.e., the total numbers of persons with each type of support.

[continued]

Table VII-2 [continued]

	Index of return among				Total number of respondents			
	Students in		Stay-ons in		Students in		Stay-ons in	
	United States	France	United States	France	United States	France	United States	France
3. Host country								
a) Government	1.28	1.26	-.89	-.67	(165)	(91)	(28)	(16)
b) University where respondent studied	.95	-	-.12	-	(350)	(2)	(131)	(2)
c) Private, such as foundations	1.57	-	-.29	-	(116)	(4)	(22)	(2)
B. Sources of support acquired after start of foreign study:								
1. International and regional organizations	1.42	-	-	-	(36)	(7)	(2)	(3)
2. Home country								
a) Government	1.81	1.62	1.00	-	(82)	(56)	(8)	(0)
b) Private, including universities	1.80	-	-	-	(49)	(5)	(0)	(0)
3. Host country								
a) Government	1.39	1.45	-.59	-1.00	(126)	(53)	(25)	(13)
b) University where respondent studied	1.06	-	-.28	-	(334)	(3)	(106)	(5)
c) Private, such as foundations	1.46	-	-.60	-	(104)	(3)	(25)	(0)

ordinary pledges without financial penalties. In our data, bonds are reported by most nationalities and particularly by persons from Brazil, Colombia, Venezuela, Iran, Turkey, Sri Lanka, and Thailand. A pledge to return but without a bond is most common in Brazil, Venezuela, all of Africa, and Tunisia. The nationalities most often free of obligations are West Indians, Mexicans, Lebanese, Egyptians, Indians, Koreans, and Filipinos--i.e., nationalities with high rates of emigration in Table III-1.

The specialties where bonding is most common are agriculture, biology, mathematics, and physical science. Specialties with the highest proportions reporting non-financial pledges to return are agriculture, arts, home management, and journalism. The specialties with the fewest bonds and non-financial pledges are architecture, business management, and philosophy.

In Table VII-3, bonds and pledges are clearly associated statistically with higher rates of return. Bonds are more effective than non-financial pledges among the nationalities going to the United States. But among the foreign students in France and Canada, the two methods are equally effective. Obligated students in Canada plan to return at nearly the same rates as those in the United States and France. One difference in the Canadian data is the much higher rates of emigration by the private and unobligated students; another reason for the higher overall rates of emigration in Canada is the higher proportion of students without any obligation.

Discussion about the brain drain often depicts widespread "skipping bond." According to Table VII-3, few bonded students expect to emigrate permanently: either skipping bond is rare, or few persons answering questionnaires confess it. Some persons with bonds can be found abroad after completing studies, but many expect to return after this additional period of work experience. In our surveys of students, about 210 were bonded, and 36 planned to work abroad temporarily after study, a number far higher than the prospective permanent emigrants among the bonded. Of the 370 stay-ons in our data so far, 18 had been bonded while students and 6 of these were still planning to return home. In our surveys of returnees so far, 515 had been bonded and 34 of them had worked abroad before return.

Bonds compel some persons to return against their will, but the proportion is considerably below that of the bonded returnees going home voluntarily. In our surveys of students, stay-ons, and returnees, about 6 per cent of the bonded planned to return home despite a preference to remain abroad. About 3 per cent of the unbonded were returning involuntarily. Therefore, bonding may increase return slightly, but most persons entering into bonds would return home anyway.

Table VII-3

Type of Obligation and Long-Run Plans of Students

	Index of return among students in			Total number of respondents		
Obligation	United States	Canada	France	United States	Canada	France
Bond	1.78	1.62	1.71	(141)	(78)	(23)
Pledge, no bond	1.54	1.67	1.63	(301)	(89)	(102)
None	.89	.10	1.02	(996)	(696)	(289)

The table is confined to the three surveys of students. Questions were asked also in the surveys of stay-ons and returnees as well, and the complete findings are summarized in the text.

In an earlier chapter, we reported that women are more likely to emigrate than men. When they first go overseas, women are less often obligated to return. In the surveys of students, the proportions are:

Obligation	Men	Women
Bond	9%	6%
Pledge, no bond	19	16
Army service	1	--
None	71	78
	100%	100%
Total number of respondents	(2234)	(476)

Guarantees of a job are associated with higher return

If a student from a developing country has a job waiting at home, he is much more likely to return than if he does not. Table VII-4 reports the results in the three surveys of students. Guaranteed employment produces a high rate of return even in the survey of students in Canada, who otherwise often consider emigration. About one-fifth of foreign students in the United States have jobs waiting for them at home--a proportion higher than in either of the other surveys of students--and this fact is one reason the general rate of return from the United States is higher than many readers might have expected. Earlier surveys of foreign students have also discovered that assurance of a job at home is strongly related to return.[4]

[4] Myers, Education and Emigration (op. cit., fn. 1), pp. 261-265; Oh, The Role of International Education in the Asian Brain Drain (op. cit., fn. 2), pp. 125-128; Cortes, Factors Associated with the Migration of High-Level Persons from the Philippines to the U.S.A. (op. cit., fn. 1), pp. 65-66; Jayme, Demographic and Socio-Psychological Determinants of the Migration of Highly Trained Filipinos to the United States (op. cit., fn. 1), p. 31; Ritterband, The Non-Returning Foreign Student: The Israeli Case (New York: Bureau of Applied Social Research, Columbia University, 1968), pp. 113-115 and 164; and Man Singh Das, "Brain Drain and Students from Less Developed and Developing Countries," Transactions of the Seventh World Congress of Sociology, 1970, Volume I, pp. 183-194, Table 6.

Some stay-ons have jobs waiting too: one-fifth of the stay-ons in the United States are on leave. (This is rare in France, since many stay-ons are refugees.) Guarantees of a job attract some stay-ons home eventually, but not all: of the 67 stay-ons on leave from jobs in the American survey, 33 per cent expect to return home, 16 per cent are undecided, and the rest will emigrate. Of the 217 foreign students in the United States on leave from jobs, 13 per cent expected to stay on temporarily to work and then return home permanently; almost all the others expected to return at once.

The nationalities who most often study abroad while on leave from jobs are Brazilians, Ghanaians, Thais, and Ceylonese. The specialists most commonly on leave are in agriculture, biology, home management, journalism, and mathematics.

Fewer women than men have jobs waiting for them at home, while they study abroad. In the samples of students, 21 per cent of the women and 26 per cent of the men had jobs at home.

Table VII-4

Employment at Home and Long-Run Plans of Students

Guarantees of jobs	Index of return for students in: United States	Canada	France	Total number of respondents: United States	Canada	France
Can recover old job	1.77	1.66	1.77	(284)	(115)	(22)
Had job, but no official leave	.92	.11	.91	(76)	(66)	(18)
Quit old job	.87	.51	1.36	(478)	(312)	(48)
No job	1.05	.29	1.18	(702)	(344)	(327)

Wording of the question: "In order to go abroad for study, did you have to resign from your old job in your country of origin?" The responses were "Does not apply, since I did not have a job." "Yes," and "No, I had a job but did not have to resign." A further question asked "If 'no,' are you on leave of absence

[continued]

Table VII-4 [continued]

from your old job in your country of origin, which you can recover after completing your studies abroad?" Those on formal leave presumably have firmer assurances than those without formal leaves. The latter must renegotiate their status with their employers. The table is confined to the three surveys of students. Questions were asked also in the surveys of stay-ons as well, and the complete findings are summarized in the text.

Few persons are contacted by employers while they are abroad, but such persons are more likely to return

Programs to reduce brain drain often set up channels to inform foreign students and foreign workers of the employment situation at home and to convey specific job offers. Merely displaying some interest in the student is thought to encourage return. And guarantee of a satisfactory job at home should overcome fears of unemployment that might induce the foreign student to seize upon any job abroad.

Communication with employers at home. At least three-quarters of each sample said they had not been informed either of job prospects generally or of particular job openings by any government agencies while abroad;[5] among some nationalities, less than one-fifth had ever been contacted in any way while abroad by any private employers from home. More persons had been contracted before departure: these were the students who had lined up jobs that awaited their return.

Although contacts from home are too few for firm conclusions, apparently they are associated with higher rates of return. In the surveys of students, the proportions who intended to return were 82 per cent among those who had been contacted by government agencies and embassies while they were abroad, and 60 per cent among those never contacted.

---

[5] Wording of the question: "How often did persons in the government agencies, personnel registries, embassy or consulate of your country of origin contact you about job opportunities and your career plans while studying abroad?"

Proportions of students planning to return were 77 per cent among those who had been contacted while abroad by private employers from home and 62 per cent among those never contacted.[6]

<u>Effectiveness of official programs</u>. Several national groups in our survey of stay-ons in the United States come from countries with special programs to publicize openings and to place applicants:[7]

> <u>India</u>. The Council of Scientific and Industrial Research of the Government (CSIR) maintains an "Indians Abroad Register," con-

---

[6]Our findings confirm earlier research: students and stay-ons are rarely contacted by their embassies or by prospective employers; but those who receive information on job offers are more likely to return. John Niland, <u>The Asian Engineering Brain Drain</u> (Lexington: Heath Lexington Books, 1970), pp. 47-49; John W. Orton, "An Interview-Based Study of Pakistanis Employed in the Professions in the United States" (New York: Institute for International Education, 1965), pp. 41-48; and Godwin C. Chu, "Student Expatriation: A Function of Relative Social Support" (<u>op</u>. <u>cit</u>., fn. 2), p. 178. An enquiry by the National Association of Foreign Student Affairs several years ago found that few embassies in the United States regularly informed their nationals about job opportunities at home, and probably the number has risen only slightly. Gregory Henderson, <u>Emigration of Highly-Skilled Manpower from the Developing Countries</u> (New York: The United Nations Institute for Training and Research, Research Report Number 3, 1970), pp. 138-140.

[7]The programs are discussed in Committee on the International Migration of Talent, <u>The International Migration of High-Level Manpower</u> (New York: Praeger Publishers, 1970), pp. 143-146, 246-252, 388-393, and 474-475; Prakash Awasthi, "An Experiment in Voluntary Repatriation of High-Level Technical Manpower: The Scientists Pool," <u>The Economic Weekly</u> (Bombay), Vol. XVII (18 September 1965), pp. 1447-1452; Walden F. Bello and others, "Brain Drain in the Philippines," in <u>Modernization: Its Impact in the Philippines IV</u> (Quezon City: Ateneo de Manila University Press, 1969), p. 127; and Henderson, <u>Emigration of Highly-Skilled Manpower from the Developing Countries</u> (<u>op</u>. <u>cit</u>., fn. 5), pp. 140-142.

sisting of persons with higher education from foreign universities. At the time they fill out the questionnaires, most respondents are still studying or working abroad. Information about the registrants is circulated to prospective employers in the public and private sectors, and some registrants receive notices of jobs that are available.

Since 1958, CSIR has operated the "Scientists Pool." The best young professionals become temporary officers of CSIR. The foreign-trained are guaranteed a salary as soon as they return, since they are on the CSIR payroll. Efforts are exerted to find them satisfactory employment, either in government or in private enterprise.

Argentina. The National Council for Scientific and Technical Research (Consejo Nacional de Investigaciones Scientificas e Tecnicas) offers jobs in Argentina. Returnees receive the fare, moving expenses, and a little extra money. Repatriation subsidies are offered to Argentinian universities for the employment of research personnel who currently work abroad.

Republic of Korea. The Korean Institute of Science and Technology occasionally contacts some Korean scientists in the U.S.A. with job offers.

Iran. Occasionally an official from Iran tours campuses or Iranian clubs in the United States, to describe job opportunities and to urge Iranians to return.

Philippines. The Philippine Social Science Council has tried to set up communication and placement centres that link Filipino students abroad to job opportunities in their special fields at home.

How effective are these programs? How many persons have heard of them? Table VII-5 summarizes the stay-ons' knowledge and experience with these activities while studying or working in the United States. (This information was elicited by personal interviews and therefore was not obtained from the entire sample of stay-ons, since most received their questionnaires by mail.)

The Indian and Korean programs are well publicized, and most respondents had heard of them. Other nationalities were unaware of the efforts of their governments; even many stay-ons from India and the Republic of Korea needed reminders from the interviewers. Less than half had ever been in touch with any program, and few were entered on registers. Only one person out of the seventy-five asked these questions had ever learned of any jobs through these channels.

Respondents who had been in touch with these programs were asked to evaluate their effectiveness. Everyone thought that such machinery was a good idea, particularly for persons definitely committed to return. Returning without a guaranteed job is unsettling; searching in a country with scarce openings (like India) is depressing for the young and previously optimistic returnee; and therefore such programs could be helpful to the professionals. These methods also could help the employer by directing to him the persons most suitable for his needs.

Most persons answering our questions were skeptical about the effectiveness of these programs. Employers had not yet learned to specify their personnel needs clearly or to evaluate the dossiers of candidates. In countries with large numbers of jobseekers, such as India, too many employers still depended on personal applications initiated by the candidates, instead of investigating the value of the official registries. A few critics among the Indian stay-ons feared that the salary guarantees of India's Scientists Pool might discourage ambition.

Table VII-5

Experience of Stay-Ons* with Placement Programs

	India	Republic of Korea	Iran	Philip-pines	Argen-tina
"Does your country have any method for offering jobs to persons while they are studying and working abroad?"					
Yes	20	4	2	0	4
No	13	2	1	15	9
Don't know	3	0	0	0	2
(Total number of respondents)	36	6	3	15	15
(Interviewer then reads a description of the program and asks): "Do you recall hearing of this program?"					
Yes	33	6	2	0	5
No	3	0	1	15	10
(Total number of respondents)	36	6	3	15	15
(Persons who recall hearing of the program were asked): "Have you ever been contacted by officers administering these programs?"					
Yes	11	2	0	--	1
No	21	4	2	--	4
Respondent wrote to program but got no answer	1	--	--	--	--
(Total number of persons who knew of program)	33	6	2		5

* Data from stay-ons in the United States. Figures are numbers of persons, and not percentages. The numbers are not weighted.

[continued]

Table VII-5 [continued]

	India	Republic of Korea	Iran	Philip-pines	Argen-tina
(Persons in touch with the programs were asked): "Have you registered your name in any of these programs?"					
Yes	5	1	--	--	1
No	6	1	--	--	0
(Total number of persons in touch)	11	2			1
(Persons registered with the programs were asked): "Did you learn of any jobs through these programs?"					
Yes	0	1	--	--	0
No	5	0	--	--	1
(Total number of persons registered)	5	1			1
(Persons who learned of jobs were asked): "Did you actually obtain any jobs through these programs?"					
Yes	--	0	--	--	--
No	--	1	--	--	--
		1			

Several Indian and Argentinian respondents thought that greater precision and better communication should be introduced. Employers should learn how to state their needs more clearly and how to estimate in cost-benefit terms the gains from hiring a particular foreign-trained person, even if his starting salary is higher than that of domestically educated persons. Candidates should specify their skills and future career aims better in their applications. And employers and candidates should exchange more numerous and more exact letters before the professionals return home, in order to improve the matching. Some Indians thought that the registries and the Scientists Pool should be more selective; some favored higher salaries for Pool officers. One of the South Koreans had heard of India's Scientists Pool and thought it a good model for his country, since a returnee without a job guarantee is taking a risk.

Implications for policy. So far, contacts by governments and employers and organized hiring programs reach few people. Managers of these programs know they are busy corresponding with and hiring many applicants, but the numbers are small proportions of the total.

Expansion of these contacts and programs would improve morale of students and professionals overseas and would probably increase return. At present, students and overseas professionals from several countries with tight markets at home worry about their prospects if they return, unless they are on leave from a job. An important reason why some stay abroad temporarily after completing study is to wait for an attractive job to open at home, according to Table VIII-6, *infra*. If they were fully informed of opportunities at home, they might return sooner. If they remain out of touch, as under present conditions, many may become integrated into life and work abroad, thereby nullifying their preferences and intentions to return.

Private employers could make use of these programs for publicizing and filling jobs far more than heretofore. If these employment systems are perceived as too "official," associations of private employers might set up their own, to contact students and stay-ons abroad.

Efforts should be increased to inform stay-ons of opportunities at home. They are at a point in life when their skills have matured and can be used at home, but they are also at a point where they can become integrated into life abroad and thereby lost to the home country. At present, it is much easier for home governments and employers to communicate with students, because students are members of organizations with lists.

Persons receiving more letters and publications from home are more likely to return

Maintaining personal and professional communications with home while the person is abroad is associated with a greater tendency to return. According to Table VII-6, the more frequent the letters from family and friends, the greater the intention of students to return and stay. Persons without ties--i.e., no family or friends or no letters from the family and friends that are at home--are the ones least likely to return.

The nationalities that get letters from home most often--i.e., at least half receive letters once a week or more frequently from family members--are Mexicans, Brazilians, Colombians, Argentinians, Peruvians, Indians, Pakistanis, Ceylonese, Thais, and Iranians. The nationalities that correspond most often with friends at home are Mexicans and Africans.

Channels for keeping up with professional developments. Table VII-7 lists several channels for learning about professional developments at home. Some are used more than others: correspondence with friends and other professionals is most common, documents from embassies and correspondence with employers are least common. But for all channels, the greater the use, the greater the intention to return--i.e., the higher their index numbers of return.

Table VII-6

Personal Letters from Home and Long-Run Plans

Wording of question: "How often do you receive letters from your country of origin?"	Index of return among students giving each response to the question about letters from:		Total numbers of students	
	Family	Friends	Family	Friends
"At least once a week"	1.00	1.09	(1,087)	(441)
"About once every two weeks"	.96	1.07	(1,005)	(637)
"About once a month"	.61	.80	(493)	(835)
"Less often than once a month"	.11	.57	(204)	(747)
"Never"	-.69	-.09	(23)	(144)
"Does not apply, since I do not have family or friends there"	-.51	-1.15	(61)	(23)

First, respondents were classified by their answers to the question about receiving letters from family and friends. The totals are in the right-hand columns: for example, 1,087 students said they got letters from their families at least once a week and 441 said they got letters from friends at least once weekly. Numbers in the first two columns are the indexes of return for the categories in the right-hand columns. The numbers rise as one ascends the column, showing that increased numbers of letters are associated with more plans to return. The calculations combine all respondents from the surveys of students in the United States, Canada, and France. Returnees are not included in this table; so many of them exchanged letters at least once a week that we lack the variations essential to measure effects on return.

The nationalities that relied on each channel most often were:

Popular magazines: Senegal, Ivory Coast, Cameroon, Tunisia
Professional journals: Brazil, Senegal, India, Republic of Korea, Philippines
Correspondence with professionals: Jamaica, Mexico, Brazil, Colombia, Senegal, Ivory Coast, Republic of Korea, Philippines, Thailand
Correspondence with employers: Mexico, Pakistan
Correspondence with friends: Brazil, Argentina Venezuela, Africa in general, Pakistan, Thailand
Publications from embassy: Jamaica, Ghana, Pakistan

Table VII-7 distinguishes between persons who received communications and felt them "important," those who received communications and deemed them "not so important," and those who received none. Plans to return decrease with each category. Those receiving letters and publications considered "important" probably included many already strongly disposed to return. But those receiving communications believed "not so important" include many whose initial commitment is uncertain. Sending documents to them, merely as a reminder of interest from home, can pay off in higher return, compared to those who recall receiving nothing. And, ultimately, anyone who receives enough pertinent publications about his field and about the market for his skills may begin perceiving them as "important" means for establishing contacts at home.

Newspapers from home. Certain other ties with home are not so effective in fostering return. For example, the mere frequency of reading newspapers and magazines from home is not associated with higher return. Such reading is not completely voluntary, nor is it a "stimulus" easily controlled by the home society. Rather, newspaper reading at present varies too much by the efficiency of delivery methods, proximity, and the student's location.

Also, the frequency of reading newspapers and magazines may not clearly predict emigration because of the functions it performs. Few people quit

Table VII-7

Professional Communications from Home and Long-Run Plans

Wording of question "While you were abroad, did you keep up with developments in your special field of work in your country of origin through any of the following methods?"	Index of return among those giving each response to the questions about communications with home: "Yes, and important to me"	"Yes, but not so important to me"	"No"	Total number of respondents: Yes, and important	Yes, but not important	No
"Popular magazines from there"	1.25	.93	.73	(690)	(982)	(3,940)
"Professional journals from there"	1.06	.85	.76	(1,207)	(759)	(3,700)
"Correspondence with professionals there"	1.10	.99	.70	(1,528)	(840)	(3,304)
"Correspondence with employers there"	1.47	.96	.72	(639)	(517)	(4,306)
"Correspondence with my friends there concerning developments in my special field"	1.11	.91	.53	(2,207)	(1,428)	(2,236)
"Publications and documents by my embassy"	1.12	.98	1.03	(533)	(673)	(3,572)

Respondents in the surveys of students, stay-ons, and returnees were asked whether they received each of the communications listed on the left. The responses were "Yes, and [receiving them was] important to me," "Yes, but not so important to me," and "No" (i.e., I did not receive them). The total numbers falling into each category appear in the three right-hand columns, and the indexes of return are in the three left-hand columns. The table combines all persons from the surveys of students, stay-ons, and returnees.

their home societies completely and irreversibly. Most who emigrate remain curious about events there. So, potential emigrants and long-term non-returnees --as well as the potential returnees--often read the press from home, whenever they can find it.

Marrying a countryman--particularly before departure abroad--is associated with return

Time of marriage. Several close personal ties to the home society bring persons back after study and work abroad. If the person was married before going abroad for foreign study, that person is more likely to return than a single person.[8] If a returnee, the individual is more likely to remain in the home country if married before foreign study. Table VII-8 shows that marriage before departure predicts return for women as well as for men. Otherwise, the women who were single on leaving were more likely to emigrate than the single men, particularly the women who married foreigners or who remained single for several years.[9]

---

[8]The same relationship between marital status upon arrival and migration was noticed by Ritterband, The Non-Returning Foreign Student (op. cit., fn. 4), pp. 112-113 and 130; Cortes, Factors Associated with the Migration of High-Level Persons from the Philippines to the U.S.A. (op. cit., fn. 1), p. 77; and Jayme, Demographic and Socio-Psychological Determinants of the Migration of Highly Trained Filipinos to the United States (op. cit., fn. 1), p. 31.

[9]Differentials in the educational experiences and career plans of men and women in our project are reported by G. Christopher Habers, Brain Drain and the University Minority: Women Students from Developing Countries (New York: essay for the M.A. in sociology, Columbia University, 1972). Slightly higher migration rates for women can be found in earlier studies in the United States, such as Myers, Education and Emigration (op. cit., fn. 1), p. 103; Thames, Korean Students in Southern California (op. cit., fn. 1), pp. 106-115; and Cortes, Factors Associated with the Migration of High-Level Persons from the Philippines to the U.S.A. (op. cit., fn. 1), pp. 61-62. Surprisingly little research has been conducted about differences between men and women in the experiences and careers of foreign students. Nearly all tables in earlier publications have combined them.

Table VII-8

Time of Marriage and Long-Run Plans

Marital status of respondent	Index of return		Total number of respondents	
	Men	Women	Men	Woman
Student:				
Married before departure	1.53	1.42	(306)	(55)
Married abroad	.86	1.08	(224)	(44)
Single or engaged at time of survey	.90	.57	(1,228)	(274)
Stay-ons:				
Married before departure	-.11	-.18	(110)	(8)
Married abroad	-.53	-.66	(184)	(14)
Single or engaged	-.75	-.15	(54)	(8)
Returnees:				
Married before departure	1.30	1.16	(925)	(83)
Married abroad	1.24	1.17	(954)	(116)
Single or engaged	1.19	1.10	(509)	(212)

The data are summarized for three separate groups: the student surveys from the United States, Canada and France; the stay-on surveys from the United States and France; the returnee surveys from India, Sri Lanka, Republic of Korea, Greece, Ghana, Brazil, Colombia, and Argentina.

Nationality of the spouse. One of the most common explanations of brain drain attributes it to cross-cultural marriage.[10] Foreign study is said to provide opportunities to marry North Americans or Europeans who do not wish to settle in the developing country and who persuade the student to live abroad. Table VII-9 in our data confirm that marriage to a foreigner is strongly associated with emigration: in all three surveys and for both men and women, persons married to a foreigner are far more likely to plan permanent emigration than those married to fellow citizens. Marriage to a foreigner is associated not only with higher proportions planning to emigrate but also with higher proportions who were uncertain.

Marriage to a countryman--and other ties to the home country--"add" something to intentions held before arrival

Ties to home are associated with high return, and newly acquired connections with the host country are associated with lower return. Possibly connections are determined by the person's plans as much as plans are influenced by connections: persons who originally intended to return might maintain ties with home, persons who originally intended to emigrate might abandon contacts with home and establish new ties abroad, and therefore new programs to promote return might be wasted. Probably original intentions are related to later patterns of social relations and communications, but these ties do add something to original plans.

---

[10] Confirmed in Das, "Brain Drain and Students from Less Developed and Developing Countries" (*op. cit.*, fn. 4), Table 4; Cortes, *Factors Associated with the Migration of High-Level Persons from the Philippines to the U.S.A.* (*op. cit.*, fn. 1) p. 77; Jayme, *Demographic and Socio-Psychological Determinants of the Migration of Highly Trained Filipinos to the United States* (*op. cit.*, fn. 1), p. 31; Oh, *The Role of International Education in the Asian Brain Drain* (*op. cit.*, fn. 2), p. 211; and Geoffrey Oldham and Oscar Gish, "Survey of Immigrant Professionals in Fields of Science and Technology" (Brighton: Science Policy Research Unit, University of Sussex, 1970), pp. 22-23.

Table VII-9

Marriage to a Foreigner and Long-Run Plans

Index numbers of return	Men: Married or engaged to a foreigner	Men: Married or engaged to home countryman	Men: Single	Women: Married or engaged to a foreigner	Women: Married or engaged to home countryman	Women: Single
Students	.21	1.02	.84	-.53	1.07	.57
Stay-ons	-.77	-.04	-.88	-1.12	.42	-.16
Returnees	.97	1.29	1.21	.47	1.18	1.15
Total numbers of respondents						
Students	(245)	(732)	(1,041)	(56)	(155)	(214)
Stay-ons	(133)	(181)	(41)	(13)	(9)	(8)
Returnees	(161)	(1,926)	(368)	(23)	(213)	(193)

In our surveys, we asked both the number of years the respondent had expected to stay abroad when he arrived and the number he actually plans to stay now. If the contracts experienced during study and work abroad have no effect and were merely the result of earlier plans, everyone should increase his length of stay abroad by the same amount. But in our data, persons with weaker ties from home and stronger connections abroad are slightly more likely to change their intentions from return to emigration and (among persons who ultimately return) have slightly longer stays abroad. In other words, ties with home preserve original plans to return and limit the time abroad.

A good example of this process is marriage to a foreigner. Many observers have questioned whether this really makes a difference: persons who marry countrymen may have expected to return anyway; those who plan to emigrate may tend to marry foreigners. But our data show that if a student or stay-on marries someone from a country other than his own, he is more likely to change his plans from a short visit to permanent emigration.[11] Among those who had never decided to become an emigrant either earlier or now--i.e., those who gave a specific number of years in answer to both questions--those who married a foreigner reported the largest increase. The figures are in Table VII-10.

Other ties. The other contacts with home or with host countries also "add" to original migration intentions, although the statistical patterns usually are not as strong as in marriage to a compatriot or foreigner. Persons with closer ties to home usually show fewer cases of changes of mind from temporary to permanent stays abroad; and ties to home are associated with shorter stays among the students and temporary stay-ons.

[11]In his survey of Peruvian students in the United States, Myers concluded that marrying a foreigner does not "add" anything to the migration tendencies already operating. Education and Emigration (op. cit., fn. 1), pp. 260-261. Ritterband's data--and ours--suggest that the spouse's influence is an additional inducement for emigration. The Non-Returning Foreign Student: The Israeli Case (op. cit., fn. 4), pp. 120-123.

Table VII-10

Marriage to a Foreigner and Increased Length of Stay

	Married or engaged to foreigner	Married or engaged to countryman	Single
A. Student surveys in the United States and France			
(i) Became emigrant	10%	3%	2%
Remained emigrant	2	1	1
Became prospective returnee	2	1	1
Expected limited stay both times	86	95	96
	100%	100%	100%
(Total number of respondents)	(153)	(503)	(779)
(ii) Among those who expected limited stay both times, the median increase in number of years	+4	+2	+3
B. Stay-on surveys in the United States and France:			
(i) Became emigrant	46%	21%	42%
Remained emigrant	7	2	13
Became prospective returnee	3	1	4
Expected limited stay both times	44	76	41
	100%	100%	100%
(Total number of respondents)	(74)	(85)	(24)
(ii) Among those who expected limited stay both times, the median increase in number of years	+24	+17	+11

[continued]

Table VII-10 [continued]

Wording of the questions: "When you first went abroad for higher education, approximately how many years did you intend to stay abroad?", "What is your present expectation about the total number of years you will stay in this country, either for study or for work" (survey of students), "Approximate length of time you will stay abroad until returning to your country of origin" (survey of stay-ons), and several other items that measured length of study, date of survey, and other periods of time abroad. In Section (i) of each part of the table, "Became emigrant" refers to persons who gave a fixed number of years at arrival but now plan to remain permanently. "Remained emigrant" refers to those who answered both times that they planned to stay permanently. "Became prospective returnee" are those who planned to remain permanently when they arrived but now will return after a fixed number of years. "Expected limited stay" refers to those persons who planned to return home within a definite number of years. Section (ii) of each part of the table includes persons with definite plans to return both times; but the figures about increased length of stay show that the numbers of years increased between the two times. A "median" is a half-way point in a distribution: half the respondents expected more than that number of years, half expected less. The data are not weighted.

Table VII-10 appears to report fewer long-term emigrants than our other tabulations for several reasons. The items about length of stay were not included in the questionnaires used in Canada, a country with many respondents planning to emigrate. Not all our other respondents provided all the answers about numbers of years needed for our calculations.

Members of national clubs are more likely to return

A foreign student and professional can preserve his ties with home through his selection of friends. If his hours of recreation are spent among persons from his home country, he is more strongly committed to return.

Many nationalities organize clubs during study abroad. They are most common among Trinidadians, Jamaicans, Tunisians, Lebanese, and Indians; they are least common among Haitians, Mexicans, Brazilians, Colombians, Venezuelans, Ghanaians, Turks, Ceylonese, and Indonesians. (I.e., many of the former and few of the latter report the clubs exist.) Where nationality clubs exist among students, membership is highest among Ghanaians, Senegalese, Ivoirians, Indians, Pakistanis, Koreans, Filipinos and Thais; and membership is lowest among Mexicans, Peruvians, and Iranians. (I.e., among those reporting the clubs exist, many of the former but few of the latter are members.)

According to Table VII-11, membership in such clubs while a student is associated with return: persons who belong are more likely to return, those who could join but refuse are most likely to emigrate. (These patterns are clear in the student and stay-on surveys. Slightly stronger intentions to remain home by former members of student clubs can also be seen in the data from returnees, but the statistical relation between ties and remaining home is weaker than among the students and stay-ons.)[12]

[12]This weakening of the statistical relationship by returnees is common among the ties with home described in this chapter, because the questions about contacts refer to experience <u>during study abroad</u> and the question about their migration plans refer to the future <u>after they have already come back</u>. The returnee's future plans now are governed by many new attitudes and influences, such as growing family obligations and the mere difficulty of pulling up roots and going abroad again. Some ties during study described in this chapter persist, so the statistical relationships with present migration plans remain, although they are weaker.

Clubs also exist among professionals employed overseas, particularly among Indians, Iranians, and Filipinos. Among all the stay-ons, membership correlates with migration plans in the same manner as membership in nationality clubs during study: members of clubs have the most frequent intentions to return home; those who refuse to join clubs that are available have the lowest rates of prospective return; and those who do not belong because no nationality clubs exist near them have rates of return midway between the other two groups.

Table VII-11

Membership in National Clubs During Study and Long-Run Plans

Belonged to club	Index of return for: Students	Stay-ons	Returnees	Total number of respondents: Students	Stay-ons	Returnees
Yes	1.03	-.17	1.29	(897)	(225)	(936)
No, club did not exist	.95	-.66	1.21	(1,168)	(84)	(1,376)
No, refused to join	.25	-.87	1.22	(822)	(84)	(612)

Wording of the question: "Did you belong to a club or association largely consisting of persons from your country of origin while you were a student abroad?" Possible answers were: "Yes," "No, it did not exist where I lived," and "No, it existed there, but I did not join." The students were asked about membership at the time of the survey. The table combines three surveys of students (from the United States, Canada, and France), two surveys of stay-ons (from the United States and France), and eight surveys of returnees (from India, Sri Lanka, Republic of Korea, Greece, Ghana, Brazil, Colombia, and Argentina).

Friendship with compatriots is associated with return, while many persons with friends from the host country emigrate

Maintaining close personal ties with fellow countrymen while one is abroad is associated with higher return. The data are in Parts A and C of Table VII-12. In Part A, persons in the surveys of students and stay-ons who saw their countrymen frequently are most likely to return and stay. The relation is even more clear in Part C: those who saw fellow countrymen more often than anyone else are most likely to return; those who associated with countrymen less often than with other nationalities had the lowest plans to return.

Becoming absorbed into the culture and peer groups of developed countries is associated with lower rates of return. According to Part A of Table VII-12, if a student sees host-country nationals "frequently" or "occasionally," he is less likely to return than if he associates with them "rarely" or "never." And, according to Part C, he is much less likely to return and stay if his friends were drawn primarily from the country of study or from the country of work abroad: among the students and stay-ons in Part C, persons are less likely to return if host-country nationals are their principal friends or if their contacts are a mixture, including host-country people but omitting their fellow countrymen.[13] Among the returnees, the persons most likely to emigrate now are those whose friends earlier came primarily from the country of study.

In many cases, avoidance of fellow-countrymen is voluntary. In other cases it results from the composition of the campus. We asked all respondents whether they had a circle of friends from home while

---

[13] One of the few surveys that ever asked the nationality of friends of foreign students or of foreign stay-ons also discovered that return is less likely if friends are drawn primarily from the host country. Oldham, "Survey of Immigrant Professionals in the Fields of Science and Technology" (op. cit., fn. 10), pp. 16-17 and 20.

they were abroad; if they did not, they were asked whether they missed their countrymen. In the student surveys, the proportion planning to return home in each category was:

	Plan to return home
Had a circle of friends from home country	68 per cent
No such circle but missed it	48 per cent
No such circle and did not miss it	36 per cent

Even among the returnees, the weakness of ties with fellow citizens while abroad predicts later commitment to remain after return: those who had no circle of friends from home while abroad and did not miss it had a lower rate of intention to remain home (73%) than those who had such a circle (81%) and those who had no such circle but missed it (85%).

<u>People from home advise the student to return, while persons abroad often advise them to emigrate</u>

The students and stay-ons were asked about advice from relatives, friends and professional associates at home and abroad. Persons still in the home country strongly recommended return, particularly relatives, friends, employers, and former teachers in the surveys of students. Employers and professors in the host country recommended that the person stay abroad.

Two groups with strategic influence are friends and relatives from the home country who are living abroad: they have much in common with the foreign student and professional, and they have the advantage of proximity. Our respondents indicated high respect for these advisors. These persons recommended emigration more often than return to their common home. Even though most students from developing countries plan to return, they often grumble about prospects in conversations about home. Therefore, many foreign students claim that their friends abroad from their home countries advise them not to return and will emigrate while the respondents themselves plan to return.

Table VII-12

Friendship with Persons from Home Country and from Country of Study and Long-Run Plans

	Index of return for			Total number of respondents		
	Students	Stay-ons	Returnees	Students	Stay-ons	Returnees
A. While abroad, saw persons from home country:						
Frequently	1.03	-.21	1.27	(1,544)	(181)	(1,503)
Occasionally	.56	-.41	1.26	(917)	(154)	(838)
Rarely	.32	-.95	1.19	(353)	(46)	(439)
Never	.67	-1.17	1.36	(76)	(11)	(88)
B. While abroad, saw persons from host country:						
Frequently	.70	-.47	1.18	(1,524)	(278)	(1,820)
Occasionally	.74	-.31	1.27	(947)	(102)	(798)
Rarely	.96	.22	1.38	(339)	(7)	(217)
Never	1.09	-	1.69	(61)	(3)	(29)
C. Principal group of friends:						
Fellow countrymen	.96	.09	1.38	(717)	(40)	(583)
Host country	.25	-.73	1.17	(512)	(123)	(653)
Other foreigners	.70	-1.33	.96	(99)	(6)	(72)
Mixed, fellow countrymen included	.94	-.28	1.24	(1,279)	(206)	(1,229)
Mixed, fellow countrymen not included	.51	-.54	1.11	(286)	(20)	(391)

[continued]

Table VII-12 [continued]

Wording of questions in student and stay-on surveys: "How often do you see each of the following groups of people socially outside of school or working hours?" Wording in returnee survey: "How often did you see each of the following groups of people socially while you were abroad outside of school or working hours?" The categories were "People from my country of origin," "people from the country where I studied," and "other foreigners, but neither from my country of origin nor from the country where I studied." (In the stay-on survey, the second category was "people from this country"--i.e., the country of work.) For each category, one of the following responses was checked: "frequently," "occasionally," "rarely," "never." As usual in such tables, respondents were first classified by their answers concerning types of friends, and the total numbers of persons are in the three right-hand columns; the index of return for each category is in one of the three left-hand columns. The table combines the surveys of students in the United States, Canada, and France; stay-ons in the United States and France; and returnees in India, Sri Lanka, Republic of Korea, Greece, Ghana, Brazil, Colombia, and Argentina.

Advice from the spouse. The most influential advisor is the husband or wife, according to our comparisons of the several types of counsel and the respondents' migration plans. One reason why the nationality of the spouse relates so strongly to migration plans is his (or her) advice: fellow nationals from home are much more likely to advise return; when foreign spouses give advice, on balance they recommend emigration. The data appear in Table VII-13. One result of this influence is the higher emigration rates of women. Compared to a man married to a foreigner, a woman is far more likely to follow him to his home country, as Table VII-11 showed.

Table VII-13

Nationality of Spouse and Advice

Type of survey and nationality of spouse or fiancée	Type of advice: Return home	Stay abroad	None		Total number of respondents
Students:					
Home country	49%	26	25	100% =	(759)
Foreign	15%	31	54	100% =	(251)
Stay-ons:					
Home country	25%	38	36	100% =	(164)
Foreign	9%	53	38	100% =	(126)

Wording of question: "Since you arrived in this country did any of the following persons advise you where to go during the coming years?" Included in the battery of ten persons were "husband or wife" and "fiancée (or fiancé)." The responses were: "Advised me to return to my country of origin." "Advised me to stay in this country," and "Gave me no advice." The question appeared in the student and stay-on surveys, but not in the returnee survey. The table combines the student surveys from the United States, Canada and France, and the stay-on surveys from the United States and France. Respondents are omitted if they have neither spouse nor fiancée.

Teachers in developed countries. Policymakers in development affairs often recommend that faculty members in developed countries guide foreign students toward the best contributions they can make at home.[14] In practice, teachers seem more interested in the development of their own fields than in the development of the foreign students' home countries: they do not provide overwhelming advice for return and, in a few of our samples, slightly more teachers recommend staying abroad. The results are in Table VII-14.

Table VII-14

Advice from University Professors in Developed Countries

Advice of teachers in country of study	Students in United States	Students in Canada	Students in France	Stay-ons in United States	Stay-ons in France
Return home	10%	5%	9%	13%	12%
Stay abroad	11	13	9	24	14
None	79	82	82	63	74
	100%	100%	100%	100%	100%
Total number of respondents	(1,550)	(890)	(407)	(325)	(60)

14 Malcolm S. Adiseshiah, "Brain Drain from the Arab World" (Cairo: Eighth Arab Cultural Conference on the Training of Scientific Workers in Arab World, 1969); Ashok Parthasarathi, "Some Suggestions for National and International Action to Combat the Flight from Developing Countries" (paper at the 19th Pugwash Conference on Science and World Affairs, 1969); and many other writers. A minority view is that the foreign student and persons from his home country should make these deccisions themselves, and that foreign student advisors and professors should be free to point out opportunities abroad. Howard J. Caquelin, "Exchange or Immigration: The Phony Controversy," NAFSA Newsletter (National Association for Foreign Student Affairs), Volume XVII, Number 1 (October 1965), pp. 2-3.

Because, in so many instances, no advice is given by professors abroad, advice from this source is proportionately less than from any other source.

Implications for policy. If educational exchange is supposed to encourage the return and best use of foreign students, faculty members need to be involved better. An earlier section of this chapter showed that many foreign students and stay-ons receive scholarships from the universities abroad on the recommendations of faculty members, and these grants reinforce any advice to migrate. At present, universities in developed countries are working internally at cross-purposes: foreign student advisors may encourage students' repatriation, but the teachers may urge different decisions.

Trips home do not increase rates of return

A common belief in discussions about the brain drain is that visits home decrease changes of permanent emigration. During the visits, the person can get a job and renew his personal ties. So, one recommendation has been to sponsor inexpensive trips home during summer vacations and before the time for long-term commitments.

At present, trips home during foreign education are rare. They are largely a function of distance: half the students in France are able to visit their nearby homelands; but only one-third of the students in the United States and one-fifth of those in Canada report visits. Between graduation and the start of work abroad, many more visit home; three-quarters of the stay-ons have been home at some time.

From a statistical standpoint, visits home do not seem to increase the likelihood of return: whether a student or professional had ever visited home during study or work, he was equally likely to return home and stay. In most surveys of returnees fewer than 20 per cent had ever visited home; but all the respondents had returned anyway. In distant countries like Korea and Ceylon, no more than 10 per cent had ever visited home during study or work abroad. (The Greeks are exceptional and are virtually international commuters. Over three-quarters visited home while they were studying or working abroad.)

Respondents were asked whether the visits had increased or decreased their intentions to return. The increases outnumbered the decreases; but in some samples, considerable numbers said the trips had no clear effects. Therefore the net gains associated with visits were modest.

Among those who had ever visited home and became more committed to return, the principal reasons were: recognition that they had more in common with their home cultures than with the developed countries; renewal of ties with family and friends; and a feeling that their countries needed them. Among those whose plans to return were weakened by visits home, the principal reasons were: finding few job prospects; difficulties in readjusting to the country after time abroad; and (in a few countries) distasteful political conditions. Few checked one possible response that is often thought to be a common cause of brain drain, viz., "I found my training was not relevant to the work in my field."

Even though visits may not reduce brain drain now, organized programs and special fares might still be worthwhile. Perhaps the most important function of visits at present is to keep the student and stay-on in touch with developments, so he can adjust more easily if and when he returns. Special new programs might be organized to introduce the student to employers and to inform him of new trends in his field at home. This will improve utilization, even if it does not raise the return rate. Once started, organized programs might encourage return more successfully than the present informal family visits.

In summary, persons with the strongest attachments to home are the most likely to return

Chapters III and IV mentioned a battery of questions about those ties with home that created adjustment problems during study and work abroad. The ability to adapt abroad varies according to the country of origin: the least adaptable groups have the highest rates of return. Barriers to assimilation vary among developed countries: the most hospitable have the highest rates of immigation.

When individuals are classified by their own adjustment capacities abroad, their migration plans are strongly related. Table VII-15 is confined to the surveys of students, but the data from the stay-ons and returnees show the same patterns. If the person's ties with home were so strong that he missed his family, friends, and home culture, so that he was lonely abroad, and so that his marriage plans were hampered, then he was far more likely to return. If the educational system and languages at home were so different that he had difficulty adjusting abroad, then he was more likely to return.

Table VII-15

Adjustment Problems During Study Abroad and Long-Run Plans

Problems during study abroad	Index of return among students whose scores on each cluster are		Total number of students	
	High	Low	High	Low
Separation from home	1.06	.55	(1,313)	(1,602)
Loneliness	1.14	.54	(1,064)	(1,851)
Educational and Linguistic difficulties	.88	.72	(793)	(2,122)
Delay in marriage	1.09	.74	(132)	(2,783)

The battery of 26 items asking about adjustment problems during study was reduced to main clusters by the method cited on page 90, footnote 1, supra. For each cluster, an additive index was created, based on respondents' answers to the items belonging to that cluster. A cluster was "high" for a respondent in our calculations, if his score showed predominant

[continued]

Table VII-15 [continued]

ratings of the items as "very important," "important," and "of slight importance." A cluster was deemed "low" if his score showed predominant ratings of "unimportant" and "does not apply." This table uses only the four clusters that bear upon attachments to home. Columns 3 and 4 give the total numbers of respondents who ranked "high" and "low" on each cluster. Columns 1 and 2 give the index numbers of return for each "high" and "low" category. The table combines the surveys of students in the United States, Canada, and France.

Implications for policy: strengthening ties with home

Selecting those most likely to return. If an educational exchange program tries to maximize return, certain types of persons would be preferred. Those most likely to return grew up in the majority groups of the society, spoke the vernacular languages at home, are married to members of the majority groups, have strong family ties, and have tastes in reading and recreation closely associated with their own countries,cultural traditions.

But, of course, any such narrow selection method has serious disadvantages. Talented members of minority groups will resent being shut off from foreign study and will be even more likely to emigrate. Excluding them from foreign study is too crude even for purposes of maximizing return: many return at present.

Various considerations might argue against recruiting foreign students from certain social groups rather than from others. Some policy-makers might say that educational exchange should optimize the preparation and utilization of manpower throughout the world; therefore all citizens of every society should be available, even if market forces induce some to work abroad rather than at home. Others might oppose any categorical restrictions on the rights of persons to travel, study, and work wherever they wish, as a violation of the Universal Declaration of Human Rights.

<u>Controls by the home country</u>. The closer the student's ties with his home country, the more likely he will return. A trend among developing countries is to increase controls over foreign study: more students are sponsored, more have obligations to return, and more have jobs waiting upon return. These traits are strongly associated with return, in part because the persons who obtain these arrangements have the other motives and characteristics of returnees, and in part because any organized program reduces the uncertainties that lead to emigration.

Some governments place great faith in the efficacy of bonds and develop a considerable apparatus to administer them. But financial bonds and simple pledges may be equally effective in ensuring return. Both are associated with higher return than no obligations at all. One reason for their strong association with return is probably self-selection: persons secretly contemplating emigration do not get involved in such arrangements. While stories about persons skipping bond are common, actual occurrences may be rare. Bonds and pledges may reinforce the effects of an organized program: in addition to the obligations, many of these persons were carefully screened for overseas study and have jobs waiting.

Of course, even if the net effect due to bonds is statistically small--i.e., if only a few persons are compelled to return who otherwise would have emigrated--the result is still profitable to a country that can afford no losses at all. But the small gains are profitable only if the entire bonding system is cheap to administer and only if involuntary returnees are productive. The best method is to motivate people to return enthusiastically.

<u>Adjustments to the country of study</u>. International exchange programs are usually concerned that the foreign student will adjust successfully to the host country, that the society will be hospitable, and that he will think well of it in the future. But at first sight, this seems to contradict a goal of encouraging return: the persons most likely to return are those least able to adjust to the host country. They suffer from pulls from the home coun-

try, such as separation from family and friends. They suffer from pushes from the host country, such as language barriers, educational difficulties, loneliness, and racial discrimination. The more successful a developed country in the tolerance of cultural diversity and in the acceptance of foreigners (e.g., Canada), the fewer the adjustment problems and the greater the migration intentions of its foreign students.

Maintaining contact with home. If the goals of educational exchange include both encouraging return and improving morale abroad, one solution is better organization of the community of foreign students. Some nationalities in some places abroad have clubs, but some do not. Many persons miss not being reached by clubs or by organized recreation. Participants in these activities and those who get letters and literature from home are more likely to return than others. Some developing countries (such as India) foster extensive social and cultural contacts with their compatriots overseas, but most do not, and recreation is left to the organizational efforts of the students and foreign student advisors themselves. Much more can be done by the home governments and by their embassies overseas.

Of course, not every student can be reached. Some wish to live more closely with persons from the host country and avoid clubs of their fellow countrymen. If someone has strong family ties and his marriage has been postponed until his return, no club can make him feel less lonely. But existing arrangements can be improved, clubs and mass media distribution can be created on campuses that lack them, and individuals presently overlooked and isolated at large universities can be encouraged to participate.

Existing publications about professional developments at home should be distributed more widely and more promptly among students and stay-ons overseas. Some countries have magazines about engineering, agriculture, and the sciences for their foreign-trained returnees, and perhaps these or specially written new journals should be sent to students and stay-ons overseas. Some journals for returnees are published by the embassies of developed countries that gave many fellowships for foreign study, although the editors and contributors are the returnees themselves.[15] Developed countries could make a great contribution by supporting special professional journals for overseas students and stay-ons and by helping create voluntary registries of foreign manpower.

[15] For example, Participant Journal (New Delhi, India) and Renew (Tehran, Iran).

Chapter VIII

THE DECISION TO STUDY ABROAD

Many attitudes and influences induce the student to study abroad. Some are aspirations, others are personal influences. Some are pushes out of the home country, others are inducements from foreign countries. Some are short-term stimuli, others are long-range expectations of benefits. One or two motives are not enough to explain the decisions of so many different persons. Each individual acts on the basis of a combination of strong and weak pushes and attractions, and the combination varies throughout the world.

To capture the principal motives and influences that anyone might have, we asked each respondent to rate how each of thirty-seven items affected his decision to study abroad in general and to study in his first foreign country in particular. We devised the following accounting scheme to explain the decision to study abroad, and we wrote questionnaire items indicating whether the individual was affected by each of its dimensions:

1. Academic:
   - (a) Pulls from the foreign country
     - (1) Quality of education
     - (2) Scholarships available there
     - (3) Advice by persons abroad: family there, teachers, friends
   - (b) Pushes from the home country
     - (1) Positive stimuli:
       - (a) Scholarships for foreign study from home country
       - (b) Advice by persons there: spouse, family, teachers, friends

(c) Value of foreign training after return
(2) Negative pushes
(a) Inferiority of domestic education
(b) Not accepted by domestic universities

2. Economic:
(a) Pulls from the foreign country:
(1) Opportunities to work
(2) Quality of professional environment there
(3) Living conditions
(b) Pushes from home country:
(1) Positive stimuli: value of work experience abroad after return
(2) Negative stimuli: limited career prospects at home

3. Personal:
(a) Pulls from the foreign country:
(1) Congenial personal environment, presence of relatives and friends
(2) Personal freedom
(3) More attractive political situation
(4) Explore prospects for permanent emigration
(b) Pushes from the home country:
(1) Discrimination
(2) Political situation
(3) Gain freedom from family

The precise wording of each item appears in Table VIII-1. The respondent could check whether each factor in his decision was "very important," "important," "of slight importance," present but "unimportant," and absent and therefore "did not apply." We tried to anticipate all possible reasons for the decision, and few persons felt it necessary to add anything in the thirty-eighth category, viz., "other reasons (please specify)." All respondents--whether student, nonreturnee, or returnee--answered the battery; minor variations in wording adapted the questions to each group.

For all respondents together and in the separate

samples, the answers fell into seven main clusters[1]:

1. Academic benefits from foreign study
2. Value of foreign experience after return
3. Opportunity to work abroad
4. Escape from controls at home
5. Influence of family, friends, and connections abroad
6. Academic pushes from the home country
7. Explore prospects for permanent emigration

Table VIII-1 gives the proportions of respondents who said that each attitude, experience, and influence was "very important" or "important" in their original decisions to study abroad. The questions were not answered in the order they appear in the tables, but they are rearranged by cluster.[2]

Educational benefits are the most important reasons for study abroad

Educational benefits. So much has been said about study abroad as an ulterior channel of emigration that the strength of purely educational motives may be surprising. But, according to Table VIII-1, the attractions of curricula and facilities in developed countries are the most common reasons for studying abroad--i.e., items a and b in Cluster 1 have the highest percentages in each column. The other educational reasons in Cluster 1 also are

---

[1]The problem is to classify a question in one or another cluster, according to answers by all respondents. While we wrote each question to fit a category in our original accounting scheme--described in previous paragraphs--the problem in research is what the items measure in practice. Our summaries of all such batteries in this manuscript classify the items according to the clusters derived from the actual responses. The method of grouping questions into clusters is described in the sources on page 90, footnote 1, *supra*.

[2]Therefore we list items in clusters where they were assigned by the psychological processes of our respondents, even when some of those assignments--such as items 2(c), 5(i), and 6(d)--differed from the intent of our original accounting scheme.

given by substantial proportions of respondents. In previous surveys of foreign students, educational benefits also are given by far most often as reasons for studying abroad.[3]

Other benefits. Another well defined cluster of responses is similar to the educational reasons but is distinct in the type of gain foreseen: high proportions say that the prestige of education abroad and the experience of having been abroad are beneficial (Cluster 2). Fewer give as reasons the desire to work abroad (Cluster 3), but these items are mentioned by between a fifth and a third of all respondents. Working abroad is not the same as permanent emigration but often means acquiring skills for eventual use at home, as we shall see later in this chapter. Consequently, in Table VIII-1 the proportions of persons who went abroad because of employment prospects (Cluster 3) greatly exceeds those who were taking the first step in emigration (Cluster 7).

Academic pushes from home. In two previous surveys of the reasons for study abroad, many respondents had been pushed: they preferred to study at home but were unable to do so, because they were not admitted or received no scholarships.[4] Several governments with large secondary school enrollments and limited university openings suspect many of their students are being pushed abroad. Some wish to re-

---

[3]Paul Ritterband, The Non-Returning Foreign Student: The Israeli Case: (New York: Bureau of Applied Social Research, Columbia University, 1968), Ch. II; Robert G. Myers, Education and Emigration (New York: David McKay Company, 1972), pp. 266-267; Keshav Dev Sharma, "Indian Students in the United States," International Educational and Cultural Exchange, Volume IV, Number 4 (Spring 1969), p. 47; and Tai Keun Oh, The Role of International Education in the Asian Brain Drain (Madison: dissertation for the Ph.D. in Industrial Relations, University of Wisconsin, 1970), pp. 79-91 passim.

[4]Tai Keun Oh, The Role of International Education in the Asian Brain Drain (op. cit., fn. 3), pp. 83-85; and Paul Ritterband, "The Determinants of Motives of Israeli Students Studying in the United States," Sociology of Education, Volume 42, Number 4 (Fall 1969), pp. 335-347.

duce this involuntary movement, since it uses up scarce hard currency, revolutionary sentiments may be learned abroad, and some students may become part of the brain drain. So, these governments recently have planned expansion of their universities, despite the danger of overproduction of professionals.

In our data, simple academic pushes are not common. Some students from Iran, Thailand, Turkey, Lebanon, Ghana and Trinidad studied abroad because they were refused entry or scholarships at home, or because they feared refusal. But the proportions are low. Simple pushes are even more rare from other countries (Cluster 6 in Table VIII-2).

While simple academic pushes are unusual, more sophisticated pushes are common: large proportions of foreign students could have studied in universities at home but preferred going abroad to benefit from a wider choice of fields, specialized curricula not available at home, and better facilities (items a, b, e, and h in Cluster 1).

Reasons for study abroad vary among countries

Each nationality is affected by certain reasons more strongly than by others: when students are compared by home country, motives that are strong for some are weak for others. The following paragraphs summarize nationalities with highest scores on certain reasons for study abroad. In addition, Table VIII-2 shows the extreme cases, viz., those nationalities who gave a reason much more often and much less often than the average. Since the table is confined to the extreme cases, the text describes some patterns that do not appear in the table.

Table VIII-2 resembles Table VI-2 on page 104: the symbols permit the reader to pick out the extreme cases very quickly. The first column shows the average percentage and the symbols show the largest deviations. By reading down each column, one can see the reasons that affect persons from each country to an unusual degree. By reading across each row, one sees the countries that are affected far more or far less than the average for each reason.

[Text continues on page 184]

Table VIII-1

Reasons for Study Abroad

Reasons	Students %	Stayons %	Returnees %
1. Academic benefits:			
a) "In my special field and at my level, I felt that training abroad was superior to that offered in my country of origin"	50	72	73
b) "In my special field and at my level, I felt that facilities abroad were superior to those offered in my country of origin"	56	72	71
c) "I wanted to study in a particular school abroad"	34	38	39
d) "In my special field and at my level, it would take less time to earn a degree abroad than in my country of origin"	15	18	16
e) "I could get a wider choice of fields abroad than in my country of origin"	43	51	43
f) "I could get more contacts with members of my profession abroad"	27	38	39

Proportions are all respondents who said each reason was "very important" or "important" in their decision. The difference between each number and 100 per cent is the persons who said the reason was "of slight importance," who said it was "unimportant," who checked "this factor did not apply to me, since it was not present when I made my decision," or who did not check a box. Persons who omitted the entire battery are excluded. Since some respondents omit check-marks rather than answer "unimportant" or "does not apply," we interpreted "no answer" in this battery as a negative response--provided the respondent checked some other boxes. The text along the left-hand margin gives the exact wording of the thirty-seven items. [continued]

Table VIII-1 [continued]

Reasons	Students %	Stayons %	Returnees %
g) "I obtained a scholarship to study abroad from a source (or sources) in my country of origin"	17	12	22
h) "There were no courses or facilities for studying my special field in my country of origin"	36	42	50
2. Value of foreign experience after return:			
a) "Prestige attached to foreign training after my return to my country of origin"	36	54	41
b) "In my special field, a degree from abroad is worth more <u>in my country of origin</u> than a degree from my country of origin"	29	47	39
c) "I wanted a chance to see the world"	53	59	45
3. Opportunity to work abroad:			
a) "I needed the qualifications to have a good career abroad, in case I stayed there"	34	39	17
b) "I hoped to obtain profitable employment abroad and save money after my study there"	21	24	8
c) "It seemed easier to support myself while studying by means of a job abroad than in my country of origin"	30	45	18
d) "Practical experience of working abroad in my specialty is important, and the only way I could get it was by a visa as a student here"	22	25	27

[continued]

Table VIII-1 [continued]

Reasons	Stu-dents %	Stay-ons %	Re turnees %
4. Escape from controls at home:			
a) "I thought there would be more freedom abroad in personal life"	23	27	11
b) "I thought there would be more political freedom abroad"	14	14	5
c) "I wanted to get away from family pressures in my country of origin"	11	11	4
d) "My military service was postponed when I went abroad for study"	5	1	2
5. Influence of family, friends, and connections abroad:			
a) "Friends in my country of origin advised me to study abroad"	19	13	16
b) "Relatives in my country of origin advised me to study abroad"	20	21	12
c) "Teachers in my country of origin advised me to study abroad"	15	36	29
d) "Friends or relatives abroad advised me to study there"	20	16	10
e) "My spouse decided to study abroad"	5	5	5
f) "Members of my family usually have studied abroad"	9	9	5
g) "My relatives in my country of origin promised me financial aid if I studied abroad"	17	14	11

[continued]

Table VIII-1 [continued]

Reasons	Students %	Stay-ons %	Returnees %
h) "My relatives abroad promised me financial aid if I studied there"	8	3	3
i) "I obtained a scholarship to study abroad from an overseas source (or sources)"	29	51	52
6. Academic pushes from home:			
a) "I was not accepted by a university or equivalent training school in my country of origin"	5	3	3
b) "I feared I would not be able to get into a university or training school in my country of origin because of the limited openings"	9	3	6
c) "I did not receive a scholarship to study in my country of origin"	6	5	3
d) "I was not sure what subjects I wanted to study"	7	4	3
7. Explore prospects for emigration:			
a) "I was seriously considering migrating and I thought it best to try it out first as a student"	11	9	3
b) "I wanted to establish rights of citizenship or of permanent residence abroad"	12	7	1
c) "I wanted to prepare the way for other members of my family to go abroad"	13	11	4

[continued]

Table VIII-1 [continued]

Reasons	Students %	Stay-ons %	Returnees %
d) "I originally went abroad as a tourist, and decided to stay and study here after I arrived"	5	1	1
e) "I came to my first country of study with the intention of going later to some other developed country"	8	5	5
Total number of respondents	(2,981)	(397)	(2,954)

Educational reasons are mentioned by South Americans, Ceylonese, and Thais more often than by other respondents (Cluster 1). Several countries have extensive university programs at home, but their nationals go abroad because the curricula lack the subjects they need, viz., Brazilians, Argentinians, Africans, Ceylonese, and Pakistanis (item h in Cluster 1). The mere availability of scholarships for foreign study was an important motive for Africans (item g in Cluster 1).

The prestige value of foreign degrees is greatest in Colombia, Iran, and Asia (items a and b in Cluster 2). Prestige gains are less compelling for the West Indian and African countries with new universities, such as Trinidad and Tobago, Jamaica, Ghana, and Senegal. And interest in travel for its own sake is common, particularly among Colombians, Indians, Pakistanis, Filipinos, and Thais (item c in Cluster 2).

A desire for work experience abroad was most common among West Indians, Egyptians, Indians, Pakistanis, and Filipinos (Cluster 3). (Further variations in temporary work stays among the countries with surveys of returnees were described in Chapter III, *supra*.)

[Text continues on page 190]

Table VIII-2

Reasons for Studying Abroad by Home Country *

* All respondents were combined from the surveys of students, stay-ons, and returnees. The battery was the reasons for study abroad. The wording of each item appears in Table VIII-1, *supra*. The first column of Table VIII-2 shows the proportion of all respondents who said the reason was "very important" or "important." The table shows only those national groups with at least 29 respondents and with proportions much higher or lower than the average:

++ = 20% higher

\+ = 10% higher

\- = 10% lower

-- = 20% lower

Because the table only shows the extreme values, the text describes several patterns that do not appear in the table.

Table VIII-2 [continued]

Reasons	Per cent for all respondents	Caribbean and Central America				South America				Africa				Middle East and North Africa					Asia							
		Trinidad and Tobago	Jamaica	Haiti	Mexico	Brazil	Argentina	Colombia	Venezuela	Ghana	Senegal	Ivory Coast	Cameroon	Tunisia	Egypt	Lebanon	Turkey	Iran	India	Sri Lanka	Pakistan	Korea, Republic of	Philippines	Thailand	Greece
1. Academic benefits:																									
a) Training abroad superior	57	--	--	-	-	+		+		--	--		--	-	--	-						+			
b) Facilities abroad superior	61	--	--		-					--	--	-	--	--	--		++		+						
c) Particular school abroad	39				+		+	++	-	-			-		-	+	--				-				
d) Less time abroad	15										+	++			-		-	+		-					++
e) Wider choice of fields	43	+						+																	
f) More contacts with profession	31	-	-	--			-		-		-	-		-					+	++	+	+		+	
g) Scholarship from home sources	19	-	-	-					+	++	++	++	++	+			++	-		+					
h) No courses at home	40	-			--	+	+			++	+	+	+		--			-	-	++	+	-	--	-	
2. Value of foreign experience:																									
a) Prestige of foreign training	38	-					-	++		--	--		-	-	--			+	+		+		++	+	
b) Foreign degree worth more at home	33	--	-				-			--	-	-	-	-	--	-		+	+	-		+	++	+	

[continued]

Table VIII-2 [continued]

Reasons	Per cent for all respondents	Caribbean and Central America				South America				Africa				Middle East and North Africa					Asia						Greece
		Trinidad and Tobago	Jamaica	Haiti	Mexico	Brazil	Argentina	Colombia	Venezuela	Ghana	Senegal	Ivory Coast	Cameroon	Tunisia	Egypt	Lebanon	Turkey	Iran	India	Sri Lanka	Pakistan	Korea, Republic of	Philippines	Thailand	Greece
2. Value of foreign experience:																									
c) See world	51			--				+				--	--	-	-				+		+		+	++	
3. Work abroad:																									
a) Possible career abroad	30	+	+	+	-	-				-	-	--	-		++						+		++		
b) Save money abroad	18	+	+	+		-					-	-									+		++	+	
c) Support self easier abroad	28	+	++	+	-	-	-	-	-								-		+	-					
d) Gain practical experience	23				-		+												+						
4. Escape from controls:																									
a) More personal freedom	20			+		-	-		-		+			++	++	+		+		-			+		
b) More political freedom	12			++	-							+		+	++			+							
c) Avoid family pressures	9													+		+									
d) Postpone military service	3											+		+				+							
[continued]																									

Table VIII-2 [continued]

Reasons	Per cent for all respondents	Caribbean and Central America				South America				Africa				Middle East and North Africa					Asia						Greece
		Trinidad and Tobago	Jamaica	Haiti	Mexico	Brazil	Argentina	Colombia	Venezuela	Ghana	Senegal	Ivory Coast	Cameroon	Tunisia	Egypt	Lebanon	Turkey	Iran	India	Sri Lanka	Pakistan	Korea, Republic of	Philippines	Thailand	Greece
5. Influence of persons:																									
a) Friends at home	19			–																	+				
b) Relatives at home	18	+	+	+			–													–	+			+	
c) Teachers at home	26				–					–															
d) Friends or relatives abroad	17	+	+	++							–										+				
e) Spouse studied abroad	4																								
f) Family usually studied abroad	8	+																+						++	
g) Relatives at home promised money	12	+	+	+		–			+								–	+		–	+			++	
h) Relatives abroad promised money	5			+																					
i) Scholarship from abroad	36	--	--	--	–	++	++		–		–	–	–	--	--	--		–	+			++	--		–
6. Academic pushes:																									
a) Not accepted at home	4																	+						+	
[continued]																									

Table VIII-2 [continued]

Reasons	Per cent for all respondents	Caribbean and Central America				South America				Africa				Middle East and North Africa					Asia						
		Trinidad and Tobago	Jamaica	Haiti	Mexico	Brazil	Argentina	Colombia	Venezuela	Ghana	Senegal	Ivory Coast	Cameroon	Tunisia	Egypt	Lebanon	Turkey	Iran	India	Sri Lanka	Pakistan	Korea, Republic of	Philippines	Thailand	Greece
6. Academic pushes:																									
b) Feared would not be accepted at home	7		+															+						+	+
c) No scholarship at home	5		+										+												
d) Not sure of subjects	5																								
7. Explore emigration:																									
a) Try migrating first as student	9														+	+									
b) Establish rights abroad	9		+												++										
c) Prepare way for family	10	+													+						+			+	
d) First went as tourist	3			+																			+		
e) Go to other developed country	7				+																				
(Total number of respondents)	(6,332)	(168)	(77)	(68)	(29)	(906)	(518)	(330)	(32)	(226)	(52)	(52)	(59)	(152)	(202)	(157)	(40)	(164)	(1,104)	(202)	(116)	(415)	(84)	(69)	(683)

Foreign study as an opportunity to emigrate was mentioned most often by Trinidadians, Jamaicans, Egyptians, and Lebanese (Cluster 7). The distinction between temporary stays to acquire postgraduate work experience and permanent emigration is illustrated by the responses of Asians--few said they went abroad to investigate permanent emigration, but more said they studied abroad to lay the basis for a period of foreign employment (compare Cluster 3 and 7).

A full examination of our tabulations shows that--as in many other results of our research--classification by home country reveals some essential differences between societies often considered similar. For example, students and professionals from neighboring South American countries, such as Colombia and Venezuela, answer many questions differently.

The United States attracts more students with strong academic aspirations

Reasons for study abroad vary by country of study as well as by home country: the reasons why persons go to one country differ somewhat from the reasons for going to another.

Students go abroad primarily for educational purposes, but the strength of this motive differs among sites: larger proportions of those from developing countries study in the United States for academic reasons than in the other countries. Part A of Table VIII-3 identifies the respondents who scored high on each cluster of items in the battery of reasons for studying abroad. More foreign students in the United States were high on the clusters that measured study abroad to obtain academic benefits (50%) and to gain the prestige from a foreign degree (70%).

Part B of Table VIII-3 shows the proportions of respondents in the three countries of study who said that particular academic and prestige reasons were "very important" or "important" for studying there. For the quality of training and facilities, more students pick the United States. France is picked substantially more often than the other two countries of study on two academic grounds resulting from the highly formalized character of French educational exchanges: interest in attending a particular university well known among all French-speaking countries (usually the respondent has in mind the University of Paris or one of the special schools in Paris); and receipt of a scholarship tied to study in France.

Compared to France, the United States and Canada more often (31% to 12% for Cluster 3 in Part A) attract persons who begin study as a basis for temporary work abroad.

France more often than the other two countries attracts students seeking political and personal refuge. Twenty per cent of the students in France rank high on the cluster measuring the desire to escape from governmental, personal, and family controls; the figures for the United States and Canada are 13% and 12%.

Studying abroad for academic reasons is associated with high return

Do the motives for study abroad predict whether the student will eventually emigrate or return home? If so, learning a person's reasons for study will enable a policy-maker to make a more informed guess whether the person will return to benefit the country, and therefore whether an investment in his foreign education will pay off at home.

Academic motives are associated with higher return. If persons study abroad to gain intellectual benefits or the prestige of a foreign degree--i.e., if their scores on the first two clusters in Table VIII-4 are "high"--their index numbers of return are higher than if they scored low on those motives.[5] Foreign students in the United States

[5] Although several previous studies have asked students their reasons for studying abroad, only one has traced the effects of different motives upon the decision to migrate later. [Text and footnote continue on page 194]

Table VIII-3

Reasons for Studying Abroad by Country of Study

	Proportions with high scores on each cluster among students in:		
	United States %	Canada %	France %
A. Clusters of reasons:			
1. Academic benefits	50	27	34
2. Foreign experience	70	49	39
3. Work abroad	31	31	12
4. Escape from controls	13	12	20
5. Academic pushes	5	3	2
6. Explore emigration	4	7	1
	Proportions saying reason was "very important" or "important" among students in:		
	United States %	Canada %	France %
B. Individual reasons:			
1. Academic benefits			
a) Training abroad superior	66	43	53
b) Facilities abroad superior	72	51	43
c) Particular school abroad	33	36	51
d) Scholarship from home source	16	10	38
2. Value of foreign experience			
a) Prestige of foreign training	53	27	34
b) Foreign degree worth more at home	45	23	26
(Total number of respondents)	(1,567)	(912)	(502)

The meaning of each cluster and the set of items creating it appear in Table VIII-1. For each cluster, an additive index was created, based on respondents' answers to the items belonging to that cluster. A cluster was "high" for a respondent in our calculations, if his score showed predominant ratings of the items as "very important," "important," and "of slight importance." A cluster was deemed "low" for him if his score [continued]

Table VIII-3 [continued]

showed predominant ratings of "unimportant" and "does not apply." Part A of this table gives the percentage scoring "high" on each cluster; the difference between each figure and 100% is the proportion scoring "low."

Table VIII-4

Reasons for Study Abroad and Long-Run Plans

Reasons for studying abroad	Index of return for persons with high or low scores on each cluster		Number of respondents	
	High	Low	High	Low
Academic benefits	.95	.76	(2,694)	(3,549)
Foreign experience	.92	.74	(3,539)	(2,704)
Work abroad	.36	1.10	(1,349)	(4,894)
Escape from controls	-.09	1.05	(547)	(5,696)
Academic pushes	1.25	.98	(173)	(6,070)
Explore emigration	-.37	1.01	(180)	(6,063)

The method of calculating an individual's score on each cluster of reasons was described in the footnote to Table VIII-3, supra. The total numbers falling "high" or "low" on each cluster appear in the third and fourth columns. The index of return for persons in each cluster is in the first and second columns. All respondents are combined from the surveys of students, stay-ons and returnees, but the patterns are the same in the surveys of students alone.

have a higher rate of return than those in Canada, because they score higher on the academic and prestige clusters, which measure the value of foreign education for return.

The strongest relationship is an obvious one: if a student went abroad because schooling gave opportunities to investigate the possibility of emigration, he is more likely to go permanently than if these ideas never motivated him. In the sixth cluster in Table VIII-4, the index of return is -.37 for those with higher scores on this group of reasons, indicating a substantial tendency to emigrate. For persons not so motivated before studying overseas, the index is 1.01, showing strong plans to return. But, as the numbers in the third and fourth columns reveal, few persons study abroad primarily to explore prospects for emigration, viz., only 180 out of our 6,243 respondents.

If someone goes abroad to escape from personal and political controls at home, his chances of migrating greatly increase. In the fourth cluster, the index is -.09 for those with high scores and 1.05 for persons not affected.

Even if someone goes abroad intending to return, he can become assimilated into the cultural and occupational system of developed countries, and his commitment to home weakens. Therefore, if persons originally studied abroad in whole or in part to lay the groundwork for a period of work there, many will gradually decide to stay on permanently. For the third cluster in Table VIII-4, the index of return, while positive, is lower (+.36) than the numbers for

---

It confirms our finding that academic reasons for studying abroad are associated with the greatest chances for return; and interest in foreign study as a basis for work abroad is associated with stronger migration plans. Josefina Cortes, Factors Associated with the Migration of High-Level Persons from the Philippines to the U.S.A. (Stanford, School of Education, Stanford International Development Education Center, Stanford University, 1970), p. 82.

persons ranking high on academic motives. Persons not motivated by such foreign occupational plans have a much higher index of return (+1.10).

The highest rate of return in the survey occurs among persons whose academic motivations for foreign study were involuntary, viz., by the persons who studied abroad because they could not find openings or scholarships at home. They never wanted to go abroad in the first place, and they have the highest index of return (+1.25).

In an earlier chapter, we reported that women are more likely to emigrate than men. This intention was more evident among the students. Fewer women than men go overseas for academic reasons. In the academic cluster summarized in Tables VIII-3 and VIII-4, 43 per cent of the male students and 32 per cent of the women had high scores. In the cluster concerning the value of foreign experience for employment at home, 55 per cent of the male students and 39 per cent of the women had high scores.

Motives for study abroad and staying abroad temporarily

Going to developed countries for academic reasons is associated with immediate return home after obtaining a degree, without an intervening period of work abroad, according to further tabulations not presented here. Foreign study to gain the prestige of foreign experience is associated with staying abroad temporarily thereafter--53 per cent of the students ranking high on that cluster expected to become stay-ons--but nearly half of these stay-ons plan to return.

The cluster of motives about gaining foreign occupational experience, of course, strongly predicts a period of work abroad. But the numbers exceed the total of permanent migrants. Three-quarters of the students with high scores on these motives plan to stay abroad to work after study; but of this group planning to work abroad, only 38 per cent intend to remain permanently. (38 per cent expected to return home eventually, and the rest were undecided.)

Foreign students in developed countries rarely consider study in developing countries

If the students and professionals had not gone to their actual countries of study, the alternatives would have been other highly developed countries. Very few pick other developing societies. Certain countries with regional universities well suited for "third-country" training--Chile, Jamaica, Uganda, Senegal, Singapore, and Lebanon--are rarely mentioned. For students in the United States, the second choice would have been Great Britain; for students in Canada and France, the second choice is overwhelmingly the United States. (The data are in Table VIII-5.) Effective programs of "third-country" education will require attractive facilities and persuasive explanation, in view of the present biases toward education in highly developed societies.

Many persons work abroad after study to gain practical experience before return

Work abroad by professionals from developing countries need not be brain drain. For many, it is a form of post-graduate education that is preparation for return rather than for permanent settlement abroad.

The strongest reasons for staying on for limited periods are educational (Cluster 1 in Table VIII-6).[6] After concluding didactic instruction in classrooms and libraries, many persons desire practical training on the job. In addition, work is an opportunity to visit leading installations in one's field, to attend conferences, and to meet other professionals who will be less accessible after the student returns home. Some respondents were able to obtain post-doctoral fellowships, which are a "halfway house" between graduate study and conventional

[6]One of the few surveys ever conducted of stay-ons also discovered that educational gain was a common reason for working abroad after the conclusion of academic preparation. Research in Great Britain, reported in Geoffrey Oldham and Oscar Gish, "Survey of Immigrant Professionals in the Fields of Science and Technology" (Brighton: Science Policy Research Unit, University of Sussex, 1970), p. 18.

Table VIII-5

Other Possible Countries for Study

	Students in			Stay-ons in	
	United States	Canada	France	United States	France
Proportions who considered study in another country	50%	70%	45%	40%	48%
(Total number of respondents)	(1,547)	(883)	(450)	(333)	(60)
Number of persons picking each alternative country:					
United States		394	102		23
Canada	127		24	9	4
United Kingdom	478	293	55	27	4
France	163	112		15	
Federal Republic of Germany	228	85	48	14	1
Australia	38	19	--	3	--
Other European countries	248	93	64	17	6
Other developed countries	23	10	2	3	--
Other developing countries in:					
North America and Caribbean	22	14	1	--	--
South America	27	7	--	--	--
Africa	8	4	4	--	--
Middle East and North Africa	25	16	14	1	1
Asia and Pacific	17	8	3	--	--
(Total number of respondents who named other countries)	(816)	(595)	(200)	(41)	(29)

Respondents were asked to list the other countries where they might have studied. The table lists the second and third as well as the first alternative. Data are not weighted.

employment. Common in the United States, these fellowships enable the visitor to work on research projects or action programs at a university or laboratory.

Accumulating money is a reason mentioned less often, but it is important to nearly half. Savings abroad will be handy after return. Few mention a reason often thought to influence stays overseas, viz., acquiring foreign consumer durables that are scarce or prohibitively expensive at home (Cluster 2).

One-third use foreign employment as a base to wait for the job market to improve at home (item 4a). About a quarter are avoiding distasteful governments (item 4b).

Variations by home country. In tabulations not presented here, additional practical experience for educational purposes is a motive common to nearly all nationalities.

Earning money to use at home and repay debts is important for nationalities beset at home with low pay and depreciated currencies, such as Ghanaians, Pakistanis, Filipinos, and Jamaicans. This reason is less important for stay-ons from the more prosperous developing countries, such as most South Americans, Iranians, Lebanese, Tunisians, and Turks.

Variations by specialty. Persons in several of the "hard" sciences and applied fields were most interested in more preparation overseas through employment, viz., agriculture, engineering, mathematics, and physical science. Additional experience was less important for the specialists in health and language in our samples. Professional contacts before returning home were sought particularly by artists and mathematicians but seemed much less important to the educators, health specialists, and journalists.

Earning money for use at home most strongly motivated persons in agriculture, business, and law. It had less effect on the architects, doctors, and linguists.

[Text continues on the middle of page 200]

Table VIII-6

Reasons for Temporary Work Abroad After End of Study

Reasons	Students %	Stayons %	Returnees %
1. Professional experience:			
a) "Obtain additional professional training"	86	87	88
b) "Obtain experience on job"	87	85	90
c) "Make professional visits and contacts abroad"	55	51	47
2. Save money for use at home:			
a) "Save money for personal use after my return to my country of origin"	54	57	39
b) "Earn money for my family in my country of origin"	34	38	24
c) "Repay debts incurred because of my study abroad"	25	21	19
d) "Save money to invest in a business or in my work in my country of origin"	33	19	8
e) "Buy consumer goods that are not available in my country of origin"	6	8	21
3. Save money for use abroad:			
"Save foreign exchange for personal use abroad in the future"	34	15	13
4. Await developments at home:			
a) "Wait for a good job in my country of origin"	43	52	36
b) "Wait for the political situation to improve in my country of origin"	26	18	12
Total number of persons who will or have worked abroad and then will or have returned	(837)	(98)	(537)

Wording of the question: Survey of students: "If you expect

[The footnote to the table continues on the top of the next page]

Table VIII-6 [continued]

---

to stay abroad for a while after completing your present studies in this country, instead of returning to your country of origin at once, please answer the following questions. Which of the following reasons will probably influence your decision to stay abroad this additional time?" Survey of stay-ons: "Which of the following reasons influenced your decision to stay abroad for an additional time after completing your studies?" Survey of returnees: "Please answer [the question] if you worked abroad six months or longer after completing your studies and before returning here. . . . Which of the following reasons influenced your decision to stay abroad for an additional time after completing your studies?" The left-hand column gives the exact wording of the items. The questionnaire included other items not presented in this table.

Proportions are all respondents who said each reason was "very important" or "important" in their decision. Remaining are persons who said the reason was "unimportant in my decision" or who checked "these factors do (did) not exist for me." Persons are excluded if they did work abroad or did plan to work abroad. Tabulations of students and stay-ons are confined to those who expect to return or who are uncertain.

[Continuation of the text from page 198]

Persons in agriculture, biology, mathematics, and the physical sciences more often than other stay-ons were waiting for good jobs at home. The stay-ons in architecture, arts, and fields related to health were much less motivated by this reason.

Journalists and social scientists were more often political exiles, who waited abroad until the situation improved at home. Politics affected agriculturists and biologists much less than the average for other specialties.

Motives for study abroad and their implications for policy

Reasons for study abroad. Fears about motivation behind foreign study do not seem justified. The great majority of students go abroad for academic reasons. Not many say that they go abroad as students in order to explore prospects for emigration.

A second chance abroad. Some prefer to study at home but are not accepted in the smaller or more competitive university systems there. Because they have many more openings, the universities of the developed countries are less selective than their counterparts in these developing countries. The developed countries thereby increase the stock of manpower with higher education in those developing countries beyond the latter's own conceptions of their national needs.

Providing a second chance for students shut out from home can be defended as well as criticized. Maximum opportunity to enable the individual to develop his own potentialities in his own way free of restrictions can be justified as a human right. The international market rather than the capacities of organized educational services at home would determine whether enough or too many persons are receiving higher education. Individuals who cannot satisfy at a young age the screening procedures of a university system with limited capacity might profit from higher education and make important contributions after the second chance. If some scarce openings at home are awarded by political or personal favoritism, superior ability can be developed only through foreign study.

On the other hand, educational and manpower planners might argue that the admissions policies should be coordinated by bilateral agreements between developed countries and those developing countries whose students often seek a second chance abroad. Some recent analyses of the brain drain attribute it to the overproduction of university graduates by developing countries.[7] By educating persons who were not accepted at home, the developed countries thereby encourage a preoccupation with university-level education in developing countries,

---

[7] Committee on the International Migration of Talent, The International Migration of High-Level Manpower (New York: Praeger Publishers, 1970), pp. 685-689 and 703-704; and George B. Baldwin, "Brain Drain or Overflow?" Foreign Affairs, Volume 48, Number 2 (January 1970), pp. 358-372.

when restrictions on openings might be necessary to divert competent persons into essential applied training and middle-level work.

The search for better courses and facilities. Many students could have studied at home but went abroad in search of an education available at present only in a developed country. If a developing country could duplicate these programs, perhaps more of its citizens would study at home. But the costs make this impossible, and the small student bodies make it impractical. And the benefit might not be large decreases in emigration: unlike the involuntary foreign students who go abroad in response to closed opportunities, many students searching for better curricula have other strong reasons for studying abroad; a considerable part of the brain drain today consists of persons who studied entirely at home, and improved curricula might only raise their confidence in their marketability abroad.

One solution to the expensive problem of improving curricula is regionalization. A school of high quality would be created in a developing country, with a curriculum appropriate to all the neighboring societies. The student body would be drawn from that region.[8] But, as Table VIII-5 reported, most foreign students currently in a developed country considered only other developed countries and rarely thought of the regional universities presently available on their home continents. Future research should study more precisely the conditions that might induce persons to study at home or in regional universities rather than in North America or Europe.

Reasons for working abroad temporarily. As Chapter II reported, many persons work abroad without intending to emigrate. Such practical experience is an essential part of their education, as demonstrated by tabulations in this chapter.

[8] Many observers have recommended creation of regional educational centers for developing countries, such as A. B. Zahlan, "Wanted: A Great University," Mid-East, Volume IX, Number 1 (January-February 1969), pp. 10-14.

But while policy-makers in educational exchange have thought much about university programs abroad, they have devoted hardly any planning to the post-graduate on-the-job experience that the professionals themselves consider as important as the formal training. Particularly if the professional is sponsored from home or will return to a particular job, his employment might be selected and organized to ensure the best fit with conditions at home. But overseas work might be planned even for the other temporary stay-ons, who do not yet know how they will apply their experiences at home. Since so many foreign-educated professionals will be managers or leaders at home, they might rotate through several working conditions abroad, instead of the stable long-term assignment that characterizes the typical employee at present. The proper location of the job might also be re-examined: at present, most stay-ons work in the larger cities of the developed countries where they were educated, but the practical experience most relevant for home comes from third countries that are developing successfully.

Chapter IX

LOSSES AND GAINS FROM BRAIN DRAIN

The ablest seem neither more nore less likely to return

Probably the greatest anxiety about brain drain from developing countries is loss of the ablest persons, who can make the greatest contributions to domestic growth. Two opposing hypotheses appear in the literature. One belief is that the ablest persons return, since they can get the best jobs and since public and private employers make the greatest efforts to attract them. The less able have greater difficulties winning scarce opportunities at home and need to save themselves by going abroad. On the other hand, some observers believe that universities and employers abroad spot the ablest foreign students and offer them good jobs. The ablest might prefer North America and Europe, since facilities, research work, and the intellectual milieu are seen as less attractive in developing countries.

All our respondents were asked to give their average grades while university undergraduates at home (if they ever studied there) and abroad. So far, our data show no clear-cut relation between ability and migration plans: as persons are ranked by their grades either at home or abroad, their plans to return neither increase nor decrease. There appears a very slight tendency for persons with the lowest grades to return home and stay.

Other measures of ability also fail to show clear relations to emigration. For example, all respondents were asked: "How easy or difficult has it been for you to meet the academic standards of the schools you attend while a student abroad?" Whether students, stay-ons, or returnees reported great or no difficulty lacked association with migration plans.

Countries do not lose most of their highly specialized persons

Chapter V showed that emigration and return vary by specialty. But there is no simple tendency for students to become overspecialized during foreign study and thereby unfitted for return. The fields with the higher losses include both technical specialties and more general areas. So many other occupational and personal influences affect migration decisions that degree of specialization alone is not the dominant cause.

Performing doctoral work in an advanced field depending on complex facilities does not always unfit persons for employment in more general areas. Within developed countries, it has always been common to study topics at the graduate level more specialized than the person's later work. What is important is versatility and ability to adapt knowledge to new situations.

Many returnees at present go back with advanced skills that outstrip current technology and labor markets. Some are willing to accept less complex assignments and wait until their knowledge can be fully used. They become potential resources for their countries. For example, one returnee told our interviewers:

> On balance, I am completely satisfied with my education abroad. At the moment, my field of specialty is of limited interest to the country, but with the progress of technology, my field will be of extreme importance in the future.

Some stay-ons with skills attuned to the developed countries--such as aero-space engineers--told our interviewers that they could not return, since their careers would end and there seems no chance to create these jobs at home. But other specialized stay-ons are waiting for the day when the call will come from home:

> I feel in the coming years that food industry research is going to open up. And I would desire to help by setting up training programs, processing new techniques, things along those lines. I feel that in five to ten years, that all my skills are going to be needed, and I will find a most rewarding position. Rewarding not in money, but in personal gratification that cannot be measured in terms of money. The chance to teach and stimulate people and educate people in the food industry presents a momentous challenge to me, that I could not achieve here in the United States. Therefore, speaking of income, I'd be better off in the United States, but speaking in terms of personal success, I'd be better off home, but I will stay at least ten years here in the United States until I have a more vast amount of experience and knowledge.

<u>Some professionals send remittances home, and some amounts may be substantial</u>

Even if a country loses a skilled person, it might gain in the long run if he sends back a large amount of hard currency that can be used for valuable capital imports. Perhaps he can earn more for his home country abroad if he can be employed more profitably there. Remittances by migrant workers are important sources of total national income and of hard currency for the developing countries of the Mediterranean and the West Indies. Is work abroad by professionals equally profitable? Some observers have thought that remittances might compensate developing countries for the losses of their human capital.[1] Are such remittances large and widespread enough?

---

[1]Papers by Harry G. Johnson and Kenneth Boulding in Walter Adams (editor), <u>The Brain Drain</u> (New York: The Macmillan Company, 1968), pp. 83 and 117.

Proportions who send money home. In the data delivered to us so far, questions about remittances were answered by the stay-ons in the United States and by the returnees in India and Greece. Seventy-five per cent of the stay-ons in the United States, 46 per cent of the returnees in India, and 12 per cent of the returnees in Greece had ever sent money home from developed countries. More Indians than Greeks work abroad and therefore more Indians send money back.

The proportions of each nationality in the American stay-on survey that had ever sent money home were:[2]

	Percentage	Number of person answering the question
India	84	(196)
Korea	86	(21)
Philippines	74	(14)
Iran	(4)	(8)
Brazil	39	(31)
Argentina	46	(28)
Colombia	(7)	(9)

The specialists most often sending money home were biologists, mathematicians, and physical scientists.

Earning money and then sending it home is an important reason for working abroad temporarily after the end of foreign study, although it is not as strong as educational reasons. Figures were given in the second cluster of items in Table VIII-6, supra. If persons plan to emigrate permanently, one reason is to earn money for the family at home, but the proportions are lower than among the students and stay-ons who expect to work abroad temporarily. Numbers are the percentages saying each reason was a "very important" or "important" reason for working abroad:

[2] For the two nationalities with so few members that computations might not be reliable--Iranians and Colombians--the figure in the first column is the actual number who remitted money, rather than the proportion.

Reasons for working abroad	Students' plans		Stay-ons' plans	
	Emigrate permanently	Work abroad temporarily	Emigrate permanently	Work abroad temporarily
	%	%	%	%
Remit money home for personal use	24	54	27	57
Remit money home for family	22	34	25	38

Amounts of money. The amounts of money are reported in Table IX-1. The "median" is the half-way point: half sent less and half sent more. The "mean" is larger because it is increased over the median by the few persons who transmitted very large sums. The total amounts sent by all respondents in the survey may be calculated by multiplying the mean times the number of respondents. "Amount per year" is calculated for each person by dividing his total remittances by the number of years in employment overseas.

At first sight, the total amounts do not appear high. But many stay-ons work abroad for only short periods, and therefore the annual remittances--in columns 3 and 4 of Table IX-1--seem more substantial. A considerable amount of hard currency might be earned by the home country if all stay-ons continued to send money home for long periods at these rates.

The amounts vary among nationalities in the American stay-on survey (Part 1), but the groups may be too small to yield firm estimates about cross-national differences.

Parts (2) and (3) in Table IX-1 report the money from Indians and Greeks. Indians sent far more money from the United States than from Great Britain, their two principal countries of foreign employment. The Greeks sent more money from West Germany than from the United States.

Although more Indians than Greeks were employed

abroad, the average Greek remittance was slightly higher. Part (2) is given in Indian rupees and Part (3) in Greek drachmas and the two can be compared directly by dividing each figure in Part (3) by four, since each rupee is equal to four drachmas. Or, both currencies can be converted into United States dollars, according to the exchange rate in the footnote to Table IX-1. In dollars the median remittances from the United States were about $667 for Indians (equal to the 5,000 rupees given in the table) and $1,000 for Greeks.

Amounts of money sent by temporary and permanent stay-ons. A developing country would gain much if it received both the stay-on's money and then himself. But it might be compensated for non-return if the remittances were very high. One might pose opposite hypotheses: the future returnee may send more money home, because he has closer family ties and because he creates a nest egg for himself; the permanent nonreturnee may send more money home, because he has a more properous career abroad than the temporary stay-on and because (in some cases) his work abroad is designed to help his family more than he could at home. Following are the average total remittances of stay-ons in the United States, classified by long-run migration plans:

Expectations	Mean	Median	Number of respondents
Home	$2,462	$1,500	(60)
Uncertain	2,027	1,300	(50)
Abroad	3,714	2,000	(108)

Those expecting to stay abroad permanently send far more money than those who will return home. The reason is that many of the temporary stay-ons have low-paying jobs or post-doctoral fellowships, in order to gain practical experience after classroom education, and this income usually is barely enough to cover their households abroad. But the permanent nonreturnee acquires better paying jobs and a regular savings schedule. Future research should learn whether the long-term stay-on maintains his annual

Table IX-1

Remittances During Study and Work Abroad

	Total amount		Amount per year of work abroad		Total number of professionals
	Mean	Median	Mean	Median	
(1) Stay-ons in the United States in American dollars:					
Indians	3,082	2,000	600	366	(153)
Koreans	3,221	2,000	1,080	483	(19)
Filipinos	3,605	2,000	2,988	1,150	(14)
Iranians	2,503	1,750	1,304	1,000	(9)
Brazilians	4,966	1,750	2,867	544	(10)
Argentinians	2,070	1,750	514	393	(10)
Colombians	4,400	3,000	1,050	763	(5)
(2) Returnees in India, in rupees:					
All respondents	10,348	5,000	2,523	1,228	(253)
From United States	11,963	5.000	2,900	1,339	(162)
From Great Britain	5,118	3,500	955	719	(54)
(3) Returnees in Greece, in drachmas:					
All respondents	67,747	30,000	19,493	6,667	(63)
From United States	60,000	30,000	22,875	4,000	(26)
From West Germany	65,263	50,000	7,560	5,938	(19)

[continued]

Table IX-1 [continued]

Wording of the question: "Did you ever send money to your country of origin while you were working or studying abroad, either to support your family, as gifts to your family or friends, for deposit in your account or for purchase of assets? If so: How much money altogether, expressed in the currency of the country abroad? How much altogether, expressed in the currency of your country of origin?" Persons who sent no money or who sent money without specifying the amount are omitted from the table. Annual payments during work (columns 2 and 3) are calculated by dividing total remittance by the number of years worked abroad. The annual payments during full-time employment are slightly high estimates, because some persons sent money home during part-time employment while students. "Total amount" includes all money sent home at any time.

The median is the half-way point in the distribution: half earned more and half less. The mean is calculated by dividing the total number of professionals into the total payments reported by all. At the time of the survey, the official exchange rates were U$S 1 = 7.5 Indian rupees and 30 Greek drachmas.

remittance rate during his later years abroad or transfers his savings to the developed country, as his roots there deepen.

Losses and gains, and their implications for policy

Ability. The ablest are neither more likely than others to return from study abroad, nor less likely. Therefore, since most foreign-trained persons plan to return, developing countries do not lose large proportions of their most skilled persons in this group.

However, this is a statistical relationship: developing countries lose some of their abler foreign-trained people; but the proportions lost are no higher than among the other foreign-trained. Nevertheless, a developing country may not be able to spare any of its people; it may need a much higher return by its ablest. Therefore, the significant finding for policy-makers may be that fewer than all able persons return, and therefore special efforts may be needed to identify and attract back the remainder. Locating them will require extra work, some exceptional persons may not have seemed so promising while at home but flourished under the stimulation of study abroad, and therefore policy-makers and employers at home need to learn about them.

Our data show only that the abler foreign-trained are no more likely to emigrate than the less able foreign-trained. The question of ability and emigration has another side: does the total stock of a country's professional manpower show higher losses among the ablest because the ablest have higher chances of studying abroad? A hypothetical example demonstrates this possibility: suppose a country has 1,000 able professionals and 10,000 less able; 500 of the best and 1,000 of the others study abroad; the return rate is equal for both (e.g., 80 per cent); 400 of the ablest and 800 of the less able return; foreign study has resulted in retention of 98 per cent of the less able (9,800/10,000) but only 90 per cent of the ablest (900/1,000). We can learn about this only through new research about all professionals in a country, asking whether the ablest are more likely to study abroad and whether the less able who have studied at home have lower rates of emigration than the more skilled.

Specialties. Some specialties have higher rates of return than others. Whether study abroad in certain fields is wasteful can be decided only by comparing the numbers in each field with the opportunities available at home. Policy-makers must then decide whether the enrollments in a field can be expanded or contracted most effectively in domestic universities or in study abroad. Perhaps education in a developed country is so valuable for the further growth of an overcrowded field that enrollments should not be curtailed overseas, but students at home should be encouraged to enter other careers.

Specialization in very technical or very narrow fields abroad does not increase brain drain. Rather the problem is whether these are the most appropriate skills that returnees should bring home. Some skills might be useful in the future, when the country's development generates those requirements. If a returnee has received very specialized education that may become useful to the country, it is important that he keep abreast of developments after his return. Otherwise, he will be too "rusty" when the demand for his skills arises.

Some very specialized persons are working abroad in jobs that do not exist at home, but they look forward to the opportunity to return when they are needed. It is important for employers to know the qualifications and whereabouts of such potential leaders who are awaiting offers. The stay-ons can then develop skills that will be most useful at home. While abroad, their expert advice and sources of information can be tapped when plans are made to organize and equip their special fields at home. While still abroad, such stay-ons can locate fellow nationals with similar experience, and therefore employers might attract back entire teams.

Remittances vary widely, and the average transfer home may be modest in lifetime total but high in annual rates. A large number of short-term stay-ons could contribute much collectively to a developing country's income of hard currency. Some nationalities send more, others little. Like the intention to return itself, this depends on the strength of ties with home; persons with a family and with confidence in the future of the country more often send money. As in other respects, a country will benefit by strengthening relations with its expatriates.

Some individuals might be persuaded to invest much money at home. But the many temporary stay-ons getting essentially the pay of post-graduate students probably can spare little cash. If a country succeeds in getting back all of its foreign students almost immediately after their education, obviously it will earn little money from remittances. They will not have had the chance to accumulate earnings abroad. If a country wishes to benefit from overseas employment by its professional labor from its earnings of hard currency--as some do in the case of less skilled workers--it would have to arrange stable and well-paid employment in the receiving country and to reward those remittances that pass through legal channels.

To judge net losses from brain drain, much more evidence about the lifetime flow of remittances is necessary before we can judge whether the home country's total accounts are compensated for the costs of the emigrant's upbringing and education. Some individuals emigrating permanently send nothing or too little to "compensate" their home countries for the loss, but others send quite a bit during the first years of work abroad. If they maintain their annual rates, some persons may indeed "repay" their home countries for themselves. But it is not likely that they will send back a surplus large enough to "pay" for every emigrant.[3]

---

[3] The complex task of estimating the net gains and net losses from the international flow of professionals is being explored in new research: The Reverse Transfer of Technology:

<u>Economic Effects of the Outflow of Trained Personnel from Developing Countries (Brain Drain)</u> (Geneva: Intergovernmental Group on Transfer of Technology, Trade and Development Board, United Nations Conference on Trade and Development, TD/B/AC.11/25, May 1974); Edwin P. Reubens, "The New Brain Drain from Developing Countries: 1960-1972," in R. D. Leiter (editor), <u>Costs and Benefits of Education</u> (New York: Twayne Publishers, 1975); and Jagdish Bhagwati and Martin Partington (editors), <u>Taxing the Brain Drain</u> (Amsterdam: North Holland Publishing Company, 1976).

Chapter X

CONCLUSION

Losses of foreign-educated[1] professionals are small proportions of the total. But whether the losses are serious must be judged in the light of each country's situation.[2] Losses are much larger from some nations than from others. A loss from a country with underemployed or unemployed professionals may be less serious than from countries where everyone is fully employed or where some jobs are unfilled.[3] The needs of each country and the harm due to emigration must be studied in depth, and accurate generalizations about the costs and benefits of brain drain cannot be made on the basis of statistics or surveys applying to all countries.

---

[1]From this survey, we can generalize only about students and professionals who were educated abroad. Those educated entirely at home might represent losses of different sizes and types and might have different motivations.

[2]Good examples of individual diagnoses and solution of the brain drain from different countries appear in The Colombo Plan, The Special Topic: Brain Drain -- Country Papers, the Working Paper and the Report of the Special Topic Committee, Prepared for the Meetings of the 22nd Consultative Committee, 1972 (Colombo: Colombo Plan Bureau, 1973).

[3]Countries with losses that are small in both number and proportion may feel an urgent need for each individual. For example, see the survey designed to explain and prevent such exceptional -- but important -- losses from Nigeria: Oladejo O. Okediji and Francis Olu. Okediji, Nigerian Trained Personnel in the United States of America: Problems and Prospects of Their Recruitment for Posts in Nigeria (Lagos and Ibadan: Universities of Lagos and Ibadan, 1972).

Permanent emigration must be distinguished from working abroad temporarily after the conclusion of study. Many persons work abroad but intend to return. Ties with home and barriers to assimilation are strong enough so that some of the "permanent" stay-ons can be induced to return. The fact that so many stay-ons are temporary reduces the net outflow below the totals who live abroad.[4]

Ties with home remain strong for most persons, and few feel completely at home abroad. Except for members of minority groups that never became fully integrated at home and are now being forced out, few persons sever their ties with home completely. These contacts provide powerful levers for inducing persons to return after study and work abroad. And the ties can persuade even many permanent stay-ons to provide valuable services for their home countries.

Present connections with students and stay-ons can be strengthened, resulting in higher morale while overseas, greater and quicker return, and closer coordination between overseas experiences and the needs of employers at home. Journals and news about work and life at home can be circulated more widely and more promptly. National clubs can increase their membership overseas and can supplement their present recreational functions with information about development and employment at home. Such clubs can hear guest speakers, circulate literature, and show movies about work at home. Communication channels can be improved, so that the student and professionals overseas can learn more about the job market and can transmit his qualifications to employers.

Since staying on temporarily for work abroad is so common, experiences should be planned better for the benefit of the home country. Some persons can

---

[4]Estimates of return flows reduce considerably the losses of persons educated entirely at home, in the calculations by Anthony Scott, "The Brain Drain: Is a Human-Capital Approach Justified?", in Conference on Research in Income and Wealth, Education, Income and Human Capital (New York: National Bureau of Economic Research and Columbia University Press, 1970), pp. 262-266.

receive more varied work assignments, so that they are better prepared for management and innovation at home. Temporary work in rapidly developing societies ("third countries") or in frontier regions of developed countries might be more valuable for the home country than the current pattern of narrow assignments in the big cities of developed societies. Suitably coordinated with the needs of the home country, staying on temporarily abroad might be preferable to immediate return after the completion of formal education.

Some methods of inspiring return are appeals by effective leadership rather than monetary rewards. If a country's political and professional leaders project an image of growth, purpose, pride, and toleration, its students and professionals overseas will be eager to return.

Working conditions need to be organized better at home, in order to improve morale and increase return. Nearly everyone would be happier with more time for research and better opportunities to keep in touch with new developments overseas. Where only a few leading jobs sit atop a broad pyramid, with many junior persons awaiting promotion by seniority, the structure of ranks and salaries needs to be widened, so that more people feel they have opportunities to rise and can change employers safely. Although everyone would like higher pay, real incomes may be reasonably high for most professionals, and great increases in pay may not be necessary to combat brain drain. Continued increases in pay may create problems by reducing money available to improve facilities, widen employment, and generate national economic growth.[5] Improving laboratories, equipments, communications with professional workers abroad, and research opportunities would raise productivity and morale.

---

[5]On the harmful effects of general salary increases, see Charles R. Frank, "The Problem of Urban Unemployment in Africa" (Princeton: Princeton University, Woodrow Wilson School, Research Program in Economic Development Discussion Paper No. 16, 1970).

Certain specialties seem particularly troubled, have higher than average losses, and require urgent remedies. They include biology, teaching of languages, teaching of the handicapped, and certain other fields. These specialists feel they need higher pay, better facilities, better contacts with their counterparts overseas, and more recognition at home. Even though general pay increases for everyone would reduce investment in facilities and might not motivate higher return, higher pay might be justified for the troubled specialties.

To increase return, countries must think of the professional's family as well as of the professional himself. At present, many persons return primarily because of family ties, even when working conditions are unsatisfactory. A country must assure a hopeful setting for the professional's children as well as for himself, or else losses will increase. Foreign spouses should be welcomed hospitably and be assured of work permits. Countries should make clear that binational children of professionals have as bright a future as any citizens.

Professional persons working overseas might become more valuable resources for the home country. They might provide higher remittances or loans for development at home. They can help students and temporary stay-ons adjust to life abroad without forgetting home. They can advise employers at home about promising students and stay-ons and about the newest equipment and organizational forms. Some might organize new international firms in collaboration with returnees.

Developing countries need persons -- whether educated at home or abroad -- who will serve their fellow citizens patriotically in all sectors of the society. The country is not well served by emigrants who remit no benefits from abroad. It may be served as badly by returnees who concentrate in the largest cities, provide services only within the élite, press for higher salaries to pay for high living standards that depend on scarce imports, and raise self-centered children. The internal brain drain is as detrimental to orderly development and the general welfare as the international brain drain. A general problem is to select, motivate, and sponsor those students for both domestic education and for international exchanges who will serve all regions and classes.[6]

Selection, appeals, and subsidies to individual students and professionals who would most help development at home need not result in complete control over educational exchanges. Many individuals will continue to study abroad without obligations. Some have potentialities for service at home or overseas that might be overlooked by an official selection system. Official programs can be kept "on their toes" through independent efforts by private organizations and individuals. Even if some unregulated and unsponsored persons emigrate after study abroad, this channel enables rebels and members of minority groups to exercise their human right to make a new start in a more hospitable society. In many cases, the cost of their higher education is borne by the country of study, and the home society loses little.

Study abroad will always give professional persons skills and perspectives wider than those available at home. Every country needs leaders conversant with the international trends in professional fields.

But, in addition, every country needs professionals intimate with its own needs. Educational and manpower planning should coordinate more closely the numbers and types of entrants to universities and the employment prospects in the society, for both the near future and the more distant future. Curricula and work-study programs should stress applications of the professional fields to circumstances in that country. Foreign study should be integrated more closely with study at home; probably students can gain the most from study abroad if they

[6]The harm from the internal -- as well as the international -- brain drain is described in Frederick H. Harbison, Human Resources as the Wealth of Nations (New York: Oxford University Press, 1973), Ch. 5; and Colombo Plan, Brain Drain (op. cit., fn. 2), p. 230.

have had some of their higher education at home. Bilateral arrangements between governments and universities at home and abroad might enable students to "commute" back and forth, gaining academic credits in both places and acquiring the mix of skills most valuable for home. The more meaningful is education for work at home, then probably the lower the brain drain and the greater the effective utilization of the student at home.

FURTHER ANALYSIS OF THE DATA

Despite its length, this report is a simple overview of the main findings of the survey. The aggregate responses to many separate parts of the questionnaires have been summarized, but a great deal of space has not been devoted to a thorough explanation of any one aspect. The data can be used in many ways other than their use in this report to explain the reasons for migration and return or to explore analytical problems in the social sciences. (Appendix F lists subjects in the social sciences that can be studied with our data.)

UNITAR sponsorship. While UNITAR was responsible for the conception and launching of this project, and has taken an active role in arranging for the surveys in different countries and comparative analysis of the results of the surveys, it cannot with its limited financial and manpower resources continue to act as a management center for worldwide research in this field. The Institute, however, encourages continuation of the project. The Center for the Social Sciences at Columbia University will continue to act as the central data depository for purposes of cross-national comparison, subject to the same procedures and safeguards already enforced.

In particular, UNITAR hopes that funds will eventually be made available for cross-national comparison of the surveys currently under way, to permit the carrying out of relevant surveys in additional countries, and to facilitate further multivariate analysis of the data. UNITAR will consider publishing any future report or reports based on the data generated by the project. The four areas below are of special interest to policy-makers concerned with the implications of the findings of this report.

Stay-ons. The analysis at present suffers from inadequate facts about the central group of stay-ons in developed countries who are the actual members of the brain drain. Cooperation of governments and of other organizations is needed in order to draw good samples of stay-ons and to conduct surveys in ways assuring high completion and data of good quality.

Multivariate analysis. As has been said throughout the manuscript, certain factors help explain migration and return, but individually they do not explain everything. In order to explore intensively how the results combine into patters, some combination of factors should be developed by techniques of multiple regression, discriminant function analysis, and so on. The elements in each combination and the structure of the relationship will vary, depending on the home country, the stage of the person's career (whether student, stay-on, or returnee), and other conditions.

Particular topics could be studied in greater depth than was possible in this manuscript. Our data show that income relates only slightly to migration, but since "everyone knows" that money is the chief cause of brain drain the data could be ransacked to learn whether income is a stronger cause under certain circumstances or if measured in different ways--or if, indeed, its influence is only moderate under all conditions.

Another promising subject for more thorough analysis is comparison between men and women in foreign study and in the brain drain. Hardly anything has been published about the special experiences of female students abroad.[7] In our data, we have re-

[7] One of the few books and articles ever published about women in educational exchange is Loan Eng Tjioe, Asiaten über Deutsche: Kulturkonflikte ostasiatischer Studentinnen in der Bundesrepublik (Frankfurt am Main: Thesen Verlag, 1972).

peated the familiar finding that women students are slightly more likely to emigrate than men. In future work, we hope to explain this result more thoroughly.

National reports. Throughout the manuscript, certain answers have been given more often by persons from certain countries and rarely by citizens of other countries. The report has had to deal with so many items and so many nationalities that we could not devote the space and special effort to explain systematically the differences among countries on any one question. Nor could we draw different parts of the survey together to describe and explain the entire combination of attitudes, experiences, and career plans for one nationality.

Thorough understanding and explanation of these patterns require a series of national reports to summarize the many findings for each country's students and professionals, cite significant deviations from patterns common to the rest of the project, and explain distinctive results according to the economic and social characteristics of each country concerned. A few of our participating research centers are preparing basic summaries of the findings in their surveys of returnees, but considerable new effort is needed to derive explanations from the characteristics of the countries themselves.

Substantial numbers of the nationals of some countries appear in the surveys of students and stay-ons. Therefore, national reports can examine not only the motivations of the returnees but can generalize about persons overseas as well.

Nationalities in sufficient numbers in two or three of our surveys to permit thorough national reports are Argentinians, Brazilians, Filipinos, Ghanaians, Greeks, Indians, Iranians, Koreans, Pakistanis, Trinidadians, and Tunisians.

A final edition with all our data. The present monograph is a progress report based on tabulations from slightly over half of all the data we will obtain eventually. The simplest extension of the report, if new funds can be obtained, is a second edition when all data have been delivered from all participating countries. If the same patterns continue in data that are so numerous and come from so many countries, we can be confident that our general conclusions will indeed apply to others.

Appendix A

DESIGN AND CONDUCT OF THE SURVEY

The project aims to explain why persons from developing countries study in developed countries, why some stay on to work, and why others return home. It compares the effects of different experiences at home and abroad. The extensive literature and the studies already done supplied us with many hypotheses and with many of the building blocks for our research design.

THE QUESTIONNAIRES

Eliciting reliable data about reasons for a decision is one of the pitfalls in survey research. The only reliable method is to present to all respondents lists of the principal (or all possible) reasons for a decision according to some theoretical accounting scheme. Each respondent then indicates the role of each reason in his decision--such as the decusion to study abroad or the decision to return home. Statistical techniques then identify types of respondent and patterns of response. The techniques of "reason analysis" have guided us in both the writing of the questionnaires and in the analysis of the data.[1]

[1]The theoretical approach and earlier research about other sorts of decisions are summarized in Charles Kadushin, "Reason Analysis," International Encyclopedia of the Social Sciences (New York: The Macmillan Company and The Free Press, 1968), Volume 13, pp. 338-343. On the difficulties in asking about decisions in questionnaire surveys, see Paul F. Lazarsfeld, "The Art of Asking Why," National Marketing Review, Volume I, Number 1 (Summer 1935), pp. 32-43.

When making any decision, a particular individual is affected by a number of variables: the positive characteristics of the object chosen, the negative characteristics of the alternative, information about the general situation, the advice or inspiration of other persons, and so on. Different individuals may make the same choice for a somewhat different combination of reasons. Other individuals make different choices for substantially different reasons. The problem in a survey is to induce the respondent to identify all the possible reasons that affected him; the problem in analysis is to identify the various combinations of motives and influences that are the principal determinants of decisions. Therefore, our questionnaires contained many long checklists to elicit all the pushes, pulls, and barriers that affected each decision.

We have assumed that decisions are not only due to a combination of attitudes and influences at the time of the choice, but they grow out of earlier decisions as well. The kinds of reasons leading to foreign study will predict many persons' decisions whether to emigrate permanently, return home promptly, or work abroad temporarily. For other persons, experience as a student may be a better predictor of later decisions than the original set of reasons. Therefore, our questionnaires asked respondents to reconstruct past decisions as well as current ones, and considerable information was sought about social origins, educational history and occupational career.

As a result of our multivariate and processual conceptions of decisions, we wrote a very long questionnaire. Several earlier surveys had left issues unsettled because their questionnaires were too short, so we tried to cover very many variables in the same instrument. We risked a high refusal rate and lower quality of responses, but we hoped that the sponsorship by the United Nations would motivate cooperation. We believe that length was not a substantial cause of refusal in most countries, and that the large gain in information offsets any losses of respondents.

The kind of statistical analysis foreseen required maximum standardization and comparability of the data. Therefore, all questionnaires in all countries were nearly identical. During prolonged periods of visits and correspondence between UNITAR and the participating research centers in 1968 and 1969, and by means of pre-tests in several countries, we tried to adopt topics, concepts, and wording that would fit all countries in the project. Minor variations in wording adapted the standard questionnaires to each country.

Questionnaires have been administered in English, French, German, Spanish, Portuguese, Korean, Greek and Farsi. Wording and spelling in English and Spanish followed usage in each country.

After filling out questionnaires, many stay-ons and returnees answered short interviews. Questions dealt with such subjects as experiences at home and abroad and were more flexible than the fixed format required in self-sdministered questionnaires.

DEFINITION OF GROUPS SURVEYED

The design called for questionnaires from three comparable groups:

Students from developing countries matriculated, at the time of the survey, as undergraduates, graduate students, or special students in institutions of higher learning in developed countries;

Returnees -- professional persons working in their home countries at the time of the survey, who had received all or most of their higher education in a developed country;

Stay-ons or nonreturnees -- professional persons from developing countries working in developed countries at the time of the survey, who had obtained some or all of their higher education in a developed country.

The sample of students consisted of:

- persons who had received all or most of their secondary education in a developing country;
- graduate and undergraduate students with at least one year of academic studies in a developed country.
- students in all of higher education, except for medicine and related fields;
- students from a wide range of universities and of comparable professional and advanced training institutions:
  - institutions of varying quality, including both high and low;
  - large and small institutions;
  - institutions in different regions of the host country.

The samples of <u>returnees</u> and <u>stay-ons</u> consisted of:

- persons who had received all or most of their secondary education in a developing country;
- those who completed their higher education in 1960 or later;
- those who had received a degree, diploma, or at least two years of higher education in one of the developed countries we planned to include in the study;
- all fields of specialization, except for medicine and related fields. Some of our research centers in developing countries took "extra" samples of doctors for their national reports.

All three groups--students, returnees, and stay-ons--included men and women, those who went abroad on personal funds or on scholarships, and those who were bonded to return or were unbonded. Professionals who migrated to industrialized countries after obtaining all their education in their home or another developing country are not included in the survey. Professionals in practical training programs run by industrial firms or by government agencies were excluded. Professionals otherwise eligible for the survey were not excluded if they had acquired citizenship in a developed country.

In addition, employers in several developing countries who were in a position to hire foreign-trained professionals have answered questionnaires and have been interviewed. So far, the surveys have been conducted in Brazil, Ghana, India, Republic of Korea, Sri Lanka, and Trinidad and Tobago. It has not been possible to report on those surveys in this volume.

SELECTION OF COUNTRIES

Adequate coverage of students, stay-ons, and returnees required matching surveys in some developed and some developing countries. At the least, we needed developed countries with large numbers of foreign students and with many foreign-born professionals, such as the United States. Various developed countries were invited to take part, because they had many foreign students and because adding more sites for education would strengthen our conclusions about general principles and cross-national variations. The list grew as research centers in additional developed countries became interested in the subject and in participation in an international survey.

Our basic task was to assess the effects of education in developed countries upon the careers of professional persons from developing countries. Therefore, we needed at least a few developing countries that sent their students to several different developed countries, such as India. We expected motivations, influences, and decisions to vary widely among countries, and therefore conclusions would be unreliable if we surveyed only a few. So we sought a considerable range of developing countries according to the following criteria:

different regions of the world;
high and low rates of return for foreign-trained professionals;
various types of educational systems;
traditional orientations toward some of the developed countries (e.g., French-oriented, British-oriented, American-oriented) or orientation toward no one developed country;
different adaptability of the elites to life abroad.

If the sample designs in the student projects included many members of a particular nationality, we tried to arrange a matching survey of returnees. Research centers in some countries heard about the project and asked to join.

In each country we tried to identify and invite survey research centers that would do reliable field work and that would enjoy the trust of respondents. Some were research laboratories at universities, others were autonomous scholarly institutes. Surveys were always done by local teams, never by foreigners. The professional disciplines of the survey staffs were sociology, social psychology, education, or social statistics. In most countries, grants were provided by the government. In a few cases, funds were obtained from private foundations abroad.

This manuscript presents data from the surveys completed by the following research centers:

Surveys of students and stay-ons:

Canada: Département de Sociologie, Université de Montréal; and Institute for Behavioural Research, York University, Toronto.

France: Groupe de sociologie industrielle comparée, Centre National de la Recherche Scientifique, Paris.

United States: Bureau of Applied Social Research, Columbia University, New York; and Chilton Research Services, Philadelphia

Surveys of returnees:

Argentina: Department of Sociology, Fundacion Bariloche, Buenos Aires.

Brazil: Departamento de Pesquisas, Escola Brasileira de Administração Publica, Fundação Getulio Vargas, Rio de Janeiro.

Colombia: Instituto Colombiano de Crédito Educativo y Estudios Técnicos en el Exterior (ICETEX), Bogota.

Ghana: Department of Sociology, University of Ghana, Legon, Accra.

Greece: National Centre of Social Research (EKKE), Athens.

India: Council of Scientific and Industrial Research, New Delhi.

Republic of Korea: Central Education Research Institute, Seoul.

Sri Lanka: Colombo Plan Bureau, Colombo.

Surveys of students still in progress or incomplete:

Australia: Educational Research Unit, Research School of Social Sciences, Australian National University, Canberra.

Federal Republic of Germany: Forschungsinstitut für Soziologie der Universität Köln.

United Kingdom: Political and Economic Planning, London; and Social and Community Planning Research, London.

Surveys of returnees not completed in time for inclusion in this volume:

Iran: Institute of Psychology, University of Tehran.

Pakistan: Department of Statistics, University of Karachi.

Philippines: Statistical Center, University of the Philippines, Manila.

Trinidad and Tobago: Faculty of Social Sciences, University of the West Indies, St. Augustine.

Tunisia: Centre d'Études et de Recherches Économiques et Sociales (CERES), Université de Tunis.

Uruguay: Centro de Investigaciones y Estudios Sociales del Uruguay, Montevideo.

Research centers in other countries have expressed interest in the project, and eventually they may contribute data to the pool.

DESIGN AND REPRESENTATIVENESS OF SAMPLES

Surveys of students. In all our surveys, we attempted to give questionnaires to representative national samples. In developed countries, names of foreign students were picked randomly from lists from a representative selection of universities throughout the nations.

To acquire enough cases for comparisons, some nationalities were oversampled, provided they were among the principal nationalities in the host countries and provided that we had prospects for matching returnee surveys at home. In our analysis, we correct for such sampling variations by the use of weights.

We sought high quality in the field work and

high response rates. But it is very difficult to obtain high returns in surveys of foreign students: many change their addresses and can be traced only with difficulty; those with stable addresses are at home only for short times and most students would rather spend their time in activities other than the completion of questionnaires. Field work in developed countries took place during the early 1970's, when rumors were circulating that governments of those countries would soon reduce foreigners' right to live and work, and these anxieties were further barriers to high completion of our surveys of students.

As we said in Chapter I, the UNITAR survey was intended to cover professions other than medicine and nursing. A recent project by the World Health Organisation (WHO) concentrates on them.[2] However, some persons with future or present careers in medicine and nursing are included in our data: some students not currently enrolled in medical curricula plan to enter them in the future; some students were already qualified in medicine but fell into our samples because they were enrolled in other scientific curricula to prepare them for medical research; because of special interest in the medical brain drain, a few of our survey centers expanded their samples of returnees by adding doctors. Many of our conclusions probably apply to doctors and nurses, but one cannot be sure without new field work. Since the medical brain drain is important, we have brought our research design and findings to the attention of WHO, to assist them prepare their project.

Surveys of returnees. Representative samples of foreign-trained professionals cannot be designed easily in developing nations. Some countries can estimate numbers of professionals from the national

---

[2]A Multi-National Study of the International Migration of Physicians and Nurses (Geneva: World Health Organisation, HMD/73.5, 1973); and Multinational Study of the International Migration of Physicians and Nurses: Second Draft General Protocol (Geneva: World Health Organisation, HMD/HMP/74.1, 1974).

census or from other sources, but these figures are not broken down by place of study. All our survey centers had to spend months polling the principal employers in their countries, to create lists of the professionals educated in whole or in part in developed countries. Some added names from directories or manpower registries of professionals. These methods produced high estimates rather than complete enumerations of the population of foreign-trained, but nevertheless good samples can result. In some countries, respondents can be found easily at their home or office addresses and are cooperative, but this is not true everywhere.

Centers in developing countries drew returnees from the principal countries of study, according to their estimates of the proportions who studied in different places. A few centers added to their basic samples persons educated in developed countries (such as Belgium and Sweden) where we lack matching surveys of students.

Ideally, an explanation of decisions should use control groups of persons who did not make the decision, for comparison with those who had studied abroad. But our resources did not permit comparable surveys of those who had never been abroad.

Surveys of stay-ons. The most difficult and least satisfactory part of our work concerns the group central to a study of brain drain, viz., surveys of the stay-ons in developed countries. Several research centers concluded that no lists of any sort existed, and therefore samples could not be created. Some government agencies have dossiers on all recipients of residence or work permits but claim that rules of confidentiality forbid their use by research projects; even if these files are opened, immense work is necessary to pick out the professionals. In other countries, imperfect lists were found, but they may have omitted many permanent migrants who were trying to merge themselves into the societies of developed countries.

Stay-ons--and particularly the permanent migrants--may be suspicious of surveys, and therefore our completion rates were lower than we hoped. However, our surveys of stay-ons may yield exploratory generalizations that are stronger than mere hypotheses, even if they clearly are not fully proven conclusions. Many patterns in our surveys of stay-ons seem plausible, since they are consistent with similar relationships among the students who expect to work abroad and among the returnees who had once been temporary stay-ons.

ANALYSIS

Since the questionnaires asked questions in identical ways, the data have been coded and arranged in a standard fashion for tabulations. Each research center retains copies of its own data and--with proper safeguards concerning protection of identity of respondents--may obtain copies of data from other countries for comparative analysis.

Several research centers have written or are now writing national reports about their own surveys, viz., the surveys of students in the United States and Canada and the surveys of returnees in Brazil, Colombia, Greece, India, and the Republic of Korea. Other national reports are planned.

STATISTICAL NOTES AND TABULATIONS

Throughout the manuscript, unless otherwise indicated, all statistics are weighted to account for variations in sampling fraction among groups within each national survey.

In addition, when distributions for all students are presented in Chapter II, the respondents are weighted to take account of much larger numbers of foreign students in the United States. At the time of our surveys, the populations of students from developing countries eligible for our enquiry were: United States, 78,000; France, 14,000; and Canada, 7,000. Therefore, in combined tabulations in that chapter, the three samples are weighted 11:2:1. Without this weighting, the lower rate of return peculiar to Canada would substantially alter the total results.

In all tables, total numbers of respondents are the unweighted sums of persons.

Many tables in the manuscript are constructed like Table II-4. First, respondents are classified by their answers to one question in the survey. (In Table II-4, they are classified by answers to the questions about their own career plans, divided into (1) returning home and (2) staying abroad or uncertain about future plans.) The total number of respondents in each such classification appears in the lower half of the table in parentheses. Second, how each such category answers some other question in the survey is calculated, and those statistics appear in the upper half of the table. (In Table II-4, the figures in the upper half are the percentages of the members of each classification who named their home countries as the ideal locations for their children.)

VALIDITY OF OUR QUESTION ABOUT MIGRATION PLANS

How accurate is the information elicited for our central dependent variable, viz., the answer to the question about long-term migration plans? The wording is the following:

> What do you expect to do in the future --i.e., what do you realistically anticipate rather than prefer?
>
> I definitely will return to my country of origin
>
> I probably will return to my country of origin
>
> I am uncertain whether to return there or to stay abroad

I probably will remain abroad to live and work permanently

I definitely will remain abroad to live and work permanently

Survey of returnees:

What do you expect to do in the future -- i.e., what do you realistically anticipate rather than prefer?

I definitely will stay in this country [actual name of the country was used]

I probably will stay in this country [actual name of the country was used]

I am uncertain whether to stay here or to go abroad

I probably will go to another country to live and work permanently

I definitely will go to another country to live and work permanently

The distribution of answers to these questions appears in Table II-1, supra.

A problem is whether the question elicits accurate statements about the respondent's migration plans. Do many give false answers, so that our distribution is far from the truth? Would those who failed to fill out questionnaires give answers different from respondents, so that our completed samples do not accurately represent the populations? Are the popular legends about enormous brain drain correct while our statistics -- showing return by large majorities -- are wrong?

Proportions of students and professionals who emigrate. Earlier surveys show a very wide range in the proportions planning to emigrate. Our proportions are lower than those in some other surveys, for several reasons. We excluded certain groups with very high migration rates that predominated in some previous samples: all citizens of developed countries, all Chinese, and all Cubans. Our definition of migration was based on the long-term plans described in the question quoted above; many previous studies got higher rates because they employed much looser definitions of migration, such as any temporary work abroad or merely obtaining a residence visa.

When the same nationalities are matched -- i.e., by comparing our Table III-1 with previous surveys of the same groups -- other surveys usually showed slightly higher rates of return home. Instead of missing brain drain that other surveys have documented, we located slightly more of it.

The data seem internally consistent. Certain other variables that should correlate highly with migration plans do so, such as migration preference and influence of the spouse.

We believe we can detect concealment. We received a few questionnaires from respondents who deliberately gave mixed-up answers, and these documents read quite differently from all the others.

We have encountered some differences from earlier research. For example, age, social class and ability do not correlate as strongly with emigration as in previous surveys. But, as we noted in the reviews of the literature in our footnotes, some findings had not been as consistent as had been supposed. Some differences between our findings and these earlier studies might result from our samples: compared to earlier surveys, our samples were more heterogeneous and more representative. If our subsamples were matched more exactly with theirs, perhaps these results would be duplicated.

Is a question about migration plans sufficiently reliable that it evokes consistent answers from the same respondent at different times? The only such reliability test yet conducted showed that persons answer such a question the same way.[3]

Does any question about migration plans -- whether asked by us or by others -- produce answers that accurately predict behavior? The only follow-up study done so far established high accuracy for such a question.[4]

Cooperativeness by respondents. Our field representatives in most countries filled out forms describing their encounters with members of the samples who did and did not fill out questionnaires. The reports about the respondents are part of their machine-readable data at present, so that we can run tables comparing responses classified by respondents' attitudes toward the survey, their apparent understanding of the questionnaire, and so on. The hostile and suspicious respondents were more likely to emigrate than the others. But only small proportions were antagonistic among the respondents who answered and among the students who refused. Very few returnees refused in some countries, slightly more in others. If many of the refusals were due to hostility and suspicion toward the project, the proportions of persons in the population planning to emigrate would be somewhat higher than our estimates. But probably the difference would not be great.

Project representatives filled out a form about each person who failed to fill out a questionnaire. The behavior of the person and the reasons for non-response are entered. In research we hope to conduct in the future concerning the statistics of cross-national comparisons, we will use these non-response forms to compare systematically the

---

[3] Josefina Bulatao Jayme, Demographic and Socio-Psychological Determinants of the Migration of Highly Trained Filipinos to the United States (Pittsburgh: dissertation for the Ph.D. in Psychology, Carnegie-Mellon University, 1971), pp. 28-29.

[4] Robert G. Myers, "International Education, Emigration, and National Policy (A Longitudinal Case Study of Peruvians Trained in the United States)", Comparative Education Review, Volume XVII, Number 1 (February 1973), pp. 81-82.

characteristics of the respondents and non-respondents. Then we might estimate whether the counterparts of the non-respondents who filled out questionnaires differ essentially from the rest of the sample, so that more of the non-respondents might have altered the results. We can then estimate the statistical error when generalizing solely about respondents.

The largest numbers of refusals were encountered in the surveys of stay-ons. We will study their non-response forms carefully to estimate the proportions that might be involved in the permanent brain drain.

Missing persons on our lists. Foreign students proved more difficult to find than we had expected. Returnees were easy to find except in a few countries with considerable domestic geographical mobility. Were the persons who changed addresses or failed to keep appointments more likely to emigrate? Because of migration motives, were some trying to hide from our field staff? If we had higher completion rates, would our return rates be lower?

Our present data enable us to compare the respondents who were easy to find and elusive: the reports by the project representatives were coded, respondents can be classified as more or less difficult to find, and we have related these categories with answers on the question about migration plans. In such tables, the persons who were more difficult to locate and who were more reluctant to fill out questionnaires were more -- not less -- likely to return. The persons less assimilated into the bureaucratic ways of developed countries are the ones who change locations without leaving forwarding addresses, fail to answer their mail, forget appointments with interviewers, and avoid filling out long questionnaires. And they are more likely to return home.

In the surveys of foreign students, a number of persons on our original lists could not be found because they had already gone home; or, they left the country after our interviewer delivered the questionnaire but before he could pick it up. In the surveys of students, probably the number of "can't locates" (who may tend to return home) more than offsets the number of refusers (who may tend to emigrate).

A few parts of the project depended on mail, and we cannot guess the reasons for non-response. However, one group -- the Brazilian students in the United States -- was queried both by field representatives and by mail. Comparing the two suggests some bias from the lower response by mail: of the 110 Brazilians who answered by mail 94 per cent planned to return home; of the 170 who were contacted personally by our field staff, 91 per cent planned to return. Of the 230 stay-ons in the United States who answered by mail, 29 per cent planned to return; of the 104 stay-ons personally contacted by a representative of the project, 26 per cent planned to return. Therefore, probably the persons who failed to return questionnaires in that part of the survey conducted by mail are slightly more likely to emigrate than those who answered.

Appendix B

THE EFFECT OF REASONS ON ACTUAL PLANS TO RETURN HOME OR STAY ABROAD

Chapter VI analyzed several batteries of reasons for preferring one's home country or a foreign country. Tables VI-1 and VI-2 showed whether each reason operated on behalf of return or emigration, and whether each reason was common or rare in frequency. The next problem is the effect of each reason upon actual migration plans.

Statistical methods. Table B-1 gives the measures of association ("gamma") between each reason and the respondents' plans to return home or to stay abroad. Gamma varies between +1, if two variables are perfectly associated; 0 if they are independent; and -1 if higher values of the independent variable are associated with lower values of the dependent variable. Gamma would be +1 if every person saying that a reason induced him to return home actually returned; if everyone who said that a reason left him undecided was also uncertain about his ultimate destination; and if everyone who said that a reason directed him abroad also intended to emigrate. Gamma is 0 if the distribution of answers on the two questions--i.e., a reason for choice of countries and the persons' actual migration plans--are statistically independent. Gamma would be -1 if every person did precisely the opposite of what he said a reason induced him to do.[1]

[1] The purposes and formulae for gamma are in Leo A. Goodman and William H. Kruskal, "Measures of Association for Cross Classifications," Journal of the American Statistical Association, Volume 49 (December 1954), pp. 732-764. Comparisons of gamma and of the other common measures of association that we

All the gammas in Table B-1 are positive, indicating that all reasons are associated with migration plans: if persons say that a reason directs them home, they usually plan to go there; if they say that a reason influences them toward foreign countries, enough go there to reduce the skew toward return in the general distribution of our data;[2] persons not affected in either direction on a reason are often undecided about their actual plans. Gamma is a measure of consistency and reversals in the order between two variables, and the large positive numbers in Table B-1 mean that the foregoing pattern is followed far more often than it is reversed. Very strong association (i.e., a number close to 1.00) is not achieved for any reason, in large part because of the bias (the "skew" in the statistics) toward permanent return: many respondents are not affected by a reason or say it influences them to emigrate, but they return nevertheless. Very strong disassociation (i.e., a number close to -1.00) is not achieved, because this would mean that nearly everyone does the opposite of his inclinations.

In the first three columns of Table B-1 are the measures of association between each reason and migration plans at each stage in study and in professional careers. The first column combines the answers by all students, by all nonreturnees, and by all returnees referring to their states of mind during or at the end of study abroad; these respondents appeared previously in Table VI-1. The second column combines the answers of all stay-ons and by those re-

---

calculated to confirm its results appear in ibid.; in Herbert L. Costner, "Criteria for Measures of Association," American Sociological Review, Volume 30, Number 3 (June 1965), pp. 341-353; and in Jae-On Kim, "Predictive Measures of Ordinal Association," American Journal of Sociology, Volume 76, Number 5 (March 1971), pp. 891-907.

[2] A persistent statistical complication in our data is the skewed distribution of many answers. Far more persons plan to return than to emigrate. On most reasons for migration or return--as Table VI-1 showed--the numbers giving one answer about a country are far larger than the numbers giving the other response. (I.e., the "home" percentage is much larger than the "abroad" percentage, or "abroad" is much larger than "home.")

Table B-1

How Reasons Predict Plans at Different Stages of the Professional's Career

Reasons	Answers of all respondents: During or at end of study	Answers of all respondents: During or at end of work	Answers of all respondents: After return	Answers about state of mind at time of survey by: Students	Answers about state of mind at time of survey by: Stay-ons
1. Working conditions:					
a) Contribution to profession	.42	.32	.41	.48	.22
b) Income	.48	.38	.52	.54	.35
c) Quality of jobs	.49	.36	.52	.54	.34
d) Number of jobs	.48	.34	.47	.57	.40
e) Housing	.26	.28	.27	.36	.17
2. Professional needs:					
a) Contacts	.31	.27	.39	.30	.12
b) Sufficient time	.33	.33	.32	.42	.38
c) Libraries	.22	.28	.37	.19	.11
d) Equipment	.26	.17	.36	.30	.11
e) Space	.26	.17	.27	.30	.26
f) Status of professionals	.31	.26	.36	.40	.34

Complete wording of the items is in Table VI-1. The numbers are Goodman's and Kruskal's gamma. A full explanation of this table is in the text of Appendix B.

Contents of each column... First column: all respondents from all surveys, based on answers by students about their current thinking, and on the recollections by stay-ons and returnees as they were finishing studies. Second column: all stay-ons in the United States and France, and returnees who worked abroad; the stay-ons answered about their thinking at the time of the survey and the returnees told how they thought as they were finishing work abroad. Third column: all returnees from India, Sri Lanka, Republic of Korea, Ghana, Greece, Brazil, Colombia, and Argentina. Fourth column: all students from the United States, Canada, and France. Fifth column: all stay-ons from the United States and France.

[continued]

Table B-1 [continued]

Reasons	Answers of all respondents: During or at end of study	During or at end of work	After return	Answers about state of mind at time of survey by: Students	Stay-ons
3. Colleagues:					
a) Fellow workers for discussion	.24	.24	.35	.27	.25
b) Assistants	.21	.14	.28	.27	.17
4. Societal setting:					
a) Cultural level	.24	.25	.21	.34	.51
b) Challenge of life	.21	.40	.32	.50	.37
5. Alienation and discrimination:					
a) Feel strange	.41	.52	.24	.48	.55
b) Discrimination	.25	.41	.14	.32	.57
6. Politics:					
a) Political conditions	.41	.45	.31	.45	.26
b) Language policies	.43	.53	.40	.42	.36
7. Citizenship:					
a) Maintain existing rights	.49	.43	.19	.59	.31
b) Acquire new rights	.65	.56	.25	.71	.54
8. Influence of others:					
a) Patriotism	.50	.51	.26	.64	.62
b) Obligations to family	.38	.40	.16	.58	.43
c) Influence of family	.37	.40	.10	.57	.48
d) Influence of friends	.35	.20	.28	.52	.33
9. Interests of spouse and children:					
a) Spouse feelings	.47	.36	.41	.63	.24
b) Education of children	.51	.59	.40	.59	.44
c) Careers of children	.55	.65	.41	.62	.40
d) Marriage of children	.39	.34	.20	.51	.53
Total number of respondents	(5,981)	(922)	(2,819)	(2,765)	(386)

turnees who worked abroad, where the reasons referred to the state of mind during or at the end of work abroad; these respondents have not been combined in any earlier table, but they were described separately on earlier pages of Chapter VI. The third column is based on the answers by all returnees concerning influences at the time of the survey. Columns four and five of Table B-1 are confined to students and stay-ons separately and refer to current states of mind. Column three might be repeated as if it were a "column six": it reports the current state of mind of the returnees and therefore is a counterpart to the fourth and fifth columns.

Within each column, the highest numbers identify the reasons that best predict migration plans. Certain reasons seem leading predictors at all stages, although some weaken in the survey of returnees. Several reasons fluctuate in importance at different stages.

Differences in strength of reasons. Several reasons in the cluster concerning working conditions are associated strongly with migration plans at the end of study and after return, notably opportunity to contribute to one's profession, income, quality of jobs, and number of jobs (items 1a, 1b, 1c, and 1d). But other motives and influences seem stronger at the stay-on stage.

The items in the cluster concerning influences of others predict migration plans strongly in the stages of foreign study and work overseas, but they weaken after return. Patriotism has some of the highest gammas at the stage of foreign study, at the stage of work abroad, in the student survey by itself, and in the stay-on surveys (items 8a, 8b, and 8c in the first, second, fourth and fifth columns). The influence of friends is a strong predictor in the survey of students (item 8d, with a gamma of .52). The weakening of these reasons among returnees is due to the increased strength of other reasons keeping them home; gamma is lower for returnees (item 8d is .28) because, in the increasingly rare cases when a returnee says these reasons operate on behalf of emigration, the proportion of such persons planning to go abroad is lower than among persons giving these as reasons for foreign stays in the surveys of students and stay-ons.

The education and careers of children are strong predictors of migration plans in all stages and in all surveys (items 9b and 9c). The marriage prospects of children are moderately related to migration plans of the students and stay-ons but weaken in the survey of returnees (item 9d). As in other items involving influences of family and children the weaker power of prediction results from the fact that, when returnees believe the children would be better served by life abroad, many expect nevertheless to continue living in the home country. The feelings of the wife or husband are strong predictors for everyone except the stay-ons, among whom they have slightly weaker influence: among some stay-on, foreign spouses will return against their wishes; while some spouses from the home country will stay abroad unenthusiastically (item 9a).

Several other reasons are strong or moderate predictors at different stages as well: feelings of unfamiliarity with one or another country during study and during work abroad (for item 5, gamma = .41 and .52), a sense of discrimination either during or at end of work abroad (among stay-ons for item 5b, gamma = .41), political conditions during the student and stay-on stages (items 6a and 6b), and interest in maintaining old citizenship rights or acquiring new ones at the student and stay-on stages (items 7a and 7b). Except for government language policies, which have arisen recently and affect returnees as their children become old enough to attend school (item 6b), all these reasons are weaker predictors for the returnees than for others. The explanation is that a number of returnees who say these causes by themselves would attract them abroad nevertheless plan to remain home for other reasons.

Opportunities for professional development are a moderately strong predictor of migration plans (item 2b), but the other reasons referring to professional needs and colleagues (Clusters 2 and 3) are among the weakest predictors in the battery. Most respondents deem these strong attractions of developed countries but return home nevertheless for other reasons. Unlike other predictors in the battery, the gammas are higher for returnees than for students and stay-ons among many items in Clusters 2 and 3. The explanation is a greater convergence between perceptions and plans: an increased number of those returnees planning to stay think the facilities and personnel are good enough at home; an increased number who are critical of the facilities and personnel become disillusioned and decide to leave for these and other reasons.

Appendix C

CALCULATION OF INCOME DIFFERENTIALS AND THEIR EFFECTS

Measurement of expected income differences. To make estimates, the questionnaires asked for respondents' monthly income estimates -- combining salaries, fees, profits, fringe benefits, and free services -- for the following situations and times:

(1) During any work at home:

(a) in first year of full-time employment or (among returnees) next year

(b) five years thereafter

(2) During any work abroad:

(a) in first year of full-time employment or (among stay-ons) next year

(b) five years thereafter

(3) If the stay-ons did not expect to return or if the returnee expected to leave, the minimum income that would induce him to work at home

(4) If the stay-ons expected to return or the returnee expected to stay, the minimum income that would induce him to work abroad

(5) And several other items.

Every respondent gave estimates for both his income expected either at home or abroad and the hypothetical income he would earn in the other location. Each answered in two currencies, viz., the salary rates at home and in the foreign country where he studied or worked. At the time of writing, we have over 6,000 answers in nearly all the currencies of the world.

A variety of investigations can be pursued in our data.[1] Chapter VI contained an introductory summary of findings about the sizes of income differences and their relationship to long-term migration plans. The data were obtained from the following questions:

Survey of students:

(a) If you return to your country of origin after completing your studies here, what is about the average income you can obtain five years [after the first year of full-time employment], expressed in the currency of that country?

(b) If you stay in this country, what is about the average income you can obtain here five years [after the first year of full-time employment], expressed in the currency of this country?

Survey of stay-ons:

(a) If you return to your country of origin now, what is about the average income you

---

[1] For example, in one of the few analyses of the effects of income on brain drain, John Niland used as his central variables (1) the ratio between income expected at home and the minimum offer from home guaranteeing return; and (2) the ratio between income expected at home and minimum offer from abroad guaranteeing emigration. John Niland, The Asian Engineering Brain Drain (Lexington: Heath Lexington Books, 1970). We can make similar analyses with more respondents and nationalities, since we asked the same questions.

can obtain five years [after the first year of full-time employment] expressed in the currency of that country?

(b) If you stay in this country, what is about the average income you can obtain here [six years from now], expressed in the currency of this country?

Survey of returnees:

(a) If you stay in this country, what is about the average income you can obtain [six years from now]?

(b) If you had stayed in the foreign country where you were educated, what is about the average income you could obtain there five years [after the first year of full-time employment], expressed in the currency of that country?

The data were coded in the original currencies. By computer programming, we first converted all into the American dollar, according to the free (or official) exchange rates prevailing when the data were collected. For example, if country X has an official exchange rate of four units to the dollar, we first divided its citizens' estimates of future income by one-fourth. If the surveys of students and returnees were conducted at different times and the members of the same nationality fell into both, two conversion rates were used, depending on when the respondent filled out a questionnaire.

If the conversions did not go beyond exchanges with the dollar, the difference between country X and the United States would be exaggerated. The United States seems to offer much higher salaries and -- if citizens expect to return to country X and accept so much smaller incomes -- it appears as if large salary differences have weak effects on migration. But the true difference between the United States and country X is smaller, if the cost of living is much higher in the United States. We need a conversion system based on purchasing power equivalents among all countries in the world, but this requires a research project by itself.[2]

We attempted to deflate the currencies of the countries with more expensive living costs by means of the system of retail price comparisons devised by the United Nations to determine salary differentials of its officials.[3] The result is a standard currency unit that pays for equivalent goods and services in different countries at similar prices. High salaries in expensive countries thereby move closer in the conversion to resemble low salaries in countries with low prices. High salaries in inexpensive countries remain high; low salaries in expensive countries stand out as unusually low in international comparisons. Our conversion methods are imperfect and will be refined in our future analysis.

Expected monthly incomes. Table C-1 shows the median predictions of monthly salaries five years after the next year of full-time employment, converted into standard currency units. The column headed "abroad" for students and stay-ons gives the rates expected in each of those countries -- i.e., all students in the United States were referring to American employment; all stay-ons in France gave prospective

[2] Such as the extensive work done for earlier periods and for fewer countries by Morton Gilbert and Irving B. Kravis, An International Comparison of National Products and the Purchasing Power of Currencies (Paris: Organisation for European Economic Cooperation, 1954); Stanley N. Braithwaite, "Real Income Levels in Latin America," The Review of Income and Wealth, Series 14, Number 2 (June 1968), pp. 113-182; and Wilfred Beckerman and Robert Bacon, "The International Distribution of Incomes," in Paul Streeten (editor), Unfashionable Economics (London: Weidenfeld and Nicolson, 1970), pp. 56-74. Professor Kravis is now developing a more up-to-date set of purchasing power equivalents that will be available to us in the future.

[3] Described in part in Retail Price Comparisons for International Salary Determination (United National Statistical Office, Statistical Papers, Series M, Number 14 (add. 3, 1962). Our calculations used the schedule of daily subsistence allowance rates outside capital cities for the second half of 1971.

Table C-1

Expected Monthly Incomes at Home and Abroad

	Expected monthly income		Total number of respondents answering the question	
	At home	Abroad	At home	Abroad
All respondents	256	414	(5,202)	(4,654)
Students in:				
United States	354	422	(1,385)	(1,353)
Canada	161	351	(632)	(656)
France	245	243	(258)	(246)
Stay-ons in:				
United States	190	615	(284)	(311)
France	468	591	(49)	(54)
Returnees in:				
India	182	420	(565)	(488)
Sri Lanka	127	320	(194)	(111)
Korea, Republic of	115	350	(243)	(232)
Greece	508	456	(410)	(300)
Ghana	198	362	(135)	(85)
Brazil	537	519	(456)	(367)
Colombia	493	450	(243)	(184)
Argentina	281	466	(348)	(267)

As explained in the text, the incomes are standard currency units, corrected for variations in living costs. If each number is multiplied by 2.9, the figures are American dollars at prices in 1971.

French wages, converted in the table into our standard units. The column headed "at home" for students and stay-ons mixes pay rates from many home countries. The column headed "at home" for returnees gives figures for each of those countries -- i.e., all Indians refer to India, all Koreans refer to Korea -- converted into our standard units. The column headed "abroad" for returnees mixes incomes from several countries of study, but half the returnees refer to the United States.

Absolute and relative differentials by home country and by country of study. Table C-2 summarizes the gains expected by respondents if they work abroad rather than at home. The left-hand side of the table shows the difference -- converted into our standard currency units per month -- between the figures foreseen at home and abroad. The numbers are medians calculated by the computer: for each group, half the numbers are larger and half are smaller. If too few students or professionals fall into a category for reliable calculations, the space is left empty.

Most numbers on the left side of Table C-2 are positive, indicating that the respondents expected to earn higher real incomes abroad. Where the numbers are negative, over half the persons in that category expected to earn a higher real income at home. If the higher salaries in developed countries had not been corrected for their higher living costs, all cells would be positive. Only 16 per cent expect to earn more at home than abroad in absolute figures; when incomes are converted into purchasing power equivalents, 30 per cent expect to earn more at home. The standard deviations and the measure of kurtosis[4] (not shown in the table) are large, indicating a very wide range. The same nationality and the same developed country appear in several places in the table:

[4] Kurtosis is the shape of the distribution of data. A large number for a statistical measure of kurtosis means that many cases of similar value are distributed widely around the average score in the data. A low number for a statistical measure of kurtosis means that many cases are bunched closely around a single score.

for example, Indian students in the United States are in Part 1, Indian stay-ons working in the United States are in Part 2, and Indian returnees educated in the United States are in Part 3.

The right-hand part of the table shows the number of times that income expected abroad exceeds the income expected at home. Numbers are median ratios. Those anticipating more at home have scores lower than 1.00. A figure like 2.00 means the foreign income is twice the domestic income.

The size of gains results from a combination of the rates expected at home and abroad. The largest increases both in absolute numbers and in relative gains are obtained by persons from low-income home countries working in high-income developed countries. For example, Indian students and stay-ons believe they can earn over three times their domestic pay in the United States, and the Indian returnees nearly three times. If a home country pays well, the gains from foreign employment are low. For example, Brazilians and Colombians believe they can earn more at home, even compared to the United States. If a developed country has a lower wage structure for all professionals or if it provides only limited opportunities for foreigners, the professional may earn more at home. For example, the average foreign student in France expects to earn about the same at home, but the figures vary widely among nationalities.

Absolute and relative gains for the same nationality vary by country of study. They can be compared by reading along the same line across Table C-2. In the developed countries with lower wage structures for foreign professionals, such as France and the United Kingdom, both the absolute and relative gains are lower than those in the United States and Canada. (I.e., the columns for France in Parts 1, 2, and 3, and the column for the United Kingdom in Part 3 show numbers lower than those in the columns for the United States and Canada.)

Comparing the American and Canadian patterns in Table C-2 is more complex because of differences between their student bodies: some foreign students

Table C-2

Expected Income Differentials Between
Developing and Developed Countries*

*The construction of the table and the entries are described in the text. In short, "absolute gain" is calculated by subtracting the income expected at home from the income expected abroad. "Proportional gain" is calculated by dividing the income expected at home into the income expected abroad. For example, the average foreign student in the United States expected to earn 99 units more a month if he stayed in the United States, and this would give him 1.29 times the pay expected at home. (First line in Part 1, first and fourth columns.) The average Indian returnee educated in the United States expected to earn 321 units more a month if he stayed in the United States, and this would give him 2.79 times the pay expected at home. (First line in Part 3, second and seventh columns.) All figures are medians: half the respondents had more and half had less.

Part 1 gives results from the surveys of students in the United States, Canada and France. The first line ("all respondents") summarizes the entire sample, but the remaining lines give only the larger nationalities. By reading down a column, one can compare different nationalities in the same survey of students. (For example, in the Canadian survey, the Indians expected to earn 2.91 times home pay each month if they stayed in Canada, and the Pakistanis expected to earn 3.44 times.) By reading across a row, one can compare the same nationality's expectations in different countries. (For example, Egyptian students expected to obtain in monthly gains over home salaries 1.90 in the United States, 2.53 in Canada, but less money--i.e., 0.76--in France.) If a nationality had too few members in one of the samples, the calculations would not be reliable, and those entries do not appear in Part 1.

[continued]

Table C-2 [continued]

Part 2 gives results from the surveys of stay-ons in the United States and France. The first line ("all respondents") summarizes the entire sample, but the remining lines give only the larger nationalities. As in Part 1, different nationalities in the same sample can be compared by reading down each column.

Part 3 gives results from eight surveys of returnees. The first and sixth columns summarize all responses from each sample. Columns two through four (and seven through ten) divide each returnee sample into the principal countries of study. By reading across a row, one can compare the same nationality's expectations in different countries. (For example, Indian returnees expected to obtain 2.79 times home salaries in the United States, 2.76 in Canada, and 1.47 in the United Kingdom.)

Table C-2 [continued]

Types of survey and home country	Absolute gain abroad in standard currency units — Country of survey			Proportional gain abroad — Country of survey		
	United States	Canada	France	United States	Canada	France
(1) Surveys of students from:						
All respondents	99	192	-12	1.29	2.21	0.95
India	310	246	250	3.36	2.91	2.77
Pakistan	167	264		1.98	3.44	
Korea, Republic of	285	284		3.02	4.94	
Philippines	145			1.93		
Tunisia			63			1.28
Egypt	195	215	-64	1.90	2.53	0.76
Iran	-30	68	-121	0.92	1.25	0.70
Lebanon	151	84	-49	1.54	1.30	0.83
Greece	22			1.05		
Ghana	253	132		1.94	1.70	
Senegal			8			1.05
Ivory Coast			-56			0.76
Cameroon			50			1.17
Brazil	-51			0.88		
Colombia	-69			0.83		
Argentina	-122			0.80		
Trinidad	229	128		1.97	1.66	
Jamaica	59	7		1.14	1.03	
Haiti	-64	180		0.83	2.42	

[continued]

Table C-2 [continued]

Types of survey and home country	Absolute gain abroad in standard currency units: Country of survey		Proportional gain abroad: Country of survey	
	United States	France	United States	France
(2) Surveys of stay-ons from:				
All respondents	394	148	3.36	1.34
India	455		3.92	
Korea, Republic of	489		4.26	
Iran	-269		0.66	
Tunisia		278		2.15
Brazil	63		1.11	
Argentina	-12		.98	

[continued]

Table C-2 [continued]

Types of survey and home country	Absolute gain abroad in standard currency units					Proportional gain abroad				
	All respondents in each survey of returnees	Countries where respondents were educated				All respondents in each survey of returnees	Countries where respondents were educated			
		United States	Canada	France	United Kingdom		United States	Canada	France	United Kingdom
(3) Surveys of returnees from:										
India	223	321	301	105	89	2.24	2.79	2.76	1.59	1.47
Sri Lanka	174	256	288		100	2.35	3.34	3.68		1.86
Korea, Republic of	238	239		51	352	2.94	3.00		1.30	3.87
Greece	-38	50		3	-33	.93	1.11		1.00	0.92
Ghana	127	243	152		103	1.69	2.18	1.79		1.55
Brazil	-67	-125	47			.88	0.80	1.12		
Colombia	-49	-56		31	-63	.92	0.89		1.09	0.84
Argentina	176	228		72	242	1.59	1.79		1.34	2.40

going to Canada have income expectations at home lower than the prospects of their compatriots studying in the United States. (Table C-1 shows the lower income expectations of the foreign students in Canada.) Consequently, while Pakistanis, Koreans, Egyptians, and Iranians expect higher incomes in the United States than in Canada, their compatriots in Canada have lower domestic starting points and predict larger proportional gains. The economic attraction of Canada is not only a wage structure that resembles the United States more closely than Europe, but also prospects for large pay increases for those with moderate economic expectations.

Absolute and relative differentials by specialty. Domestic expectations, absolute gain, and proportional gain vary by specialty, according to tabulations that we shall not present here. The highest incomes at home are earned by doctors, business managers, architects, and social scientists (particularly economists). The lowest are received by home managers, biologists, agricultural specialists, physical scientists, and specialists in languages. Some, but not all, of the low-paid specialties report the highest gains from careers abroad, viz., the biologists, agricultural specialists, and physical scientists. Some specialties paid well at home -- such as architects and business managers -- have the lowest relative gains abroad.

The financial situation of the biological scientists and the specialists in languages is part of their discontent, described earlier in Chapter V. They believe they lack facilities, colleagues, contacts with developments elsewhere in the world, stimulating colleagues, and recognition. They believe they earn too little money in developing countries, and our data show their incomes are indeed comparatively low and would be much higher abroad. Consequently, their emigration rates exceed those of other specialties.

Effects of income differentials on migration plans. Table C-3 relates migration plans to the proportional gains reported in the two previous tables. Entries are the coefficients for describing the linear relationship between plans (the dependent variable) and proportional income gains (the predictor). Similar correlations and similar variations among samples result when respondents' plans are associated with absolute gains in expected income between home and abroad.

The first two columns of Table C-3 describe how migration plans can be predicted from expectations about income gains. Positive relationships exist, but they are weak. Because so many other variables determine migration, income gain alone is not sufficient to predict the respondent's ultimate destination: for non-monetary reasons, many persons return home despite much lower pay, while some leave home despite only moderate gains abroad. The correlation coefficients are often "statistically significant" because of the large numbers of cases and are no weaker than most other simple zero-order relations in the social sciences, where multivariate relations abound, but they fall short of the widespread assumption that higher income offers from abroad should produce greater brain drain.

In the first two columns of Table C-3, income gains predict migration better in some samples than in others. The correlations and the proportions of total variance accounted for by income are largest among students in the United States and Canada, stay-ons in France, and returnees in Korea. In no sample does income gain explain more than four per cent of the total variance. The relationships are weakest among the students in France and the returnees in Brazil and Argentina: prospective stay-ons among the foreign students in France expect to earn only slightly more or even less abroad; many Brazilians expect to earn more money at home and also most expect to remain there, so the returnees are too uniform to allow enough statistical variation; the Argentinian returnees show a wider range in income expectations, but it is the small number of potential migrants who expect the least financial gains abroad.

The third and fourth columns of Table C-3 show the form of the relationship that best describes the effects of income on migration plans. They give the coefficients A and B for the regression equation and regression line Y = A + BX, where Y refers to migration plans and X refers to proportional gains in income. Y can vary between 1 and 5, corresponding to the codes for responses to the question about migration plans in our data:

Y equals	If all respondents had answered
1	Definitely return home and remain
2	Probably return home and remain
3	Undecided
4	Probably go abroad and stay
5	Definitely go abroad and stay

The "intercept" is the migration likelihood in a sample when the prospective financial gain from emigration is lowest -- i.e., when X = O, Y = A. The intercepts are largest in those samples with the strongest plans to emigrate and the weakest plans to stay, such as the stay-ons in the United States and France and the returnees in Sri Lanka and Argentina.[5]

For example, in the survey of students in the United States, Y = 1.730 + .082X. Therefore for each increment in pay abroad (X):

Gain (X)	Equation		Migration score (Y)
1	1.730 + .082(1)	=	1.812
2	1.730 + .082(2)	=	1.894
3	1.730 + .082(3)	=	1.976
4	1.730 + .082(4)	=	2.058
5	1.730 + .082(5)	=	2.140
6	1.730 + .082(6)	=	2.222
7	1.730 + .082(7)	=	2.304

In other words, offering seven times the salary expected at home by itself will decrease chances of return for the average student in the United States only slightly below the plan to return home "probably."

[5]An alternative regression equation is created by converting both variables into "standard scores". Then A = O and B (or beta) equals the correlation coefficient R.

Table C-3

Effects of Increased Gains in Expected Income Upon Plans

Surveys	Correlation (Pearson's r)	R^2--i.e., per cent of variance explained	Intercept (A)	Slope (B)	Number of respondents answering all questions
All respondents	.180	.033	1.803	0.126	(4,204)
All students	.195	.038	1.793	0.149	(1,969)
All stay-ons	.028	.001	3.270	0.018	(323)
All returnees	.078	.006	1.735	0.044	(1,912)
Students in:					
United States	.124	.015	1.730	0.082	(1,257)
Canada	.162	.026	2.398	0.136	(516)
France	.027	.001	1.584	0.059	(196)
Stay-ons in:					
United States	.098	.010	3.006	0.061	(277)
France	.201	.040	3.531	0.307	(46)
Returnees in:					
India	.104	.011	1.693	0.078	(484)
Sri Lanka	.144	.021	2.101	0.061	(110)
Korea, Republic of	.165	.027	1.330	0.063	(222)
Greece	.154	.024	1.455	0.086	(269)
Ghana	.192	.037	1.243	0.227	(82)

[continued]

Table C-3 [continued]

Surveys	Correlation (Pearson's r)	R^2--i.e., per cent of variance explained	Intercept (A)	Slope (B)	Number of respondents answering all questions
Returnees in:					
Brazil	.042	.002	1.673	0.044	(345)
Colombia	.114	.013	1.987	0.142	(177)
Argentina	.062	.004	2.102	-.036	(223)

In order to limit the effects of a few outlying cases that probably constituted response, coding, or keypunching errors, the calculations used only those proportional gains between 0.30 and 20 times income at home. If migration plans are converted by logarithmic transformation to reduce the effects of the skewed distribution, the results are virtually identical; Table C-3 uses the untransformed distribution, since the intercept and slope are in units of the codes for the original question and can be understood more easily in the text. The intercept can vary between 1 and 5 since (as we explained in the text), Y can vary between 1 (if everyone said he would return) and 5 (if everyone said he would emigrate).

How large an income offer would convert an entire group to indecision or toward emigration? In numerical terms, how large must X be in order to bring about Y = 3, or Y = 4, or Y = 5? Because the association between income gains alone and permanent migration is weak, enormous offers would be necessary.

For example, in the survey of students in the United States:

To achieve	Equation	Proportional gain required
Y = 3	3 = 1.730 + .082(X)	X = 15.5
Y = 4	4 = 1.730 + .082(X)	X = 27.7

In the survey of returnees in India in Table B-3, the following offers would be required to bring about complete shifts toward indecision and emigration:

To achieve	Equation	Proportional gain required
Y = 3	3 = 1.693 + .078(X)	X = 16.7
Y = 4	4 = 1.693 + .078(X)	X = 29.6

Variations at different intervals. Even though simple linear relationships between income gains and emigration are moderate in some samples and very weak in others, associations in another form might have greater predictive power. Perhaps higher income offers have great effects, but only after a particular threshold. However, no sudden jumps in migration plans appear consistently among samples. Shifts in plans are sometimes larger at some point, but their location varies among samples. This suggests that curvilinear regression would not be much more informative than the linear regressions reported in Table C-3.

Variations among types of people. Even if improved money offers have weak effects on most people's migration decisions, perhaps they affect some who are peculiarly responsive to money. The simplest classification is the respondent's own judgment whether money is important to him. A battery of questions about occupational values asked the respondent to "check all those characteristics of a job which are important to you, when you think of an ideal job." A category that could be checked was "good salary." The statistical results are:

Money important	Correlation (r)	Intercept (A)	Slope (B)
Yes	.209	1.813	.159
No	.128	1.716	.079

The results are expected in direction but disappointing in size. The large correlation and slope show that increased income prospects are associated with migration decisions more strongly among persons interested in money than among persons not interested. The higher intercept for persons interested in money shows them slightly more likely to emigrate even when higher prospects are very small, and the difference widens as income prospects abroad increase. But even in this group, money stimulates emigration only slightly: if they respond more strongly, the correlation coefficient would be much larger than .209 and the slope would be much larger than .159.

Economic gains to the individual through migration. Even though the association between income gains and migration is limited, it is present. Therefore migrants will earn more than returnees. Table C-4 classifies respondents by their long-term migration plans and shows the income gains possible for each category if its members worked abroad.

Prospective permanent migrants report higher gains abroad than the permanently returning persons in those samples where income differentials clearly relate to migration plans, such as the students in the United States and Canada, the stay-ons in the United States, and the returnees in the Republic of Korea, Ghana, Greece, and Colombia. (For these samples, the numbers in the first five columns tend to increase from left to right -- i.e., with firmer migration plans, the proportional gains increase.) But in other samples the differences are small or

Table C-4

Proportional Gains Expected from Foreign Employment Associated with Different Intentions

	Proportional gains for each intention					Numbers of respondents				
	Definitely home	Probably home	Undecided	Probably abroad	Definitely abroad	Definitely home	Probably home	Undecided	Probably abroad	Definitely abroad
Students in:										
United States	1.17	1.34	1.44	1.75	1.66	(644)	(336)	(159)	(103)	(44)
Canada	2.06	1.97	2.46	2.58	2.48	(163)	(89)	(81)	(106)	(90)
France	0.89	1.08	0.78	1.05	0.81	(135)	(29)	(14)	(12)	(10)
Stay-ons in:										
United States	2.91	3.31	3.42	3.36	3.80	(35)	(48)	(66)	(84)	(46)
France	----	1.71	----	1.44	1.29	(3)	(6)	(1)	(13)	(24)
Returnees in:										
India	2.12	2.23	2.52	2.13	2.11	(197)	(180)	(82)	(19)	(6)
Sri Lanka	2.30	2.36	2.29	2.88	----	(23)	(45)	(33)	(7)	(2)
Korea,Republic of	2.93	3.04	3.86	----	----	(142)	(46)	(30)	(4)	(1)
Ghana	1.57	1.75	1.96	----	----	(51)	(14)	(14)	(2)	(2)
Greece	0.86	0.96	1.06	----	----	(167)	(85)	(27)	(3)	(3)
Brazil	0.88	0.88	0.87	----	----	(160)	(140)	(51)	(4)	(1)
Colombia	0.77	0.93	1.01	1.13	----	(58)	(65)	(43)	(13)	(3)
Argentina	1.41	1.55	1.82	1.30	----	(88)	(93)	(52)	(10)	(4)

The five right-hand columns classify respondents by migration plans, and the five left-hand columns give the proportional gains if they stay abroad. For example, among foreign students in the United States, 644 said they definitely expected to return home; the median proportional gain in income expected by this group if it stayed abroad was 1.17. 44 of the foreign students in the United States said they definitely would emigrate, and their proportional gain would be 1.66.

absent, such as the Brazilian returnees, who can earn barely more abroad than at home -- i.e., on the row for returnees in Brazil, the numbers are nearly the same from left to right.

Appendix D

BIBLIOGRAPHY ABOUT THE MIGRATION AND RETURN OF PROFESSIONALS

1. General works about the "brain drain":

   a. Walter Adams (editor), The Brain Drain (New York: The Macmillan Company, 1968; London: Collier-Macmillan Ltd., 1968). Contains some provocative essays by specialists on the subject, such as Stevan Dedijer, Brinley Thomas, Harry Johnson, Kenneth Boulding, Enrique Oteiza, Charles Kindleberger, and others. A useful symposium, in that it presents rival perceptions of and remedies for the situation. Includes special studies about France, Greece, Africa, India, Western Europe.

   b. Education and World Affairs commissioned a number of national reports and committee investigations about the magnitude, causes, and cures of "brain drain":

      (1) The Committee on the International Migration of Talent, Modernization and the Migration of Talent (New York: Education and World Affairs, 1970). Summary of findings and recommendations.

      (2) International Migration of High-Level Manpower: Its Impact on the Development Process (New York: Praeger Publishers, 1970). Contains the special national reports about Taiwan, The Philippines, Japan, Thailand, Korea, Malaysia and Singapore, India, Middle East, Turkey, Iran, Equatorial Africa, Tanzania and Kenya, Latin America, Britain, The Netherlands, France, Australia.

      (3) George B. Baldwin, "Brain Drain or Overflow?", Foreign Affairs, Volume 48, Number 2, January 1970, pp. 358-372.

c. Bibliographies about the brain drain:

(1) Stevan Dedijer and L. Svenningson, Brain Drain and Brain Gain (Lund: Research Policy Program, University of Lund, 1967).

(2) Selected Publications and Research Related to the International Migration of Professional Manpower (Washington: Study Committee on the International Migration of Talent, Education and World Affairs, 1968).

(3) G. Beyer, Brain Drain/Auszug des Geistes/Exode des Cerveaux: A Selected Bibliography on Temporary and Permanent Migration of Skilled Workers and High-Level Manpower, 1967-1972 (The Hague: Martinus Nijhoff, 1972).

(4) Special issue of the International Newsletter on Migration, Volume 2, Number 3, September 1972.

(5) The Foreign Medical Graduate: A Bibliography (Washington: U.S. Government Printing Office, 1972). DHEW Publication No. (NIH) 73-440, November 1972.

d. Many reviews of the available knowledge have been written:

(1) Joseph G. Whelan, Brain Drain: A Study of the Persistent Issue of International Scientific Mobility (Washington: U.S. Government Printing Office, 1974). Prepared for the Subcommittee on National Security Policy and Scientific Developments of the Committee on Foreign Affairs, U.S. House of Representatives, by the Foreign Affairs Division, Congressional Research Service, Library of Congress.

(2) Hans Peter Schipulle, Ausverkauf der Intelligenz aus Entwicklungsländern: Eine Kritisch Untersuchung zum Brain Drain (Munich: Weltforum Verlag, 1973).

(3) Susumu Watanabe, "The Brain Drain from Developing to Developed Countries," International Labour Review, Volume 99, Number 4, April 1969, pp. 401-433.

(4) Subbiah Kannappan, "The Brain Drain and Developing Countries," *International Labour Review*, Volume 98, Number 1, July 1968, pp. 1-26.

(5) Ehsan Naraghi, "L'exode des compétences." Published in numerous places: *Politique étrangère*, July 1967; *Problèmes économiques*, 28 December 1967; *Jeune Afrique*, 1967; *Journal de Téhéran*, November 1, 2 and 4, 1967.

(6) Guy Hermet, "L'exode des cerveaux," *Notes et Etudes Documentaires*, Number 3598, 9 juin 1969.

(7) R. Avakov and V. Gavriliuk, *Pokhishchenie Umov* (Institut Mezhudunarodnogo Rabochago Dvziheniia, Akademia Nauk, Moscow, USSR, 1970).

(8) Peter Vas-Zoltan, *The Brain Drain: An Abnormal Relation* (Budapest: Academic Publishers, 1975).

(9) Walter Adams, "The 'Brain Drain': Fact or Fiction," *Population Bulletin*, Volume XXV, Number 3, June 1969, pp. 57-87.

(10) John Z. Bowers and Lord Rosenheim (editors), *Migration of Medical Manpower* (New York: Josiah Macy, Jr. Foundation, 1971).

e. Proceedings and reports of conferences:

(1) *The Special Topic: Brain Drain--Country Papers, the Working Paper and the Report of the Special Topic Committee, Prepared for the Meetings of the 22nd Consultative Committee* (Colombo: The Colombo Plan, 1972). Excellent research reports about twenty-two countries.

(2) *The International Migration of Talent and Skills: Proceedings of a Workshop and Conference* (Washington: Council on International Educational and Cultural Affairs, United States Department of State, 1966). Transcript of discussion by Americans who have done research or have made policy decisions on the subject.

(3) C.H.G. Oldham, rapporteur, International Migration of Talent from and to the Less-Developed Countries: Report of a Conference at Ditchley Park (Ditchley Park: The Ditchley Foundation, 1968).

f. Miscellaneous books and articles:

(1) F. Bechhofer (editor). Population Growth and the Brain Drain (Edinburgh: The University Press, 1969; Chicago: Aldine Publishing Company, 1969). Essays by demographers. Only a few papers deal with migration of professionals.

(2) D.N. Chorofas, The Knowledge Revolution: An Analysis of the International Brain Market (New York: McGraw-Hill Book Company, 1970).

(3) Brinley Thomas has written many articles, such as "The International Circulation of Human Capital," Minerva, Volume V, Number 4, Summer 1967, pp. 479-506.

(4) Gregory Henderson, "Foreign Students: Exchange or Immigration?" International Development Review, Volume 6, Number 4, December 1967.

(5) Richard Jolly and Dudley Seers, "The Brain Drain and the Development Process," in Gustav Ranis (editor), The Gap Between Rich and Poor Countries (London: Macmillan, 1972).

(6) Dudley Seers, "The Brain Drain from Poor Countries" (Brighton: Institute of Development Studies, University of Sussex, 1969).

(7) Saleem M.M. Qureshi, "Brain Drain from the Developing Countries," Pakistan Horizon, Volume XVIII, Number 2, Second Quarter 1965.

(8) Prakash Awasthi, "Brain Drain from Developing Countries: An Exercise in Problem Formulation," Manpower Journal (New Delhi), Volume II, Number 1, April-June 1966, pp. 80-98.

(9) Robert G. Myers, "The 'Brain Drain' and Foreign Student Nonreturn: Fact and Fallacy in Definitions and Measurements," Exchange, Spring 1967, pp. 63-73. This magazine often carries articles about the movements of students and professionals to the United States.

(10) Robert G. Myers, "Comments on the State of Research: 'Brain Drains' and 'Brain Gains'," International Development Review, Volume IX, Number 4, December 1967.

(11) A. Khoshkish, "Intellectual Migration: A Sociological Approach to Brain Drain," Journal of World History, Volume 10, Number 1, 1966, pp. 178-197.

(12) Michel E.A. Hervé, "International Migration of Physicians and Students: A Regression Analysis" (Washington: Agency for International Development, United States Department of State, 1968).

(13) George Psacharopoulos, "On Some Positive Aspects of the Economics of the Brain Drain," Minerva, Volume IX, Number 2, April 1971, pp. 231.242.

2. Research and reports by the United Nations:

a. By the United Nations Institute for Training and Research:

(1) Gregory Henderson, Emigration of Highly-Skilled Manpower from the Developing Countries (New York: United Nations Institute for Training and Research, UNITAR Research Report No. 3, 1970.) A review of the available knowledge. A shorter version is "Outflow of Trained Personnel from Developing Countries: Report of the Secretary-General," United Nations General Assembly, 23rd Session, Agenda Item 47, A/7294, 5 November 1968.

(2) The Brain Drain from Five Developing Countries: Cameroon, Colombia, Lebanon, The Philippines, Trinidad and Tobago (New York: United Nations Institute for Training and Research, UNITAR Research Report No. 5, 1971). Summary of available facts about five countries. Also issued as

"Outflow of Trained Personnel from Developing to Developed Countries: Report of the Secretary-General, with Addendum," United Nations Economic and Social Council, 49th Session, Agenda Item 9, E/4820 and E/4820/add. 1, June 1970.

(3) Summaries of the design of UNITAR's multinational questionnaire survey of professionals and students:

"Outflow of Trained Personnel from Developing to Developed Countries: Progress Report by the Executive Director of the United Nations Institute for Training and Research," United Nations Economic and Social Council, 49th Session, Agenda Item 9, E/4798, 27 March 1970, and 50th Session, Agenda Item 3, E/4948, 9 February 1971.

(4) For publications resulting from UNITAR's multinational questionnaire survey of professionals and students see Appendix E.

b. By the United Nations Educational, Scientific and Cultural Organisation:

(1) Allen S. McKnight, Scientists Abroad: A Study of the International Movement of Persons in Science and Technology (Paris: UNESCO, 1971).

(2) "Problem of Emigration of Scientists and Technologists ('Brain Drain' or Exode des compétences)" (Paris: Science Policy Division, UNESCO, SC/WS/57, 1968).

(3) Emigration of Talent (Paris: Executive Board 95th Session, 95 EX/29, September 1974).

(4) 17 C/58, 10 October 1972, Report by the Director-General of UNESCO on the answers of member States concerning the anxiety caused them by the migration of talent.

c. By the United Nations Conference on Trade and Development:

(1) The Reverse Transfer of Technology: Economic Effects of the Outflow of Trained Personnel from Developing Countries (Brain-Drain) (Geneva: Intergovernmental Group on Transfer of Technology, Trade and Development Board, United Nations Conference on Trade and Development, TD/B/AC. 11 (25, 1974).

(2) TD/B/C.6/7, 13 October 1975, A study by the UNCTAD Secretariat presented to the Trade and Development Board, Committee on Transfer of Technology, on "The reverse transfer of technology: its dimensions, economic effects and policy implications".

d. By the World Health Organization:

(1) HMD/HMP/74.8, Report of the Consultation of Experts on the Multinational Study of the International Migration of Physicans and Nurses convened by WHO in Geneva, 4-8 March 1974.

(2) HMD/75.7, Multinational Study of the International Migration of Physicians and Nurses, "Analytical Review of the Literature", prepared by Project Staff at WHO Headquarters, 1975.

(3) HMD/76.4, Multinational Study of the International Migration of Physicians and Nurses, "Country-specific migration statistics", WHO, 1976.

e. Others:

(1) Migration: Report of the Research Conference on Migration, Ethnic Minority Status and Social Adaptation (Rome: United Nations Social Defence Research Institute, 1973).

(2) E/C.8/21, 18 January 1974, Report of the Secretary-General of the United Nations to the Committee on Science and Technology for Development on the "Outflow of Trained Personnel from Developing to Developed Countries".

(3) E/C.8/34, 29 December 1975, Report of the Secretary-General of the United Nations to the Committee on Science and Technology for Development

on "Social and other aspects of science and technology - outflow of trained personnel from developing countries".

(4) NOEI/D.31, "The Brain Drain" paper by Jagdish N. Baghwati, for the ILO's Tripartite World Conference on Employment, Income Distribution and Social Progress and the International Division of Labour, and presented at the International Institute for Labour Studies' World Symposium on the Social Implications of a New International Economic Order, Geneva, 19-23 January 1976.

(5) E/CN.3/485, 28 April 1976, Report of the Secretary-General of the United Nations to the Statistical Commission on "Social and demographic statistics: Migration statistics - The improvement of statistics on the outflow of trained personnel from developing to developed countries".

(6) "Employment, Growth and Basic Needs: A One-World Problem", Report of the Director General of the International Labour Office, Chapter 8, International Manpower Movements; Vol. II on "International Strategies for Employment" contains chapters on "Migration from Developing to High Income Countries" by R. Böhnig, "The Brain Drain" by J. Bhagwati and "Transfer of Qualified Personnel to Developing Countries" by the International Committee for European Migration (Geneva: ILO, 1976).

(7) E/CN.5/545, 18 October 1976, Report of the Secretary-General of the United Nations to the Commission for Social Developments on "Outflow of Trained Personnel from Developing to Developed Countries".

(8) E/CN.5/L.421, 12 November 1976, "'Brain drain': the disengagement alternative" paper prepared by Martin Godfrey, Consultant, for the Commission on Social Development.

3. Research by the Organisation for Economic Co-Operation and Development:

a. J.R. Gass and R.F. Lyons, "International Flows of

Students," Policy Conference on Economic Growth and Investment in Education (Paris: Organisation for Economic Co-Operation and Development, 1962, Paper V).

b. F.J. Van Hoek, The Migration of High Level Manpower from Developing to Developed Countries (The Hague: Mouton, 1971).

c. The International Movement of Scientists and Engineers (Paris: Organisation for Economic Co-Operation and Development, 1969).

4. Migration and its relation to economic development:

a. Bibliographies about migration:

(1) J.J. Mangalam, Human Migration: A Guide to Migration Literature in English 1955-1962 (Lexington: University of Kentucky Press, 1969).

(2) Gunnar Olsson, Distance and Human Interaction (Philadelphia: Regional Science Institute, 1965).

b. Brinley Thomas, International Migration and Economic Development: A Trend Report and Bibliography (Paris: UNESCO, 1961).

c. Angus Maddison, Foreign Skills and Technical Assistance in Economic Development (Paris: OECD, 1965).

d. Charles P. Kindleberger, "Emigration and Economic Growth," Banca Nazionale del Lavoro Quarterly Review, Number 74, September 1965, pp. 235-254.

e. Solomon Barkin, "The Economic Costs and Benefits and Human Gains and Disadvantages of International Migration," The Journal of Human Resources, Volume II, Number 4, Fall 1967, pp. 495-516.

f. Gunnar Myrdal, Economic Theory and Under-Developed Regions (London: Duckworth, 1957). Reprinted in Myrdal's book Rich Lands and Poor (New York: Harper, 1957). How economic conditions affect migration.

g. John C. Shearer, "Intra- and International Movements of High-Level Human Resources," in Development Administration: Spatial Aspects (Durham, N.C.: Duke University Press, forthcoming).

h. W.M. Besterman, "Immigration as a Means of Obtaining Needed Skills and Stimulating Economic and Social Advancement," International Migration, Volume III, Number 4, 1965, pp. 204-208.

i. Mary Jean Bowman and Robert G. Myers, "Schooling, Experience, and Gains and Losses in Human Capital through Migration," The Journal of the American Statistical Association, Volume 62, September 1967, pp. 875-898.

j. Brinley Thomas (editor), Economics of International Migration (London: Macmillan, 1958).

k. Jagdish Bhagwati. Several works about the economic losses to developing countries and methods of compensating them.

   (1) Co-editor of Taxing the Brain Drain (Amsterdam: North Holland Publishing Company, 1976).

   (2) "The Brain Drain," International Social Science Journal, Volume XXVIII, Number 4, 1976, pp. 691-729.

5. Educational exchanges throughout the world:

   a. Ingrid Eide (editor), Students as Links between Cultures: A Cross-Cultural Survey Based on UNESCO Studies (Oslo: Universitetsforlaget, 1970). Includes reports of the UNESCO studies of returnees in Iran, India, Egypt.

   b. Otto Klineberg and J. Ben Brika, Etudiants du tiers-monde en Europe: problèmes d'adaptation (The Hague: Mouton, 1971).

   c. Statistics on numbers of foreign students in each country: Statistical Yearbook (Paris: UNESCO, annual).

d. Richard E. Spencer and Ruth Awe, _International Educational Exchange: A Bibliography_ (New York: Institute of International Education, 1970).

6. Comparative data about professional manpower:

a. Richard Layard and Jagdish Saigal, "Educational and Occupational Characteristics of Manpower: An International Comparison," _British Journal of Industrial Relations_, July 1966.

b. _Statistics of the Occupational and Educational Structure of the Labour Force in 53 Countries_ (Paris: Organisation for Economic Co-Operation and Development, 1969).

c. Charles V. Kidd, "The Growth of Science and the Distribution of Scientists among Nations," _Impact of Science on Society_, Volume XIV, Number 1, 1964, pp. 5-18.

d. Frederick Harbison and Charles A. Myers:

(1) _Education, Manpower, and Economic Growth: Strategies of Human Resource Development_ (New York: McGraw-Hill Book Company, 1964).

(2) _Manpower and Education: Country Studies in Economic Development_ (New York: McGraw-Hill Book Company, 1965).

7. The United States:

a. Immigration of professionals:

(1) "The New Immigration," special issue of _The Annals_, Volume 367, September 1966. (Philadelphia: The American Academy of Political and Social Science).

(2) _The Brain Drain into the United States of Scientists, Engineers, and Physicians_ (Washington: U.S. Government Printing Office, 1967).

(3) _International Migration of Talent and Skills_ (Washington: U.S. Government Printing Office, 1968). Hearings before a congressional committee.

(4) The Brain Drain of Scientists, Engineers, and Physicians from the Developing Countries into the United States (Washington: U.S. Government Printing Office, 1968). Hearings before a congressional committee.

(5) Some Facts and Figures on the Migration of Talent and Skills (Washington: Council on International Educational and Cultural Affairs, United States Department of State, 1967).

(6) Annual Indicator of the In-Migration into the United States of Aliens in Professional and Related Occupations (Washington: U.S. Government Printing Office, annual).

(7) Annual Report of the Immigration and Naturalization Service (Washington: U.S. Government Printing Office, annual).

(8) Report of the Visa Office (Washington: U.S. Government Printing Office, annual).

(9) Alan E. Bayer, "The American Brain Gain: The Inflow for Education and Work" (Washington: American Council on Education, 1968).

(10) Göran Friborg, Motives and Qualifications of Scientists and Engineers Emigrated from Sweden to the U.S.A. (Stockholm: Committee on Research Economics, 1969).

(11) Report of the Select Commission on Western Immigration (Washington: U.S. Government Printing Office, 1968).

b. Foreign professionals in the American labor force:

(1) Herbert Grubel has published numerous papers analyzing the characteristics of foreign-trained professionals, discussing the brain drain, and so on:

A. The Brain Drain and Foreign Scientists in the United States (with Anthony D. Scott), book in press.

B. Examples of his many articles: "The Reduction of the Brain Drain," Minerva, Summer 1968; "The Characteristics of Foreigners in the U.S. Economics Profession," The American Economic Review, March 1967; "Determinants of Migration: The Highly Skilled," International Migration, 1967; "Foreign Manpower in the U.S. Sciences," in Research in Income and Wealth (New York: National Bureau of Economic Research, 1968); and others.

(2) Tai Keun Oh, "The Asian Students in Our Labor Force: Who, What, When, Where and Why?" Business and Society, Volume 9, Number 2, Spring 1969, pp. 16-23.

(3) Richard E. Usher, The Impact of Foreign Medical Personnel in the United States (Washington: Foreign Service Institute, U.S. Department of State, 1969).

(4) Justus M. Van der Kroef, "The United States and the World's Brain Drain," The International Journal of Comparative Sociology, Volume XI, Number 3, September 1970.

(5) Scientists, Engineers, and Physicians from Abroad (Washington: National Science Foundation, 1969).

(6) Immigrant Scientists and Engineers in the United States: A Study of Characteristics and Attitudes (Washington: National Science Foundation, 1973).

(7) John R. Niland, The Asian Engineering Brain Drain: A Study of International Relocation into the United States from India, China, Korea, Thailand and Japan (Lexington, Mass.: Heath Lexington Books, 1970).

(8) Rosemary Stevens and Joan Vermeulen, Foreign-Trained Physicians and American Medicine (Bethesda: Bureau of Health Manpower, National Institute of Health, 1972).

(9) Harold Margulies and Lucille Bloch, Foreign Medical Graduates in the United States (Cambridge: Harvard

University Press, 1969).

(10) Betty A. Lockett and Kathleen N. Williams, "The Foreign Medical Graduate and Physician Manpower in the United States" (Washington: Office of International Health Manpower Studies, Bureau of Health Resources Development, Public Health Service, 1973).

(11) Barbara E. Harrison, "Foreign Doctors in American Hospitals: A Sociological Analysis of Graduate Medical Education" (New York: Unpublished dissertation for the Ph.D. in sociology, Columbia University, 1969).

c. Foreign students in the United States. Many surveys have been done about foreign students, primarily about their experiences and adjustments. Occasionally a survey asks about whether respondents intend to migrate or return.

(1) Barbara J. Walton, Foreign Student Exchange in Perspective: Research on Foreign Students in the United States (Washington: Office of External Research, U.S. Department of State, 1967).

(2) Foreign Students in the United States: A National Survey (Washington: U.S. Advisory Commission on International Educational and Cultural Affairs, 1966).

(3) Evaluation studies of the advanced training programs conducted in the United States by the Agency for International Development, for specialized personnel from developing countries:

A. Albert E. Gollin, Education for National Development: Effects of U.S. Technical Training Programs (New York: Praeger Publishers, 1969).

B. These surveys are conducted frequently by A.I.D. itself. A number of mimeographed volumes have been issued, either summarizing the survey results for that year or reporting survey results by persons who have returned to their home countries. Most questions ask about adjustment in the United States, a few ask about utilization of the training after return. Individual volumes exist about the Far East, Near East, South Asia, the Philippine Island. Copies of some volumes are available without charge from the Office of International Training, Agency for International Development, U.S. Department of State, Washington, D.C. 20520.

(4) Man Singh Das conducted a survey of foreign students in the United States:

A. Brain Drain Controversy and International Students (Lucknow: Lucknow Publishing House, 1972).

B. "The 'Brain Drain' Controversy in a Comparative Perspective," International Review of Sociology, Volume I, Number 1, March 1971, pp. 55-65.

C. "Brain Drain and Students from Less Developed and Developing Countries," Transactions of the Seventh World Congress of Sociology (Varna: September 1970, Volume 1, pp. 183-194).

D. "Brain Drain Controversy and Latin American Scholars," Sociologus, 1973.

(5) Grace Scully, "An Exploratory Study of Students from Abroad Who Do Not Wish to Return to Their Country" (New York: thesis for the Ed.D. at Teachers College, Columbia University, 1956).

(6) Steven E. Deutsch, International Education and Exchange (Cleveland: The Press of Case Western Reserve University, 1970).

(7) Jane W. Jacqz, African Students at United States Universities (New York: African-American Institute, 1967).

(8) Louise Cohen, "International Migration of Scientists Awarded Doctorates in the United States in

1958" (Lafayette, Ind.: unpublished dissertation for the Ph.D., Purdue University, 1965).

(9) _Open Doors_ (New York: Institute of International Education, annual). Characteristics of foreign students in America, based on brief questionnaire.

(10) Agnes Tysse, _International Education: The American Experience_ (Metuchen, N.J.: Scarecrow Press, 1974). Annotated bibliography.

8. Canada:

a. Harry G. Johnson, "The Economics of the 'Brain Drain': The Canadian Case, " _Minerva_, Volume 3, Number 3, Spring 1965, pp. 299-311. An important article by one of the most provocative economists who has written about brain drain.

b. Ronald M. Pavalko, "Talent Migration: Canadian Students in the United States," _International Review of Education_, Volume XIV, Number 3, 1968, pp. 300-324.

c. Louis Parai, _Immigration and Emigration of Professional and Skilled Manpower during the Post-War Period_ (Ottawa: Queen's Printer, 1965).

d. Edward I. Sheffield, "The Retrieval of Canadian Graduate Students from Abroad" (Ottawa: The Association of Universities and Colleges of Canada, 1966).

e. _Survey of Higher Education. Part II: Degrees, Staff and Summary_ (Ottawa: Queen's Printer, Catalogue No. 81-211, annual). Contains total numbers of foreign students by nationality and province, reported by Statistics Canada.

f. _Immigration, Migration and Ethnic Groups in Canada: A Bibliography of Research 1964-1968_ (Ottawa: Department of Manpower and Immigration, 1969).

9. United Kingdom:

a. Immigration of professionals:

(1) Geoffrey Oldham and Oscar Gish, "Survey of Immi-

grant Professionals in the Fields of Science and Technology" (Brighton: Science Policy Research Unit, University of Sussex, 1970).

(2) Oscar Gish, Doctor Migration and World Health (London: G. Bell and Sons, 1971). Gish has written a number of articles about foreign doctors, nurses, midwives, and others in Great Britain.

(3) Michael Thomas and Jean Morton Williams, Overseas Nurses in Britain (London: Political and Economic Planning, 1972).

b. Emigration of professionals:

(1) Brian Abel-Smith and Kathleen Gales, British Doctors at Home and Abroad (Welwyn: The Codicote Press, 1964).

(2) The Brain Drain: Report of the Working Group on Migration (London: H.M. Stationery Office, Cmnd. 3417, 1968).

(3) James A. Wilson has written several articles about emigration of British scientists and physicians. For example, "The Emigration of British Scientists," Minerva, Autumn 1966; "Emigrating British Physicians," Social Science and Medicine, 1969 (with Oscar Gish).

(4) Oscar Gish, "British Doctor Migration 1962-67," British Journal of Medical Education, Volume 4, Number 4, December 1970, pp. 279-288.

(5) Emigration of Scientists from the United Kingdom: Report of a Committee Appointed by the Council of the Royal Society (London: Royal Society, 1963).

(6) J. M. Last, "The Overseas Movement of British Doctors," Social and Economic Administration, Volume I, Number 4, October 1967, pp. 20-28.

(7) Frank Musgrove, The Migratory Elite (London: William Heinemann (1963). History of international movements by the British educated classes.

c. Foreign students in Great Britain, survey research:

(1) Michael Kendall, Overseas Students in Britain: An Annotated Bibliography (London: Research Unit for Student Problems, University of London, 1968).

(2) Colonial Students in Britain (London: Political and Economic Planning, 1955).

(3) New Commonwealth Students in Britain: With Special Reference to Students from East Africa (London: George Allen and Unwin, 1965). Survey by Political and Economic Planning.

d. Foreign students in Great Britain, total numbers:

(1) "Students from Other Countries in Universities in Britain," Commonwealth Universities Yearbook (London: The Association of Commonwealth Universities, annual).

(2) Overseas Students in Britain (London: The British Council, annual).

10. Eire:

Richard Lynn, The Irish Brain Drain (Dublin: The Economic and Social Research Institute, November 1968).

11. France:

a. J.-P. N'Diaye, Enquète sur les étudiants noirs en France (Paris: Editions Réalités Africaines, 1962).

b. Georges Tapinos, The Economic and Social Consequences, Advantages, Disadvantages and Mechanisms of Highly Skilled Migration from Developing Countries into France (Paris: Fondation Nationale des Sciences Politiques, Service D'Etude de l'Activité Economique, 1973). Prepared for the United Nations Office of Science and Technology.

c. Informations statistiques: statistiques des enseignements supérieurs (Paris: Service Central des Statistiques et de la Conjoncture, Ministère de l'Education Nationale, annual).

12. Federal Republic of Germany:

a. Emigration of professionals:

Claus Müller-Daehn, Abwanderung deutscher Wissenschaftler (Gottingen: Vandenhoeck and Ruprecht, 1967).

b. Foreign students in Germany:

(1) Prodosh Aich, Farbige unter Weissen (Cologne: Kiepenheuer and Witsch, Second Edition, 1963). English translation of much of the manuscript, "Asian and African Students in West German Universities," Minerva, Volume I, Number 4, Summer 1963, pp. 439-552.

(2) Loan Eng Tjioe, Asiaten über Deutsche: Kulturkonflikte ostasiatischer Studentinnen in der Bundesrepublik (Frankfurt/am/Main: Thesen Verlag, 1972).

(3) "Ausländische Studierende nach Ländern und Fachrichtungen im WS/SS" (Bad Godesberg: Deutscher Akademischer Austauschdienst, annual).

13. Norway:

Hans Skoie, "The Problems of a Small Scientific Community: The Norwegian Case," Minerva, Volume VII, Number 3, Spring 1969, pp. 399-425.

14. Sweden:

Göran Friborg et al., Brain Drain and Brain Gain of Sweden (Stockholm: Swedish Natural Science Research Council, 1972).

15. Asia and the Middle East:

a. Justus M. Van der Kroef, "Asia's 'Brain Drain'," Journal of Higher Education, Volume 39, Number 5, May 1968, pp. 241-253.

b. Justus M. Van der Kroef, "Asian Education and Unemployment: The Continuing Crisis," Comparative Education Review, Volume 7, October 1963, pp. 173-180.

Van der Kroef has written other articles about the educated unemployed of Asia.

c. Mary C. Hodgkin conducted a survey of returnees in Southeast Asia who had been educated in Australia:

(1) The Innovators: The Role of Foreign Trained Persons in Southeast Asia (Sydney: Sydney University Press, 1972).

(2) "The Communication of Innovations: The Influence of the Foreign Trained Returnee on Socio-Cultural Change in Developing Countries," South-East Asian Journal of Sociology, Volume 4, 1971, pp. 53-71.

d. Daphne Keats conducted a survey of returnees in Asia who had been educated in Australia:

(1) Back in Asia: A Follow-up Study of Australian-Trained Asian Students (Canberra: Department of Economics, Research School of Pacific Studies, The Australian National University, 1969).

(2) A number of articles, including "The Effectiveness of Education Abroad," in S. Bochner and P. Sydney Wicks (editors), Overseas Students in Australia (Sydney: University of New South Wales Press, 1972).

e. Special issue on brain drain and the position of professionals, Mid East, Volume IX, Number 1, January-February 1969.

f. Papers Read at the R.C.D. Seminar on Brain Drain Held at Tehran, Nov. 15-18, 1970 (Tehran: R.C.D. Section, State Organization for Administration and Employment Affairs, 1972). Essays and research about Iran, Pakistan, and Turkey.

g. A.B. Zahlan, "The Brain Drain: Lebanon and Middle Eastern Countries" (Beirut: Department of Physics, American University of Beirut, 1969; summary in "The Brain Drain from five developing countries," UNITAR Research Report No. 5, New York: United Nations Institute for Training and Research, 1971).

h. Malcom S. Adiseshiah, "Brain Drain from the Arab World" (Paris: UNESCO, 1969). Address to the 8th Arab Cultural Conference on the Training of Scientific Workers in the Arab World.

i. Tai Keun Oh, "The Role of International Education in the Asian Brain Drain" (Madison: dissertation for the Ph.D., in industrial relations, University of Wisconsin, 1970).

j. Mehri Hekmati, "Non-Returning Foreign Students: Why Do They Not Return Home?", Die Dritte Welt, Volume 2, Number 1, 1972, pp. 25-43. The full survey is reported in Hekmati, "Alienation, Family Ties, and Social Position as Factors Related to the Non-Return of Foreign Students" (New York: thesis for the Ph.D., School of Education, New York University, 1970).

16. Republic of China:

a. Charles H.C. Kao, "Brain Drain: A Case Study of China" (River Falls: Department of Economics, Wisconsin State University, 1970).

b. Yung Wei, "Socio-Psychological Variables and Inter-Nation Intellectual Migration: Findings from Interviewing Returnees in the Republic of China" (Memphis: Department of Political Science, Memphis State University, 1970).

17. Republic of Korea:

John A. Thames, "Korean Students in Southern California: Factors Influencing their Plans Toward Returning Home" (Pasadena: thesis for the Ed.D., School of Education, University of Southern California, 1970).

18. The Philippines:

a. Josefina R. Cortes, Factors Associated with the Migration of High-Level Persons from the Philippines to the U.S.A. (Stanford: Stanford International Development Education Center, School of Education, Stanford University, 1970).

b. Walden F. Bello and others, "Brain Drain in the Philippines," _Modernization: Its Impact in the Philippines, IV_ (Quezon City: Ateneo de Manila University Press, 1969), pp. 93-146.

c. Harold E. Howland, _Brain Drain--As It Affects the Philippines_ (Washington: Foreign Service Institute, U.S. Department of State, 1967).

d. Joseph T. Odenthal, _Policies and Pressures Affecting the Migration of Filipinos_ (Washington: Foreign Service Institute, U.S. Department of State, 1969).

e. Perfecto Fernandez, "Brain Drain in the Philippines" (summary in "The Brain Drain from five developing countries", UNITAR Research Report No. 5, New York: United Nations Institute for Training and Research, 1971).

f. Josefina Bulatao Jayme, "Demographic and Socio-Psychological Determinants of the Migration of Highly Trained Filipinos to the United States" (Pittsburgh: dissertation for the Ph.D., in Psychology, Carnegie-Mellon University, 1971).

19. India:

a. Emigration of professionals:

(1) Research by the Institute of Applied Manpower Research.

A. Prakash Awasthi, _Migration of Indian Engineers, Scientists and Physicians to the United States_ (New Delhi: Institute, 1968).

B. Prakash Awasthi, _Indian Scientists in the United States: A Stock Study_ (New Delhi: Institute, 1969).

C. Prakash Awasthi, _Indian Physicians in the United States: A Stock Study_ (New Delhi: Institute, 1969).

D. Prakash Awasthi, The 'Brain Drain' Study--Phase I: Analysis of Ordinary Passports Issued during 1960-1967 (New Delhi: Institute, 1970).

E. P.M. Abraham, "An Outline for a Study of Brain Drain from India," Manpower Journal, Volume III, Number 3, October-December 1967, pp. 15-44.

(2) Report of the Inter Ministerial Group on the Brain Drain (New Delhi: Institute of Applied Manpower Research, 1971).

(3) Y.D. Sharma, Brain Drain in India: An Interim Report (New Delhi: University Grants Commission, 1967).

(4) Marshal F. Merriam, Brain Drain Study at I.I.T. Kanpur: Opinions and Background of Faculty and Senior Staff (Kanpur: Indian Institute of Technology, 1969).

b. Surveys of Indian students abroad:

(1) A.K. Singh, Indian Students in Britain (Bombay: Asia Publishing House, 1963).

(2) Keshav Dev Sharma, Indian Students in the United States (Bombay: Academic Journals of India, 1970).

(3) G.C. Dorai, "Economics of the International Flow of Students: A Cost-Benefit Analysis" (Detroit: unpublished dissertation for the Ph.D., Wayne State University, 1967).

c. Foreign-trained professionals:

(1) Edward Shils, The Intellectual between Tradition and Modernity: The Indian Situation (The Hague: Mouton and Company, 1961).

(2) John Useem and Ruth Hill Useem, The Western-Educated Man in India (New York: The Dryden Press, 1955).

(3) Prakash Awasthi, "An Experiment in Voluntary Repatriation of High-Level Technical Manpower: The Scientists' Pool," Development Digest, Volume IV, Number 1, April 1966, pp. 28-35. Also in The Economic Weekly, 18 September 1965, pp. 1447-1452.

(4) P.M. Abraham, "Regaining High Level Indian Manpower from Abroad," Manpower Journal (New Delhi), Volume III, Number 4, January-February 1968, pp. 83-117.

(5) Mark Blaug et al., The Causes of Graduate Unemployment in India (London: Allen Lane, The Penguin Press, 1969).

(6) Mehdi Kizelbash, "The Employment of Returning U.S. Educated Indians," Comparative Education Review, Volume 8, Number 3, December 1964, pp. 320-326.

20. Pakistan:

a. Mohammed A. Qadeer, "A Pilot Study of the Causes of Brain Drain from Pakistan," The Pakistan Student, January 1969. Survey of Pakistani students in the U.S.

b. John W. Orton, "An Interview-Based Study of Pakistanis Employed in the Professions in the United States" (New York: Institute of International Education, 1965).

21. Iran:

a. Emigration of professionals:

(1) Habib Naficy, "Brain Drain: The Case of Iranian Non-Returnees," in H.W. Singer (editor), International Development, 1966 (New York: Oceana Publications, 1967).

(2) Iraj Valipour, "A Comparison of Returning and Non-Returning Iranian Students in the United States" (New York: thesis for the Ed.D., Teachers College, Columbia University, 1962).

b. Surveys of Iranian students abroad:

(1) Mohammed Borhanmanesh, "A Study of Iranian Students in Southern California" (Los Angeles: thesis for the Ed.D., School of Education, University of California, 1965).

(2) Morteza Nassefat, Le rôle des étudiants dans l'échange interculturel (Tehran: Institute of Psychology, University of Tehran, 1973).

c. Foreign-trained professionals:

George Baldwin, "The Foreign-educated Iranian: A Profile," The Middle East Journal, Summer 1963, pp. 264-278.

22. Turkey:

Turhan Oguzkan, The Migration of Persons with the Doctorate from Turkey to Other Nations (Ankara: Middle East Technical University, 1970, in Turkish).

23. Egypt:

Anwar Koraitem and Midhat Hamdi, Brain Drain from the United Arab Republic (Cairo: Department of Missions, Ministry of Higher Education, 1966, in Arabic).

24. Israel:

a. Paul Ritterband, "Out of Zion: The Non-Returning Israeli Student" (New York: unpublished dissertation for the Ph.D., in sociology, Columbia University, 1968). Ritterband has published several articles from this research, notably "The Determinants of Motives of Israeli Students Studying in the United States," Sociology of Education, Volume 42, Number 4, Fall 1969, pp. 330-349; and "Law, Policy, and Behavior: Educational Exchange Policy and Student Migration," American Journal of Sociology, Volume 76, Number 1, July 1970, pp. 71-82.

b. Dov Elizur, "The Return of Israel: Attitudes and Intentions of Israelis Residing in the USA: Preliminary Report," The Jewish Agency 1973 Annual.

c. Rina Shapira and Eva Etzioni, "Attitudes of Israeli Students towards Emigration," Comparative Education Review, Volume XIV, Number 2, June 1970, pp. 162-173.

d. Burton M. Halpern, "New Exodus: Israel's Talent Drain," The Nation, Volume 200, 10 May 1965, pp. 497-499.

25. Greece:

a. Evangelos Vlachos, An Annotated Bibliography on Greek Migration (Athens: Social Sciences Centre, 1966).

b. Evangelos C. Vlachos, The Assimilation of Greeks in the United States (Athens: National Centre of Social Research, 1968).

c. George A. Kourvetaris, "'Brain Drain' and International Migration of Scientists: The Case of Greece" (Department of Sociology, Northern Illinois University, DeKalb, Illinois, 1972).

26. Africa:

a. Oladejo O. Okediji and Francis Olu. Okediji, "Nigerian Trained Personnel in the United States of America: Problems and Prospects of Their Recruitment for Posts in Nigeria" (Lagos: Department of Sociology, University of Lagos, 1972). The authors have published several articles from their research, such as "Nigeria 'Brain Drain' to the United States of America: A Sociological Perspective," Journal of Eastern African Research & Development, Volume 2, Number 2, 1972, pp. 137-163; and "A Consideration of Some Factors Influencing the Loss of Nigerian Medical and Paramedical Personnel to Developed Nations," West African Journal of Education, Volume XVII, Number 1, February 1973, pp. 71-87.

b. T.M. Yesufu, "Loss of Trained Personnel by Migration from Nigeria" (Lagos: University of Lagos, 1966).

c. Paul Sack, "Formation et évasion des cadres au Cameroun" (Paris: unpublished thesis for the doctorate, Ecole Pratique des Hautes Etudes, 1968).

d. Paul Sack, "L'émigration du personnel qualifié camerounais: un cas africain d'exode des cerveaux" (summary in "The Brain Drain from five developing countries," UNITAR Research Report No. 5, New York: United Nations Institute for Training and Research, 1971).

27. Latin America:

a. Emigration of professionals:

(1) Gustavo R. Gonzalez, "The Migration of Latin American High-Level Manpower," International Labour Review, Volume 98, Number 6, December 1968, pp. 551-569.

(2) Luis Giorgi, "Extent, Nature and Causes of Loss of Scientists and Engineers in Latin America through Migration to More Advanced Countries," Final Report of the Conference on the Application of Science and Technology to the Development of Latin America (Paris: UNESCO, 1965), pp. 172-188.

(3) Mariano Ramirez and Elvidio Parra, "Algunas caracteristicos de la emigración de profesionales y tecnicos de America Latina a los Estados Unidos" (Washington: Pan American Union, 1968).

(4) G. Beijer, "Selective Migration for and 'Brain Drain' from Latin America," International Migration, Volume IV, Number 1, 1966.

(5) Glaucio Soares et al., "La fuga de los intellectuales," Aportes (Buenos Aires), Number 2, October 1965, pp. 53-66.

(6) Migration of Health Personnel, Scientists, and Engineers from Latin America (Washington: Pan American Health Organization, 1966).

(7) Alberto Sanchez Crespo, "La emigración de profesionales universitarios desde America Latina" (Washington: Organization of American States, 1969).

b. Surveys of Latin American students abroad:

Gordon C. Ruscoe, Latin American Students in United States Colleges and Universities (Washington: National Association for Foreign Student Affairs, 1968).

28. Colombia:

a. Gerardo Eusse-Hoyos, "The Outflow of Professional Manpower from Colombia" (Bogota: ICETEX, 1969; summary in "The Brain Drain from five developing countries," UNITAR Research Report No. 5, New York: United Nations Institute for Training and Research, 1971).

b. Lucia Villamizar de Hill, "Factors Influencing the Emigration of Colombian Professionals to the United States" (Washington: unpublished dissertation for the Ph.D., Catholic University, 1971).

29. Chile:

a. Inés Cristina Reca et al., Algunos aspectos teóricos y empiricos del exodo de profesionales chilenos (Santiago: Escuela Latinoamericana de Sociologia, Facultad Latinoamericana de Ciencias Sociales, 1970).

b. Sergio Guttierez Olivos, "La emigración de recursos humanos de alto nivel y el caso de Chile," Ciencia Interamericana, Volume 6, Number 2, March-April 1965.

30. Argentina:

a. Enrique Oteiza, "Emigration of Engineers from Argentina: A Case of Latin American Brain Drain," International Labour Review, Volume 92, Number 6, December 1965, pp. 445-461.

b. Enrique Oteiza, "La emigración de personal altamente calificado de la Argentina: un caso de emigración de talento de un pais dado a otro más desarrolado" (Buenos Aires: Instituto Torcuato de Tella, 1967).

c. Enrique Oteiza, "Emigración de Profesionales, Técnicos y Obreros Calificados Argentinos a los Estados Unidos --Analisis de las Fluctuaciones de la Emigración Bruta Julio 1950 a Junio 1970," Desarollo Economico (Buenos

Aires), Volume 10, Number 39-40, October-December 1970 and January-March 1971, pp. 429-454.

d. Marta Slemenson et al., "Emigración de científicos argentinos: Organización de un éxodo a América Latina" (Buenos Aires: Instituto Torcuato di Tella, 1970).

e. Morris A. Horowitz, "La emigración de profesionales y técnicos argentinos" (Buenos Aires: Institute Torcuato de Tella, 1962).

f. Nilda Sito and Luis Stuhlman, "La emigración de cientificos de la Argentina" (San Carlos de Bariloche: Departamento de Sociología, Fundación Bariloche, 1968).

31. Peru:

a. Robert G. Myers, <u>Education and Emigration: Study Abroad and the Migration of Human Resources</u> (New York: David McKay Company, 1972). The study of Peruvian students in the United States is supplemented by data about many other nationalities and by generalizations about brain drain. A follow-up survey--the only one ever to check the fulfillment of students' plans--is reported in Myers, "International Education, Emigration, and National Policy (A Longitudinal Case Study of Peruvians Trained in the United States)", <u>Comparative Education Review</u>, Volume XVII, Number 1, February 1973, pp. 71-90.

b. Santiago Segura et al., <u>Fuga de Talentos y Desaprovechamiento Interno</u> (Lima: Universidad Nacional Federico Villarreal, Centro de Investigaciones Economicas y Sociales, 1971).

32. Jamaica:

a. Jay R. Buffenmyer, "Emigration of High-Level Manpower and National Development: A Case Study of Jamaica" (Pittsburgh: dissertation for the Ph.D., in political science, University of Pittsburgh, 1970).

b. Lee R. Duffus, "Jamaica: Why the Brain Drain Continues Unabated" (Lafayette: Purdue Univeristy, 1969).

33. Trinidad and Tobago:

Leo Pujadas, The Emigration of Professional, Supervisory, Middle Level and Skilled Manpower from Trinidad and Tobago 1962-1968: Brain Drain (Port of Spain: Central Statistical Office, 1970; summary in "The Brain Drain from five developing countries," UNITAR Research Report No. 5, New York: United Nations Institute for Training and Research, 1971).

Appendix E

PUBLICATIONS RESULTING FROM THE PROJECT TO DATE

I. The project as a whole:

1. William Glaser and Annerose Schneider Hürfeld, "The Migration and Return of Professionals," UNITAR News, Volume 2, Number 3 (Autumn 1970), p. 2.

2. Mehri Hekmati and William A. Glaser, "The Brain Drain and UNITAR's Multinational Research Project on the Subject," Social Science Information, Volume 12, Number 2 (April 1973), pp. 123-138.

3. William A. Glaser, "UNITAR's Project on the Brain Drain and Study Abroad," Focus/Technical Cooperation, 1974/2, pp. 26-27. Special insert in International Development Review, Volume XVI, Number 2, 1974.

4. William A. Glaser and G. Christopher Habers, "The Migration and Return of Professionals," International Migration Review, Volume 8, Number 2 (Summer 1974), pp. 227-244.

5. William A. Glaser, "Migration of Talent," International Encyclopedia of Higher Education (San Francisco: Jossey-Bass Inc., 1977).

6. G. Christopher Habers, The Universal Minority: A Study of the Female Brain Drain of Students from Developing Countries in Three Developed Countries (New York: Essay for the Master of Arts in Sociology, Columbia University, 1972).

7. Christine Mironesco, Reasons for Studying Abroad, A Comparative Analysis of Brazilian, Iranian and Lebanese Students in the United States and France (New York:

Essay for the Master of Arts in Sociology, Columbia University, 1972).

8. William A. Glaser, "The Process of Cross-National Survey Research," in Alexander Szalai et al. (editors), Cross-National Comparative Survey Research: Theory and Practice (Oxford: Pergamon Press, 1977), pp. 403-435.

9. William A. Glaser, "The Return of the Professional: The Value of His Education Abroad". Proceedings of the inaugural conference, Center for International Higher Education Documentation, Northeastern University, Boston, 1977.

II. National reports:

1. United States: Orlando Rodriguez, Social Determinants of Non-Return: Students from Developing Countries in the United States (New York: dissertation for the Ph.D., in Sociology, Columbia University, 1974).

2. Australia:

(a) G. Lakshmana Rao, Overseas Students in Australia: Some Major Findings from a Nation-wide Survey (Canverra: Education Research Unit, Research School of Social Sciences, Australian National University, 1976).

(b) Geoff Caldwell, "Australia, Asian Students and the Brain Drain," Education News (Australian Federal Department of Education), June 1974, pp. 16-17.

3. Argentina:

Sara Pallma, Emigración y Retorno de Profesionales: El Impacto de los Estudios en el Exterior (San Carlos de Bariloche, Fundación Bariloche, 1974).

4. Brazil:

All issued by Instituto Brasileiro de Relações Internacionais and the Escola Brasileira de Administração Publica of the Fundação Getúlio Vargas:

(a) Renato Raul Boschi, *Bibliografia International Comentada sobre Imigração e Retôrno de Pessoal Qualificado*, 1971.

(b) Renato Raul Boschi, *O Estudo Pós-Graduado no Exterior: Caracteristicas por Ramo de Especialização*, 1971.

(c) Magda Prates Coelho and Elisa Maria Pereira, *O Emprego, no Brasil, de Profissionais Treinados no Exterior*, 1971.

(d) Simon Schwartzman, *Profissionais Brasileiros Treinados no Exterior--1960 a 1970*, 1971.

(e) Simon Schwartzman, *Projeto Retôrno--Avaliação do Impacto do Treinamento, no Exterior, de Pessoal Qualificado--Relatório Final*, 1971.

(f) Simon Schwartzman and Elisa Maria Pereira Reis, *Profissionais Brasileiros com Treinamento no Exterior*, 1972.

(g) *Pesquisa Complementar Projeto dos Empregadores--Relatório Final*, 1972.

5. India:

"Opinions of Indian Returnees from Abroad (An Interim Report), *Technical Manpower*, Volume XV, Number 10 (October 1972).

6. Republic of Korea:

Hyun Ki Päik, Ok Ki Kim and Young Hwan Oh, *Tunoe yuch'ul e kwanhan yŏn'gu: kwigukcha pun* (A Study on the Brain Drain: Return of Professionals) (Seoul: Korean Educational Development Institute, 1974).

7. Uruguay:

Hector J. Apezechea, Carlos Filgueira and Suzana Prates, *Estudio y Trabajo en el Exterior* (Montevideo: Centro de Informaciones y Estudios del Uruguay, 1976).

Appendix F

TOPICS IN THE SOCIAL SCIENCES

As we said in Chapter X, our data are susceptible to considerable further analysis, from the standpoints of manpower policy, education, and the social sciences. Following is a brief list of subjects that might be explored in the future by sociologists, economists, and other social scientists.

1. Reasons for decisions, using the customary techniques of reason analysis. (The methods are cited in the publications in footnote 1 of Appendix A.)

   (a) Dependent variables:

      (1) Decision to study abroad.
      Choice of a particular foreign country.

      (2) Choice of a country to live and work at different stages of one's career.

      (3) Choices at several stages can be arranged in sequences. Analyze types of sequence.

   (b) Independent variables:

      (1) Many social and economic characteristics of the respondent, as reported in his questionnaire.

      (2) Macroscopic social and economic characteristics of the countries involved in respondents' choices. Our many questions about countries are coded with numbers that permit linkages to the machine-readable macro data about countries available from the compendia of Russett, Banks & Textor, and others.

(c) Replicate on our world-wide samples the findings reported in the more specialized surveys on brain drain by Paul Ritterband, Robert Myers, John Niland, and others. Their books are cited in Appendix D.

2. Reference group analysis:

   (a) Types of reference groups: spouse, children, friends, professional colleagues, religion, ethnic group.

   (b) For most groups, information has been obtained about: degree of participation in that group, size of group, orientation of that group, effects on respondent's decisions to emigrate or return to home country.

   (c) Besides studying the effects of group characteristics on emigration decisions, one can analyze them as a separate subject. E.g., comparisons of the networks of group relations among the professionals of different societies, comparisons of participation rates, comparisons of the spouses of foreign-trained professionals, etc.

3. Communications behavior. Amount of contact with home country and with the foreign country by reading and by letters.

4. Languages spoken and read at various stages in the respondent's life. Languages spoken with teachers, colleagues, spouse. The spouse's linguistic capacities. Few surveys have obtained extensive sociolinguistic data from so many respondents.

5. Adjustments of foreigners to developed countries:

   (a) Satisfactions and complaints about relations with employers, fellow workers, and the population. Adjustments of spouse and children.

   (b) Whether maladjustments abroad are associated with adaptation or equal alienation from the home society.

   (c) Whether assimilation abroad began before departure from the home country. Whether assimilation abroad is associated with alienation from the home country.

(d) As in other topics in this survey, this subject can be analyzed by itself, independently of its effects on migration. E.g.:

(1) Comparisons of how different nationalities from developing countries adjust to developed countries.

(2) Comparisons of how different developed countries receive foreigners.

6. Comparisons of working conditions and organizational structures in different countries, according to respondents' perceptions.

7. Economic comparisons among countries:

(a) Differentials between developed and developing countries in:

(1) Rates of pay.

(2) Ownership of consumer durable goods.

(b) Increments in pay obtained in home country as a result of:

(1) Studying in developed countries.

(2) Working in developed countries.

(3) How these increments vary among different developing countries--e.g., whether study in the United States is more profitable than study in Great Britain.

(c) Macro data about countries' occupational and financial characteristics can be linked to respondents' answers.

8. Political variables:

(a) Effects of immigration and emigration regulations on the flows of students and professionals among countries.

(b) Respondents' perceptions of political conditions at home, and how these affect decisions to migrate and return.

9. Education:

(a) Respondents' educational history at home and abroad, and how this relates to choices of specialties, jobs, countries.

(b) How education abroad and degree of specialization abroad relate to the occupational opportunities and needs of the home country. Whether foreign education creates adjustment problems at home. Whether foreign education can be used at home.

(c) Relations with fellow students and faculty members abroad.

(d) Satisfaction with the curriculum abroad.

(e) Organizational characteristics of the universities abroad can be linked to the respondents' answers.

(1) The American survey of foreign students has been coded with numbers for the universities where respondents were currently enrolled. Those code numbers permit linkages to the machine-readable organizational data about American universities available from the American Council on Education.

(2) Similar organizational data about other respondents' universities can be obtained from the "Commonwealth Universities Yearbook" and from other sources.

10. Methodology of cross-national research:

(a) Develop new statistical techniques for:

(1) Comparing national samples differing in their sampling fractions and completion rates.

(2) Generalizing across several national samples. How can weights compensate for differences in sampling factions and in completion rates?

(b) Develop efficient computing techniques for merging two data files:

(1) Sample surveys of respondents.

(2) Macrostatistics about countries, communities, schools.

(c) Develop standardized monetary units in order to compare salaries in many different countries.

(d) Can scales of items that function well in one national sample be used in some or all other samples? What are the empirical and statistical meanings of cross-sample differences in the performance of scales?

(e) Summarize the organizational history of this project. Lessons for future cross-national research: what to emulate, what to avoid.

11. Policy research:

(a) Select the principal issues in international education and international migration. What inferences can be drawn from our data concerning how things work in practice, feasibility of various proposals?

(b) What styles of policy report would be appropriate for governments, private associations, and schools in various countries? What styles would be appropriate for presentation in the Economic and Social Council and in the General Assembly of the United Nations?

12. Intensive analysis of the characteristics of students and professionals of a particular nationality. We will have many national groups with over one hundred respondents.

AUTHOR'S ACKNOWLEDGMENTS

Project directors in several countries solved the difficult tasks of organizing staffs, raising funds, conducting field work, and coding, so their data could be used in this report. They are:

Argentina: Manuel Mora y Araujo and Sara Pallma, Departamento de sociología, Fundación Bariloche, Buenos Aires

Brazil: Simon Schwartzman, Departamento de Pesquisas, Escola Brasileira de Administração Publica, Fundação Getulio Vargas, Rio de Janeiro

Canada: Jacques Dofny, Département de Sociologie, Université de Montréal

Colombia: Jesus Villamizar Herrera, Instituto Colombiano de Crédito Educativo y Estudios Técnicos en el Exterior (ICETEX), Bogota

France: Paul Beaud and Alfred Willener, Groupe de sociologie industrielle comparée, Centre National de la Recherche Scientifique, Paris

Ghana: K. E. de Graft-Johnson and Tom Kumekpor, Department of Sociology, University of Ghana, Accra

Greece: Anna Amera, National Centre of Social Research (EKKE), Athens

India: P. S. Nair and Kamalesh Ray, Council of Scientific and Industrial Research, New Delhi

Republic of Korea: Kim Ok Ki and Hyun Ki Paik, Central Education Research Institute, Seoul

Sri Lanka: S. Mahendra, Colombo Plan Bureau, Colombo

At the Bureau of Applied Social Research, Columbia University, we ourselves directed the surveys of students and stay-ons in the United States. Orlando Rodriguez did much of the work.

The analysis was done at the Columbia University Computer Center (using an IBM 360/91-75 ASP system); at the Rio Datacentro of the Pontifícia Universidade Católica, Rio de Janeiro (using an IBM 370/165); and at the Instituto Brasileiro de Informatica, a part of the Instituto Brasileiro de Geografia e Estatistica, Rio de Janeiro (using an IBM 370/155). The extensive data management was performed with Utility Coder 360 and several other utilities. The statistical analysis used primarily CROSSTABS II and SPSS (Statistical Package for the Social Sciences). A project of this complexity could be carried out only by the most efficient use of third-generation computers. We could not have succeeded without the advice of Stephen Butts, computer consultant at the Bureau of Applied Social Research, Columbia University.

The costs of administering the project, managing the data, and analyzing the surveys for this manuscript were covered by Contract AID/csd 2524, Agency for International Development, United States Department of State; and by Grant 700-0062 to Columbia University from the Ford Foundation. An earlier draft was written during a seminar held in Rio de Janeiro, supported by the Foreign Area Fellowship Program. Data were collected in each country under grants made to each research center by its own government or by private foundations.

For very thorough reading of the manuscripts and many valuable suggestions for revision, we are indebted to Dr. Alexander Szalai, Special Fellow, UNITAR; Miss Margaret Croke, UNITAR; and Dr. Munir Ahmad, Department of Statistics, University of Karachi. Gregory Henderson, then a research officer at UNITAR, made important contributions during the preparatory stages of this project.

INDEX OF NAMES

INDEX OF SUBJECTS

I

J

K

L

M

N

O

P

W

Z